From Idolater to Friend of God

Studies in the Life of Abraham

by James H. Large

Published by
JOHN RITCHIE LTD.
40 Beansburn, Kilmarnock KA3 1RH

ISBN 0 946351 04 X

Copyright © 1986 by John Ritchie Ltd.
40 Beansburn, Kilmarnock, Scotland

Typeset and printed by G.T.P., 48 York Street, Glasgow

Contents

Foreword

Basing himself on the Bible's own presentation of Abraham as a historical figure (neither mythical nor legendary) Mr. Large gives us in this devotional study the results of his lifetime's interest in Abraham.

As one might expect from his background, Mr. Large is second to none in recognising that certain events in Abraham's life have significance as prototypes of greater events in the life and work of Him whose day Abraham "rejoiced to see". But his observations along this line gain rather than lose from the fact that the primary emphasis in this study is placed where it should be placed: on Abraham's own personal experience of God in the real-life circumstances through which God led him.

Cherishing every detail of the inspired record, Mr. Large has tried to penetrate the surface of things and with imagination and sympathy to enter into Abraham's mind and heart, his moods and his motives, both in his failures and in his triumphs; and so to perceive more fully the divine understanding, tact, kindness, patience and firmness with which God trained, tested and perfected Abraham's faith.

Everywhere Mr. Large tries to get us to look at the narrative reverently but realistically: to avoid investing Abraham anachronistically with a Christian halo and then criticising him for not living up to Christian standards; to avoid concentrating so much on the goal of his pilgrimage that we fail to see that he had to "tackle the very practical day-to-day problems of the management and future planning of a large enterprise while playing his proper role in a delicate domestic situation"; and to avoid being so overwhelmed by the giant stature of his faith that we fail to see — and to be encouraged by — the plain fact that he was "of the same common clay as ourselves" and therefore a realistic example for us to follow.

A certain subjective and conjectural element is inescapable in a study of this kind; but Mr. Large consciously tries to compensate for it by his lack of dogmatism and by his willingness, indeed his desire, that everything shall finally be

5

judged in the light of what the text actually says.

May God use this study widely to encourage those who because of their faith in Abraham's Seed, love Abraham and seek to walk in his steps.

David Gooding

Introduction

What is here offered for the reader's consideration contains the substance of what the writer has frequently been privileged to deal with during sixty years' ministry in all parts of Great Britain; it is now presented in expanded form to cover more fully the many wide and important issues raised by the story of Abraham. Until enforced retirement offered sufficient leisure he had never contemplated undertaking such a task and at this late date it would risk making invidious distinctions to try to recall the names of some of the writers and speakers who in the early years inspired him to research the subject for himself. However, the omission of acknowledgements, though regretted, is not serious when the vast store of exposition which has accumulated in this field has left little room for originality.

There is always fresh pleasure in retracing even well-worn paths in territory we have learned to love for its variety and beauty, for it is always possible to catch a glimpse of some feature not noticed before or to see the landscape from a different angle or in a different light. The same is true in retreading the fertile fields of Scripture.

The generous reader may think that a worthwhile effort has been made to portray Abraham as a man of like passions with ourselves, who had to cope with the stresses and strains of real everyday life in home and business, and also to examine carefully his inner spiritual conflicts and perplexities for the sake of the light they throw on the experience of twentieth-century believers. Here was a one-time idolater who, without becoming a mystic, developed in God's moulding hands into a spiritual giant and the friend of God.

This is not to say that other far-reaching implications, devotional, moral and prophetic have been neglected.

A Basic Conviction

The divine authority of Holy Scripture was at one time so generally accepted by Christians that it would hardly have been thought necessary in work of this kind to say that it was written in the conviction that the Scriptures are God-breathed, (2 Tim 3:16; 2 Pet 1:21).

To-day, however, the relentless and increasing pressure of modern thought is being brought to bear and this tends to shake the confidence of some believers — especially those who are young in the faith. This is not altogether surprising seeing that there is hardly a distinctive doctrine of Christianity which is not denied in one quarter or another — sometimes alas by men who take the position of being leaders in the church. As O.W. Hughes has quaintly but aptly said, "The cubes of truth used to stay exactly where they were put ... but now they have been so played with and worn down that they can run anywhere like marbles".

Certainly Paul and Peter, in the passages quoted above, were referring to the OT but as this is where our subject lies there is no need to go into the reasons for accepting the same as true of the NT.

Devout scholars who have ably expounded the various proofs of inspiration have rendered a valuable service particularly to young Christians who seek assurance on problems presented to them, but who hopefully will reach the stage where personal experience of the power and authority of the word of God (where there is a readiness to do God's will) imparts a conviction more satisfying than arguments (John 7:17; Hos 6:3).

More than sufficient for our present purpose is Christ's own authentication of the Scriptures. The evidence is so abundant that to avoid tedium only a small selection is made from His sayings: "Till heaven and earth pass, one jot or one tittle shall in no wise pass from the law till all be fulfilled" (Matt 5:18); "All things must be fulfilled which were written in the law of Moses, and in the prophets and in the Psalms concerning me" (Luke 24:44); "The Scripture cannot be broken" (John 10:35).

Very pertinent to our present study is His confirmation of many parts of the Genesis record, including several references to Abraham and associated events (Matt 8:11; 22:32; John 8:56; Luke 17:28-32).

Rather than embark on a treatment of alleged difficulties (which in any case have been adequately dealt with by competent scholars) we are content to know that the Saviour saw none. There we leave the matter after quoting Leon Morris' reference to the One who knew and loved and lived by the Scriptures as none else ever could: "The Bible is the only book Jesus ever quoted and then never as a basis for discussion but to decide the point at issue".

The Super-natural

To the believer convinced of inspiration the record of occurrences contrary to normal experience presents no problem. If Scripture says so it is so. Nevertheless many who accept inspiration in a general way feel uneasy about incidents involving the super-natural such as the divine appearances to Abraham. They feel relieved if they can regard them simply as stories intended to embody some spiritual meaning. Furthermore, some critics go so far as to allege that they are but refinements of crude pagan myths about heathen gods. A thoughtful reader of the Genesis record will surely sense a dignity and appropriateness which rings true, in contrast to the absurdities of pagan myths. The repetitions of myths do not tend to refinement but to degeneracy; it is far easier to believe that they are distorted variations of ancient traditions.

To automatically reject the super-natural is really to claim that we are competent to decide what is possible and what is not. After all, what do objections to the super-natural amount to? More or less, simply this:— "We have not known such things to happen —therefore they cannot have happened in the past and cannot happen in the future". This is a strange sort of logic akin to the reasoning of the scoffers to whom Peter refers, i.e. seeing that things have continued as they were from the beginning, nothing so unprecedented as the Coming of the Lord is feasible. If the premise were correct, which it is not, the conclusion would still be absurd. Obviously whatever has happened, had a first occurrence. This makes nonsense of the idea that what has not already happened cannot happen.

The times of Abraham predated written revelation and if God were minded to break into human experience it need not surprise us if He took such measures.

There still persists the ingrained idea that everything which happens in this universe must conform to the so-called laws of nature so far discovered. This implies the tremendous assumption that we are now acquainted with all the laws of nature despite the fact that present-day physicists admit that the universe is not only stranger than we imagine, but stranger than we can imagine. In any case are we to suppose that God is limited by these laws of nature which are nothing more than definitions of the way in which it normally pleases God to act?

Chapter I

Abraham's Background

Discoveries About Ur

To many of a past generation the very name of Abraham's city had an irresistible appeal. "Ur of the Chaldees" had for them a haunting cadence which seemed to epitomise the air of mystery which surrounded the city until comparatively recent times. It was known to be in Mesopotamia, as Stephen declared (Acts 7:2), but its exact location was a matter of debate.

Mesopotamia was the Greek form which the LXX gave to the ancient name of Aram Naharaim, meaning "Aram of the two rivers" in reference to the mighty Euphrates and the almost equally great Tigris which enclose with their separate courses most of the territory so named. Both are mentioned in connection with the Garden of Eden (Gen 2:14), the latter being there, and in Dan 10:4, called Hiddekel: "I was by the side of the great river, which is Hiddekel". The many passages relating to the Euphrates (sometimes simply called the river) afford an interesting study, which must not tempt us into a digression.

Both take their rise not far from each other in what is now known as Armenia. They run their separate courses in a general S.E. direction eventually joining some distance from the Persian Gulf. The Tigris has the impressive length of 1146 miles, but the Euphrates is even longer, 1780 miles; they therefore range among the major rivers of the world.

The name Aram Naharaim appears in the title of Psalm 60 indicating the extent of king David's conquests. See comments on Gen 15:18.

Excavations in Mesopotamia in the 19th century revealed much that was of great interest but archaeology then was far behind the science it has since become. Moreover the inaccessibility of the terrain with corresponding problems in transporting even modest equipment set severe limits on what could be achieved. Our later consideration of the great advances made in the early part of the 20th century should not be allowed to overshadow the value of the work done by these pioneers in difficult conditions.

Critical opinion had attacked the historical veracity of the Genesis record, and Abraham was considered to be a mythical figure invented by a late scribe to explain the origin of the proud Hebrew race. Surely a writer with such an object would not have dared to depict their revered ancestor as compromising his wife in Egypt and later in Gerah. Much less would he have exposed some of the sons of Jacob, the destined heads of several of the tribes of Israel, as an unscrupulous and murderous gang. The inclusion of such argues for an inward compulsion to record unpleasant truth.

It was alleged that this unknown author betrayed himself by his anachronisms in setting his story against a background of his own times. This despite the fact that worthy men of the past of no mean intellect, who lived much nearer the times in question, and were better acquainted with the situation, and probably had access to sources of information denied to us, accepted the record as authentic. Unless we are to make nonsense of all ancient records how can we dismiss the testimony of men of the calibre of Solomon, Isaiah, Nehemiah and Paul, to say nothing of secular writers like the historian Josephus? Yet this was done with a cool assumption of superior knowledge little short of intellectual arrogance. The Gospel record of Christ's authentication of Abraham as a real person who looked forward to Christ's day and who now was in the presence of God was likewise discounted. Cp. Luke 13:28; 20:37, 38; John 8:56.

One of the seemingly insignificant effects of the first World War (1914/18) indirectly compelled a change of opinion. Among the troops engaged in military operation in Mesopotamia were men who were sufficiently interested to keep their eyes open for signs of ancient civilisations. As news of accidental discoveries leaked out a wider circle became interested. It looked as if the distant past was ready to yield some of its secrets.

With a fresh realisation of the exciting possibilities, in 1922 the British Museum and the Museum of Pennsylvania sponsored a joint expedition under the capable leadership of Leonard Wooley. Archaeology had now become a serious science with equipment far in advance of what was available to earlier workers in the field. Partly due to the military operations already mentioned the land had been opened up in a way which made transport less of a problem. A systematic exploration over a fairly extensive area was rewarded with discoveries which at the time attracted world-wide attention. The story will entrance any one who takes the trouble to consult books available in most public libraries. The discoveries warranted sustained exploration, and in the years up to 1934 extensive ruins were excavated and an immense amount of material recovered. Evidence refuted the critics by showing that the Genesis record was in accord with the period it covered. This was not the first nor the last time that an over-ruling providence, after allowing the critics to have their say, had uncovered evidence to refute them. Whilst immature faith finds in this a welcome prop, the pleasure which this brings to those who have long known and loved the Bible is not due to a shaken faith being re-assured but to the vindication of Scripture as the Word of God.

Although our main interest now centres on a dramatic discovery of the ruins of Ur it would be inexcusable not to mention that the expedition was amazed to find that beneath the ancient city was an extensive layer of water-laid silt six feet thick. No doubt because he suspected the significance of this Wooley penetrated this layer and found beneath it the remains of a yet earlier civilisation. When it is mentioned that about the same time S. Langdon made a similar discovery about 150 miles away, the implications for the veracity of the story of the flood are obvious.

The ruins were unearthed in what is now southern Iraq at a spot about 150 miles south of Babel and about the same distance from the present shore of the Persian Gulf. It was calculated that the settlement had reached the status of a city when what later became Babylon the Great was only a village.

Many believe that it was originally much nearer the sea, but that over the past four thousand years alluvium from the combined rivers has gradually pushed the coast back to its present position; others now question this long held view.

The intensive work on the ruins of Ur made it possible to construct such a clear picture of life there thousands of years ago that many had the feeling, not easily recaptured to-day, that Abraham had stepped out of the dim shadows of the past into the broad daylight of the 20th century.

The extent of the ruins and the splendour of many of the artefacts recovered must not be allowed to obscure the immense importance of what may seem a more prosaic find —literally thousands of clay tablets. They yielded a wealth of information about the official business of the city, its religious ritual, insights into the judiciary, as well as details of caravan trade-routes from Ur. Some even showed that advanced problems in mathematics, including trigonometry, had been tackled.

The ruins were impressive — notably those of the royal palace and the temple of the moon-god. The first yielded treasures of exquisitely designed jewellery testifying to a high degree of craftsmanship, to say nothing of beautiful ornaments of silver and copper found elsewhere. The temple suggested that the moon-god was the patron deity of the city,although other gods were worshipped as well. (See Josh 24:2.) If it seems strange that people of obvious intelligence should be worshippers of the moon let us reflect that in our day educated people can be deluded into swallowing the fantastic fables invented by the founders of strange cults. In this connection it is well to ponder John 5:43; Rom 1:25; 2 Thess 2:11.

A great deal of the material recovered can be inspected in several museums but principally, of course, in the two which sponsored the exhibition. There is something very impressive about looking at objects with which Abraham would, no doubt, have been familiar nearly four thousand years ago.

The tablets indicated that commerce flourished. In addition to well-organised caravan trade-routes, a harbour and quays on the Euphrates and a connecting-canal indicated that goods were transported by sea via the Gulf, and up the Euphrates, which was navigable for vessels of considerable size for 1 200 miles.

Other canals supplied a system of irrigation which rendered the region fertile so that agriculture and cattle-rearing flourished.

By the 6th century BC the Euphrates had changed its course ten miles to the east which rendered the irrigation system useless and the site was abandoned, but the question remains why so much was left behind.

However, the result was that the desert gradually took over, and it is no doubt due to this circumstance that the ruins and their contents were preserved under the desert unseen and apparently forgotten, to judge by the valuables left undisturbed by marauders.

It is an arresting thought that the city might never have come to light again had not the impression made on history by Abraham motivated the investigations. Indeed he himself would never have been heard of if he had not obeyed the call of the God of glory —moreover the history of the world would not have been the same.

Chapter II
Abraham's Family

(Gen 11:24-32)

Since there must be some purpose in information about Abraham's family being provided in the record it ought not to be neglected; a certain amount of attention will be rewarded if it makes it easier to visualise him against a background of real life. The story of God's dealings with him becomes of greater practical value if we are able to see him, not as a recluse, but a man who had to face, as we have to do, every-day realities in a very natural family set-up.

Reaction To The Flood

Possibly the principles upon which some of the Old Testament genealogies are constructed are not perfectly understood, but if we take the tables in Gen 11 and 12 as they stand, they provide good reason to believe that Abraham's generation must have been well informed about the flood which wiped out the corrupt civilisation of Noah's day. He was descended from Noah through Noah's son, Shem, who was 98 years of age when he entered the ark (11:10). The statement that he lived for 500 years after the birth of his first child implies that he was still alive when Abraham was a young man. The details given of Shem's son, Arphaxad, and his grandson, Salar, mean that they were also contemporary for a while with Abraham. Whether or not they actually met cannot be settled, but it seems clear that Abraham's generation would not be dependent on uncertain tradition handed down through several generations.

It might have been thought that the lessons of the flood would have been taken to heart and led to reverence for God's holiness, but the prevalence of idolatry in Abraham's time is less surprising if we remember that within a comparatively short time after the flood the building of the tower of Babel was indicative of a determination to resist God's purpose. Cf.

10:25 with 11:1-8.

Babel was only about 150 miles from Ur, and communications in those days were possible on a level not generally realised. As we have earlier mentioned tablets unearthed at Ur give details of regular caravan trails between the two places.

Certainly, idolatry was well established in the days of Abraham's grandfather, and the family was involved as plainly stated in Josh 24:2: "Your fathers dwelt on the other side of the flood in old time ... and they served other gods". No doubt idolatry was, as usual, linked with immorality and this may be the explanation of Isaiah's reference to the "hole of the pit" (Isa 51:1, 2).

Abraham's Relatives

Nahor, the seventh direct descendant from Shem, was the father of Terah and therefore Abraham's grandfather. His life span of 148 years meant that he lived until his grandson was 49 years of age. After Terah, Nahor begat other sons and daughters so that Abraham had at least two uncles and two aunts, and doubtless, a number of cousins. Terah and his wife also had a son named Haran and another named after his grandfather Nahor, indicating that Abraham had at least two brothers. Terah's daughter, Sarai, by another wife, was half-sister to Abraham (20:12). Their marriage would not have been regarded as offending any moral code. The fact that she proved to be barren does not appear to have lessened Abraham's regard for her. Haran had two daughters, Milcah and Iscah, and, evidently later, a son named Lot, Abraham's nieces and nephew. Nahor married Haran's daughter, Milcah, but we gather from 22:20 that Abraham had left Ur before they had any children.

Doubtless there were other members of the various families whose births are not recorded, so it may be safely assumed that the group was of considerable size.

Involvement In The Life Of Ur

Unless we assume that Abraham and Nahor adopted a pastoral life in later years (and certainly Abraham's marked success makes this most unlikely) we conclude that they were cattle-owners from the start. This does not imply that they

2

were rustics; subsequent notices of Abraham, such as his reception in Egypt, his leading role in the alliance with Mamre, his handling of the king of Sodom and later of the Philistine king, give the impression of a man accustomed to a position of influence.

The south of Mesopotamia being fertile as the result of a very efficient irrigation-system makes it likely that the family was prosperous. Its members would be involved in business transactions in the city, and being idolaters would participate in the religious life of the city. Although their flocks would, of course, be in the surrounding country-side cared for by herdsmen, vv. 28, 31 suggest residence in the city.

The reader will be able from his own experience to form a mental picture of what life must have been like in such a family set-up and in such an environment.

A Prepared Heart?

In considering the scriptural instances of men called of God for a special purpose, it is generally possible to discover some evidence of antecedent influences calculated to prepare their hearts. This offers a useful study to those so inclined, but it must suffice here to suggest that the principle can be seen in the case of Saul of Tarsus. Tarsus was the capital of Cilicia so undoubtedly he would have been a member of the company referred to in Acts 6:9, 10 who disputed with Stephen but were not able to resist the wisdom given him by the Spirit. Moreover Saul was evidently a member of the Council before which Stephen was arraigned, otherwise he would have had no say in their verdict (8:1). He therefore heard Stephen's powerful defence, and, no doubt, like his fellows, was "cut to the heart". Despite this he took an official part in the martyrdom of Stephen (Acts 7:58; 22:20). His address many years later (now as an apostle of Jesus Christ) to the Jews at Antioch of Pisidia indicates that Stephen's theme had made an indelible impression on his mind (Acts 13:14).

The Lord's words to Saul, "It is hard for thee to kick against the pricks," surely indicate that ever since he had heard Stephen his conscience had been troubling him; the revelation of Christ therefore came when he was wrestling with the claims of Christ.

Are there reasons to think that Abraham may have had some exercise of heart which prepared him in some degree for a revelation of God? Such notices as we have about his relationships with Terah, Lot, Ishmael and Isaac argue for strongly-felt ties of kinship, so we judge he would be deeply affected by the untimely death of his brother, Haran. As he looked on the once-loved but now dead form he would realise that the real person had departed. But where? Did this cause him to reflect on the uncertainty of life and the solemn issues of the hereafter?

Furthermore Heb 11:10 suggests that he had a conviction about the transitory nature of earthly glory. Seeing that no mention is made of any city in God's communications to him it is most remarkable that "he looked for *the* city which hath *the* foundations, whose builder and maker is God". (See RV which takes account of the repeated definite article in the original.)

As he looked at the seeming splendour of Ur, had his mind gone back at times to the antediluvian civilisation, which for all its apparent stability was swept away, and perhaps to the abandoned Babel? He probably knew sufficient about the flood to know that the foundations of Ur were laid over the ruins of a condemned civilisation. Did he recognise that solid buildings were no guarantee of permanence? He would know that life had been going on as normal right up to the very day that the flood came and swept all away (Matt 24:39). Did he yearn for a city founded not on ruins but on the Rock of Ages? Did the thought of such a city make it easier for him, when the call came, to live for the rest of his life in tents with his son and grandson (Heb 11:9)? (Incidentally, let us take to heart the exhortation which seems to have some reference to this: "Let us go forth therefore unto him ... for here have we no continuing city, but we seek one to come", Heb 13:14.)

Divine Initiative

The possibility of prior preparation of heart in no way detracts from the fact that it was wholly by the initiative of God that the call came to Abraham. It was not that he chose God; God chose him (Neh 9:7). Micah says that God performed the truth to Jacob and the mercy to Abraham. Truth to Jacob because by that time God had made a covenant but God showed mercy to Abraham by choosing him before any promise was made (Micah 7:20). See also Luke 1:54, 55 RV. This, of course, is the case with every true conversion, although in many cases converts themselves have not entered into the enjoyment of the glorious fact that God broke into their lives by His own choice. Like the Thessalonians, Abraham did not turn to God because he had turned from idols; he turned from idols because by gracious divine constraint he had turned in heart to God, as they did. The gospel "came" to them in power because of the effectual call of God (1 Thess 1:4, 5).

Consideration of the manner of God's manifestation to Abraham will come later; for our immediate purpose we simply note three points in the call of God:
1. he was told to leave his country and his kindred;
2. to go to a land which God would show him;
3. obedience was linked with a promise of a great posterity.

Deliverance From Idolatry

Even allowing for the possibility that Abraham's heart had been exercised beforehand, the strength of faith manifested in his magnificent response to the divine summons is impressive. Unlike ourselves he had no Bible to instruct him, no precedent to encourage, and no fellow-believer to consult, yet he was prepared to be uprooted from a settled life in the land of his nativity (24:7 RV) among his own kith and kin and venture on a life of faith relying on God's word to him. Emigration to the antipodes to-day is child's play in comparison. If, as we shall see, his response at this stage fell short of perfection, only those who are blind to their own weaknesses would dare criticise. Characteristically Heb 11, aptly called the Westminster Abbey of the Bible, overlooks much in crediting Abraham with prompt obedience, "When he was called he went out, not knowing whither he went". From this standpoint it was a decision he had to make; from God's standpoint it was a deliverance; such is the force of the word "redeemed" as used by Isaiah in regard to Abraham (Isa 29:22). This is what Jacob meant when he spoke of being redeemed from all evil (Gen 48:16).

Being called out of idolatry was a deliverance in the same way as Paul spoke of our being delivered out of this present evil world (Gal 1:4). To a sinner aroused by the call of Christ the renunciation of a superficially attractive world is often a wrench but he learns to regard it as a deliverance.

Few now-a-days would think that idolatry could be a snare to the modern Christian, and even John's plea to Christians in his day to keep themselves from idols (1 John 5:21) sounds strange, until we remember that an idol is anything or anyone occupying the place of preeminence in our hearts which God alone should have.

God's Prior Claim

The Saviour endorsed the OT standard: "Thou shalt love the Lord thy God with all thy heart, and with all thy soul, and with all thy mind, and with all thy strength" (Deut 6:5; Mark 12:30). This involves the whole personality — affections, intelligence, will and capability. He described it as the first, principal commandment, the one from which all true life flows.

To regard this as depicting a God who demands first place for His own selfish gratification is to bring God down to the level of sinful man's egotism, and so to miss the whole point. God is the unique fount of all true blessedness so that in the very nature of things the creature's highest felicity is found in Him (see Psa 43:4). We shall not love others less because we love God best. Our love for others will be the greater when our love for God is the greatest. Thus the Saviour added, "And the second is like namely this, Thou shalt love thy neighbour as thyself, there is none other commandment greater than this". We can be properly related to others only in the measure in which we are properly adjusted to God. This, of course, is an on-going process (Phil 1:6; 3:12). When the God of glory delivered Abraham from the bondage of idolatry, it was the beginning of a process of spiritual development culminating when he became one whom God could call His friend.

Preparations for Leaving

Although immediately obedient in heart and will, it cannot be supposed that Abraham was able to drop everything instantly and leave at once. The necessary preparations would have been considerable. He would wish to settle up all outstanding business in an honourable way and this would take time. Whilst cash transactions were possible (23:16) it would have been difficult to sell up a large establishment at short notice in the hope of being able to set up again in a distant place; in any case there would be all the disadvantages of having to sell in a buyer's market and later buy in a seller's market. Farmers with experience of moving to distant parts confirm that there would be cogent reasons for retaining carefully reared flocks and herds and the services of trained herdsmen. Certainly the task would be formidable, but its feasibility is amply demonstrated in the case of Jacob who moved huge numbers of cattle a distance of 400 miles from Haran to Shechem under more difficult circumstances (Gen 31:17, 18). Nevertheless, the organisation needed would take several days, added to which would be a round of farewells, and what this could entail may be judged by Laban's proposal that at least ten days should be devoted to a farewell for Rebekah (24:55).

Neighbours' Conclusions

All this could not fail to attract the interest of neighbours, and curiosity would undoubtedly prompt enquiries as to what was afoot. It is not difficult to imagine their likely reaction if one who had been a fellow-idolater claimed that the God of glory had appeared to him, commanding him to leave his country; they probably drew not very flattering conclusions as to his state of mind. Of course, they would want to know where he was going, and when he had to tell them he did not know their suspicions would be confirmed and significant glances would be exchanged.

But Abraham was no fool to exchange Mesopotamia for Canaan and Ur for Zion, or to relinquish the fellowship of the family to become the friend of God and inheritor of eternal glory. To quote James Elliot who gave his life in the cause of Christ in Ecuador, "He is no fool who gives what he cannot keep to gain what he cannot lose", or the apostle John, "The world passeth away and the desires thereof, but he that doeth the will of God abideth for ever" (1 John 2:17). How true history has shown this to be in the case of Abraham. Ur has passed away and possibly would never have been remembered but for Abraham, and he himself would have occupied an unknown grave had he not answered the call of God. Instead his memory has been revered through all generations since. If we are wise we shall look not at the temporal but the eternal (2 Cor 4:18). No doubt many of his fellow-citizens pitied him but he could have expressed his sentiments in the hymn:

"Saviour if of Zion's city
I through grace a member am
Let the world deride or pity
I shall glory in Thy Name."

John Newton

Reaction of the Family

Even if, as we would like to think, Nahor took a more charitable view of his brother's sanity, he was clearly not impressed with the objective reality of his experience; it appears that he remained an idolater to the end. Evidently he had little sympathy because, as we shall see later, although news must have reached him from time to time, it evoked no direct response from him (see notes on 22:20).

With the father it was surprisingly different. It speaks volumes for Abraham's moral stature that Terah's affection for him was matched by confidence in his judgment; accepting his son's testimony, he was willing at an advanced age to embark on what must have struck many as an ill-advised venture.

Lot's attitude is more difficult to assess. Whether he was at that time old enough to take a responsible decision, or whether he was still young and for some reason it was not thought advisable to leave him with the family, it is impossible to say. Although he had lost his father presumably his mother was still alive, and there were his two sisters. At the time of his return from Egypt he was old enough to be the owner of a considerable establishment and the father of marriageable sons and daughters, but it would be necessary to know the length of the sojourn in Haran to base estimates on this. On this point we can only say that it must have been a considerable period judging by the fact that they succeeded in acquiring considerable substance and increasing the number of their retainers (12:5).

He had no call from God, but although he was of a pliable nature too much stress must not be laid on the fact that Terah "took him" because it is also said that he took Abraham. Once the decision to leave was made, Terah, accustomed to wielding patriarchal authority, assumed control of the expedition. He must have been optimistic, but optimism is not faith, "Faith cometh by hearing and hearing by the word of God" (Rom 10:17). True faith must have God's word to rely on and neither Terah nor Lot had a call from God.

Partial Obedience

Clearly God's command was only partially complied with, for although Abraham got out of his country he did not fully sever his connections with his kindred and his father's house. As we have already said, only those blind to their own weaknesses will be inclined to sit in judgment on him, but this need not prevent us from learning what lessons we can, for the final consequences were regrettable for Abraham and disastrous for Lot.

An effort should be made to understand the predicament he was in, remembering that believers can find themselves in situations which are not clear-cut, and even those who basically wish to do God's will find themselves the subjects of conflicting influences. Paternal authority in that age was almost absolute (see remarks on ch. 22), and Abraham would have been in a quandary about over-riding his father's decision by insisting on going out alone. Furthermore he may have been encouraged to think that his example had induced his father to abandon Ur and even to cherish the hope that he would renounce idolatry. The same hope with regard to Lot may have made him ready to have Lot join in with them. Perhaps this actually happened in his case to judge by Peter's remarks (2 Pet 2:7, 8). As so often happens in a believer's spiritual conflicts, a seemingly good case for compromise can be made, but the price always has to be paid, and sometimes it is a heavy one. On a wider scale it can be argued that the spiritual effectiveness of the church to-day has been impaired by the long-term effects of compromises made long ago, often with the best intentions.

How true it is that the flesh (which we may see represented by the old man, Terah) can mislead us by the many subtle forms it takes of seeming verity. Many a movement begun in the Spirit has lost its impetus because it has been taken over by the flesh — relying on natural capacity instead of continuing to depend totally on the Spirit's guidance and enabling. Paul agonised over the disastrous results of this blunder in the churches of Galatia where the converts had begun well through a wonderful work of the Spirit of God, and had then been misled by false teaching to think that what had begun in the Spirit could be perfected in the flesh (Gal

3:3). Far from the work being perfected it was being ruined. Yet we still see the same thing happening, the work of the Spirit being stifled by the efforts of men to mould it to their own pattern.

Imperfect Faith

Not only was Abraham's initial heart-obedience marred by compromise but his faith was also imperfect. Whilst great credit is due to him for magnificent faith and courage, yet, strangely enough, there was a niggling fear, revealed by his later confession to Abimelech (20:13). He was afraid that the beauty of his wife would attract undesirable attention which would endanger his own life; accordingly before setting out he sought her consent to a lie disguised under an element of truth. No fault can be found with consultation as to the wisest course to be taken in case of certain eventualities (e.g. 46:33), but the need to collaborate about what is to be said usually points to a desire to obscure the absolute truth. She was asked to say, if such a situation arose, that she was his sister. This would deprive her of whatever measure of protection her married condition would give her (and events proved that it was considerable), but the point was that the subterfuge might save his life (cp. 12:13). She must have been a woman of courage to embark on such an enterprise, and Peter's remarks seem to acknowledge this (1 Pet 3:6). Certainly Rebekah and Rachel were prepared to leave native-land and kindred for a new life in a distant land but with securities which made their decisions very different from hers. It would appear that she was also a woman of integrity who did not approve of the evasion, for she did not make such a misleading statement to Pharaoh but left the deception to her husband, although she kept quiet for his sake and endured the humiliation. Nevertheless it is to be noted that, for reasons we cannot conjecture, she did many years later in a similar situation say she was his sister (20:5). As happens so often, events proved that the truth would have served better. In any case such fears were strangely inconsistent with the faith and courage he showed in other ways, and yet not so strange as our readiness to trust God for eternal salvation and yet have misgivings about His ability to see us through the minor problems of daily life. And why should Abraham have feared for his life when the divine promise as to his descendants necessarily involved the preservation of his life? Consistency is not a conspicuous element in fallen human nature. We shall have cause to notice again the incongruity of trusting God in great matters and doubting Him in lesser, when we consider Abraham's attitudes to God's promises after his victory over the four kings. Only one Person was ever wholly consistent in all His ways, but this was not always apparent to His critics because His life was regulated by divine principles beyond their understanding.

The Journey Started

At last Terah, Abraham, Sarai and Lot set out accompanied by those represented by the pronoun *they*. This could refer to other members of the household, including perhaps Lot's wife, but more probably to servants who would be needed to manage the flocks and herds. By this time, having first demonstrated his willingness to step out on an unknown path, he had been told by God what his destination was, for we read, "They went forth ... to go into the land of Canaan". Prayer for guidance is not very genuine when obedience on our part depends on whether the will of God suits our inclinations. "If any man will do his will he shall know" (John 7:17). There must be the desire to *do* God's will and the readiness to take the first step on the indicated path trusting for further light as we go:

"Keep thou my feet.
I do not ask to see
The distant scene.
One step enough for me."
John Henry Newman.

The same principle is illustrated when, having decided to obey in the matter of offering up Isaac, he was told of the appointed place (22:4). When Saul of Tarsus wanted to know what the Lord would have him do he was told, "Arise and go into the city and it shall be told thee what to do". When he obeyed by going into the city, Ananias was specially sent to enlighten him, incidentally providing evidence that Saul's experience was not a figment of his imagination (Acts 9:6, 11).

The Route Taken

It would have been impossible to travel due west to Canaan, for a vast desert would have been an effective barrier. Caravans from southern Mesopotamia travelled along what was known as 'the fertile crescent' curving to the north west and then to the south west and on to Canaan and Egypt. One route passed through Babylon and then on to Damascus, but in the interests of wider trade another route diverged to the right at Babylon and passed through Nineveh and reached Damascus from the north. For some reason this longer route seems to have been chosen, possibly because it offered better facilities for the passage of flocks and herds, not by roads as we understand them, but broad tracts of mainly open country. But although the reason for choosing this longer route was valid and the ultimate intention good, the words, "They went forth ... to go to the land of Canaan," are followed by, "... and came to Haran and dwelt there", suggesting that they settled down. They had travelled something like 800 miles, necessary care in driving the cattle restricting them to something like 15 miles a day. (Deut 1:2 regards a distance of about 165 miles as requiring eleven days.) Allowing for rest-days the journey from Ur to Haran would have occupied more than two months. No doubt Terah, now advanced in years, had grown weary of the long trek and, having no consciousness of a divine call, could see no real point in pushing on for another 400 miles or so into Canaan. Haran, although far to the north, was still, strictly speaking, in Mesopotamia (24:10), and although he was now far from his former links he might have felt that crossing the border into another country would be an irrevocable step. In leaving Ur, Abraham had only partially severed his ties with his kindred, and now he failed to get completely out of his country, although admittedly he had travelled a long way from his native city.

Stopping Short At Haran

Terah had set out by a natural impulse or, as we might say in NT language, "in the energy of the flesh". In such circumstances the fancied glamour soon wears off, if we do the same in the spiritual sense we too shall weary of the pilgrimage and settle for second best. There have been impulsive individuals who, dazzled by false romance, have plunged into some special sphere of service for Christ, but, lacking the spiritual stamina imparted by a deep conviction of a divine call, have found to their dismay that the sense of romance evaporates in face of the harsh realities, and they have either returned disillusioned or, perhaps worse, have put a good face on it by doggedly plodding on in humdrum fashion devoid of spiritual freshness or vigour. Such is the tragedy of the unsent servant who might have been blessed and been made a blessing in the sphere God had appointed for him: "How shall they preach except they be sent?" (Rom 10:15).

It has been thought that Terah gave the spot the name Haran in memory of the son he had lost, indicating that his heart was still with the dead in Ur. It is possible, however, that by co-incidence the place already had the name Charan, the only difference being the harsh gutteral 'ch'. Maybe the similarity struck a chord with Terah. "Dwelt there" points to the intention of staying at least for a protracted period (cp. 13:18; 22:19). In all likelihood they were there for some years, for, as already suggested, it would take several successful seasons to gather substance, and the mention of souls probably refers to the acquisition of extra personnel to care for the enlarged flocks and herds. If Terah had felt the need to justify the decision to settle down he could very well have used the argument that their prosperity was evidence of divine approval; it is usually possible to invent some excuse for taking a course which suits us.

This dubious indicator evidently did not impress Abraham who was not tempted to remain once he was free. His justification for staying could very well have been filial duty; it would have been a very shabby thing to desert his father in his old age, leaving him to fend for himself in a new environment far from his original home. This would certainly have been a difficulty, but one of his own making. If he still felt the power of his original call, it must have meant a painful conflict of loyalties — to his father on one hand and to his God on the other. Christ who never minimised the difficulties of obedience warned that following Him could involve such clashes (Matt 10:34-38). In this, as in so many other matters, a delicate balance must be maintained, for the shouldering of proper family responsibilities can be an important aspect of Christian service (1 Tim 5:8), neglect of which can become a reproach. In Abraham's case, the dilemma would not have faced him if he had made a complete break in the first place.

Set Free

However, Terah's eventual death freed Abraham. Having attended properly to the necessary funeral, he could resume his journey to Canaan. In this connection it is useful to recall Paul's teaching about being in bondage to the flesh, and the necessity of putting our old nature to death and burial if we are to be set free to live the full life God wishes us to enjoy in the freedom of His service. (See Rom 6.)

Yet liberation from the ties of flesh was not complete while the link with Lot remained unbroken. This posed no immediate problem for Lot was prepared to go with Abraham, but in the long term it led to trouble and grief for Abraham and disaster and shame for Lot.

It is amazing how, even when the crucial decision has been taken to put our old nature in the place of death, it survives in subtle forms. Probably very few servants of Christ were more determined than Paul to crucify the flesh or succeeded to such an extent, yet even he was brought to realise that the struggle would continue while life lasted (Rom 8:23; Phil 3:12-16).

Terah's Life Span

Acts 7:4 links Abraham's departure from Haran with Terah's death, and Gen 12:4 informs us that Abraham was then 75 years of age. If 11:26 means that Terah was 70 when Abraham was born, then it follows that he died when he was 145, but in our version his age is given as 205.

Although the point does not bear on the purpose of these studies, perhaps it should be touched on in passing. In the complicated Hebrew numeration system based on the letters of the Hebrew alphabet big differences were sometimes indicated by minute marks, demanding great care and concentration in copying. If somewhere along the line a slip were made it would be perpetuated by succeeding copyists who would shrink from making any alteration.

We do not, of course, possess the original text, but one of the oldest is the independent Samaritan Pentateuch which gives Terah's age as 145, which fits the case and is more in line with the life-spans of his father and his son, 148 and 175 respectively.

It is not claimed that this settles the matter, but a fuller discussion of a point not relevant to a work of this kind is hardly called for, and must be sought in technical writings which deal with textual questions.

Chapter III
The Call Of God

(Gen 12:1-3)

A Fresh Beginning

Even without Stephen's statement in Acts 7:2, 3 it would have been clear from the terms of the command, "Get thee out of thy country and thy kindred", that it must have come to him whilst still at home in Ur. Why then is it recorded here instead of what would appear to be the appropriate place between vv. 30 and 31 of the preceding chapter, thus supplying the reason for departing from the city? There must be some reason for inserting it after the sojourn in Haran. Could it have been deliberately designed to convey the encouraging lesson that, although incomplete obedience in stopping short at Haran meant that no further revelation was given, the promises still stood available to a faith that would rise up and renew the path of obedience? God is the God of a fresh beginning (13:1).

Whilst the salutary lesson of the bitter harvest of "sowing to the flesh" must not be overlooked, yet it is heart-stirring to see how warnings conveyed by the lapses of even great men do not abandon to hopelessness those who have not heeded such warnings. It is impossible to estimate how many penitent souls who otherwise might have despaired have taken fresh courage from instances of restoration, among which one of the most outstanding cases is that of David after his grievous sin (2 Sam 12:7-14). His soul exercises as described in Psalms 32 and 51 have encouraged many to return with contrite heart to God. This he himself had foreseen, prompting him to say, "Restore unto me the joy of thy salvation ... then will I teach transgressors thy ways and sinners shall be converted (marg. return) unto thee" (Psa 51:12, 13), and in similar strain, "for this shall every one that is godly pray unto thee when thou mayest be found" (Psa 32:6). The Lord's gracious reinvestment of Peter, and Paul's recognition of John Mark's eventual usefulness point the same lesson without giving any encouragement to carelessness (John 21:15-17; 2 Tim 4:11).

The God Of Glory

Before examining the terms of God's call and the attendant promises, we must look at the divine manifestation granted to Abraham which, no doubt, invested the call with special authority and powerfully influenced him in the response he gave; the God of Glory appeared to him; and the word implies a visible appearance. It is most remarkable that this is not mentioned in the narrative — we would not have known of it but for the disclosure by Stephen, full of the Holy Spirit, in the opening words of his tremendous defence before the Council at Jerusalem. Incidentally, it is interesting to note that at the conclusion of his masterly survey of God's dealings with His people down the generations, he was himself granted a vision of the glory of God and of the Son of Man standing at the right hand of God (Act 6:5, 8; 7:2, 55).

The mention of glory naturally inclines us to think that Abraham was given a display of divine spendour, as in the case of Christ's revelation to Saul of Tarsus on the Damascus road, but this is not necessarily so. Stephen does not elaborate and, as mentioned above, the Genesis record is silent. It may therefore be well to consider whether what was revealed to Abraham was moral, as in several other compound titles of God: "The God of all grace" (1 Pet 5:10); "The God of peace" (Phil 4:9); "the God of all comfort" (2 Cor 1:3), to mention but a few.

This idea of glory implicit in the moral attributes of God is illustrated in God's response to the request made by Moses, "I beseech thee, show me thy glory". It is impossible for any mortal to see the eternal and almighty God in His very essence; as He said to Moses on this occasion, "No man shall see me and live". Compare 1 Tim 6:16, "Whom no man hath seen nor can see". Instead, God's offer to Moses was, "I will make all my goodness pass before thee, and I will proclaim the name of the LORD before thee; and I will be gracious to whom I will be gracious and will show mercy on whom I will show mercy" (Exod 33:18-23):

Great God of wonders! All Thy ways
Display Thine attributes divine,
But the bright glories of Thy grace
Beyond Thine other wonders shine.
                              Samuel Davies

John, who was very fond of the subject, said of Christ, "We beheld his glory, the glory as of the only begotten of the Father". How was that glory displayed? "Full of grace and truth". Later he adds, "No man hath seen God at any time; the only begotten Son ... he hath declared Him" (John 1:14, 18). What may be seen of God is seen in Christ, who is the brightness of God's glory and the express image of His person (Heb 1:3). The light of the knowledge of the glory of God is in the face of Jesus Christ (2 Cor 4:6). We may therefore conclude that the appearance to Abraham was one of the pre-incarnate manifestations of Christ. It seems to be a general rule that special divine revelations are suited to the particular situation at the time, or to the spiritual condition of the recipient. May it not be that Abraham was allowed to see the true beauty and glory of the divine character as opposed to the degradations which accompanied the worship of false gods and with which he would have been all too familiar?

The Terms of the Call

It will now be useful to look at the implications of the call of God for the outworking of His purposes through subsequent ages, without neglecting applications to the spiritual lives of believers to-day.

The three-fold renunciation required (thy country, thy kindred, thy father's house) has been seen as corresponding to the world, the flesh and the devil. Abraham's country could be fairly regarded as representing the world, and we have already ventured to see in Terah, the old man, an illustration of the flesh, but the interpretation of the father's house as the devil does not seem very apt. However, it is safe to look at the whole situation as involving a complete break with his former life, which is the only safe course for a child of God to-day.

A Complete Break

The Saviour's conditions for discipleship are certainly very

3

sweeping: "Whosoever ... forsaketh not all that he hath, he cannot be my disciple" (Luke 14:33). Every Christian should challenge his heart as to how far he is prepared to follow the Lord, but, as in all matters, it is important to take a balanced view lest misguided zeal turn to fanaticism (Rom 10:2). No doubt under the immediate conditions those who were prepared to accompany the Lord in His earthly ministry had literally to forsake all, but only a limited number were actually called upon to do this. There have, of course, been cases in the history of the Church, even down to the present day, where servants of Christ in special cases have been called upon to forsake all. However it is clear from the general tone of the NT that whilst complete devotion of heart should mark us all, the will of God for the great majority of believers is that they should live quietly and peaceably in all godliness and honesty (1 Tim 2:2). The Lord did not call every one of those who loved Him to follow Him in the literal sense. The cured demoniac who actually made a moving appeal to be allowed to be with his Deliverer was in fact told to return home to witness to his neighbours. This he did so effectively that he accomplished more for the glory of Christ and the blessing of others than he would otherwise have been able to do. Time given to a careful comparison of Mark 5:1-20; 7:31-37; Luke 8:37-40 will be well spent.

Get Out ... I Will: Come Out ... I Will

Quite often God's commands are linked with promises expressed by "I will". Here God's call to "get out" was coupled with wonderful promises expressed in the four-fold "I will". It will be interesting in due course to notice in more detail the fact that the call in 17:1 was followed by a seven-fold use of the same expression, but for the moment it will suffice to notice that, whereas the initial call in Ur came from God in His character as the God of glory, in ch. 17 God spoke in His character as the Almighty God. These two passages should be compared with 2 Cor 6:14-18 where the Christian is exhorted, like Abraham, to avoid any unequal yoke with unbelievers, and more specifically to "come out" from an idolatrous world. The compensations offered to Abraham had a unique character specially applicable to him, but it would be well to consider the immense rewards offered to the separated believer in the enjoyment of a special relationship with God, again expressed in a four-fold "I will"; interestingly enough, He speaks in His character as the Lord Almighty.

The First "I Will": The Land

The rather negative "get out" has a positive counterpart in "unto the land that I will show thee". The RV inserts the article — not the somewhat vague "a land" but the more definite "the land". Not any ordinary land, but "the land" for which God had a special care; His eye was upon it "from the beginning of the year even unto the end of the year", for the sake of His people, though they often failed and grieved Him. To encourage them to go in and possess the land it was described as flowing with milk and honey, watered by the rain of heaven in contrast to Egypt from which they came, where irrigation depended on the river Nile (Deut 11:9-12). No doubt it was equally fertile in Abraham's time, although in his case the contrast would be with the artificial canals running from the rivers Tigris and Euphrates. It is not known whether God communicated any of this to Abraham, but it is probable that he had some knowledge of its fertility seeing that constant caravan traffic circulated news from country to country.

The above description is borne out by evidence available to-day that Palestine was once a fertile land until (from the natural standpoint) it suffered mis-management, whilst (from the divine standpoint) it was discipline for Israel's departure from God (vv. 13-17). The amazing cultivation achieved in recent decades indicates the possibilities when the promised rainfall again becomes adequate (Isa 30:23).

Would it be wrong to think that God's special interest in the land had a deeper reason than the interests of His earthly people, namely that it was where His well-beloved Son would live that life which was wholly pleasing to His Father and die that death which would lay the sure foundation for the accomplishment of all of God's purposes for Jew and Gentile? Then God's eyes rested on it not merely from the beginning of the year to the end of the year, but were focussed for every single minute of those wonderful three and thirty years on the one Servant who, unlike disappointing Israel, never failed or grieved Him in thought or word or deed.

It is not known at what point Abraham was enlightened to foresee Christ's day, but he would have known from the promises given him that Canaan was the land God had chosen. Did he realise when walking to and fro that he was covering ground where in a far-off day the holiest of feet would tread?

The Second "I Will": A Great Nation

The second "I will" expressed God's intention to make of Abraham a great nation, amplified in 18:18 to "a great and mighty nation". In our sophisticated age when anxious uncertainty about the future tends to concentrate attention on making the most of the present, it is difficult to enter fully into what this promise meant in an age when posterity was regarded in some sense as an extension of one's personality, and the extinction of one's name through childlessness was viewed as a calamity. See remarks on 15:2. For the moment we take for granted, leaving proof until later, that the great and mighty nation was to be Israel. Her greatness, however, was not to consist in her numbers or the size of her territory but in something far more important, her destiny as a chosen people to be God's witness to the nations and a channel of blessing to the world. Many hundreds of years later Moses in his great address to all Israel (Deut 5:1) reminded them that when God chose them they were "the fewest of all people" (cp. Deut 26:5). God loved them because He loved them (7:7,8). Can we offer any other explanation for His gracious dealings with us? Why, when we were dead in trespasses and sins did He quicken us with Christ? There is no answer other than "for his great love wherewith he loved us" (Eph 2:4, 5).

The Third "I Will": Blessed And Made A Blessing

The third "I will" carries three implications:
1. Personal blessing to Abraham
   In the OT, broadly speaking material prosperity is seen as evidence of God's blessing and was so interpreted by Abraham's servant, "The Lord hath blessed my master greatly ... he hath given him flocks and herds, and silver and gold and menservants and maidservants, and camels and asses" (24:35). Cp. 26:12-14.
   However, the OT outlook is far from being materialistic. It sees the dangers of riches, if the heart turns from the God who gave them (Deut 6:10-12). Agur saw the perils

both of poverty and riches, hence his remarkable prayer to
be preserved from both (Prov 30:7-9). There is very
definite stress on the blessedness of enjoying a right
relation with God, and in having it restored when lost
through disobedience. (Cp. Psa 1:1; 32:1, and other Psalms
which commence in the same way.)

Our own experience of human nature enables us to
appreciate the mental and emotional stresses through
which Abraham passed, but it is much more difficult to
penetrate into his deeper inner spiritual exercises; however
it is unthinkable that he could fail to have been moved by
the tremendous privileges granted him in his growing
knowledge of, and fellowship with, God. His heart would
have gone with the words of Ter Steegen —

O God, Thou art far other
Than men have dreamed and taught,
Unuttered in all language
Unpictured in all thought.
Thou God art God
He only learns what that great name must be
Whose raptured heart within him burns
Because he walks with Thee.

The potential is there for us all because we have already,
in the purpose of God, been blessed with every spiritual
blessing in Christ Jesus (Eph 1:3). This epistle is a vantage
point from which we can survey our spiritual Canaan and
be challenged to walk through the length and breadth of it,
or, to use Paul's own phraseology, to "comprehend with all
saints what is the breadth and length and depth and height,
and to know the love of Christ which passeth knowledge,
that ye might be filled with (unto) all the fulness of God"
(Eph 3:18-19).

2. I will make thy name great. How different from the empty
   dream of would-be Babel builders, "Let us make us a name"
   (11:4), who only left an uncompleted city as their dismal
   memorial. God's promise was fulfilled in Abraham's
   lifetime, as witness the tributes of the children of Heth,
   "Thou art a mighty prince among us" (23:6) and of his own
   servant "he is become great" (24:35), but much more in all
   history to the present day. Not only is his name known

throughout the whole world, but it is probably true to say that no name is held in greater reverence, at least by the devout, save that of the One who is his Lord and ours. How wonderfully has the angel's promise to Mary been fulfilled, "Thou shalt call his name Jesus ... and he shall be great and shall be called the Son of the Most High" (Luke 1:31, 32).

Few Christians have attained any great degree of prominence in the world; most can aspire no higher than to be well thought of in their little spheres. Enough for them that their names are enrolled in the only place that really matters. Even to the disciples, flushed with their success in service, the Saviour said, "In this rejoice not that the spirits are subject to you, but rather rejoice because your names are written in heaven" (Luke 10:20). Whose ambition need rise higher than to be among the overcomers who confess Christ before men and whose names Christ will confess before His Father and before His angels (Matt 10:32; Rev 3:5)?

3. Thou shalt be a blessing. The RV draws attention, not so much to the divine intention as to human responsibility: "Be thou a blessing". It is wonderful to know the undeserved blessing of God, and all would echo Jacob's confession, "I am not worthy of the least of all the mercies and of all the truth which thou hast shewed unto thy servant" (32:10), but in some respects, it is an even greater privilege to be, in turn, a channel of blessing to others. This Abraham was commanded to be. Success in life is assessed by many different standards and many make personal gain their objective, only to discover when it is too late that they have made a tragic blunder. According to the only Assessor worth listening to, if it were possible for an individual to gain the whole world and in the process lose what he was really meant to be he is the sorry loser. Seeing that we have only one life to live how appalling to discover at last that we have lived for that which can never satisfy (Luke 9:25).

Although the record does not tell us all we would like to know (what a bulky volume would be needed!), we cannot doubt that Abraham walking with God must have exerted a beneficent influence on many; the sincere piety of his eldest servant brought out so charmingly in ch. 24 may be taken as an example. Nevertheless, the record does not shrink from indicating that it was otherwise when he was out of the line of God's will as in Egypt (v. 17).

Next to the satisfaction such as Enoch must have felt in receiving the assurance that he had pleased God, surely there is no greater joy in life than being used as a channel of blessing to others. A certain degree of responsibility rests on us ("be thou a blessing") not only in being willing but also in enjoying the right spiritual condition, "sanctified and meet for the master's use" (2 Tim 2:21).

The Fourth I Will

Here again there are three points to be considered:
1. "I will bless them that bless thee". Those who, favourably impressed by Abraham, wished him well would in turn be blessed by God. Abraham's son Isaac incorporated the same idea in blessing his son, and Balaam, speaking under the compulsion of the Spirit of God, applied the same principle to the nation of Israel (27:29; Num 24:9). OT history affords examples of how God's treatment of other nations depended on their treatment of Israel. During the christian era God's special relationship with Israel is in abeyance, but this does not mean that He has ceased to be interested in her welfare (Rom 11:28). In the perspective of history it is possible to see how the fortunes of some nations have been linked to their attitude to the scattered Jews. In the present kaleidoscopic political scene, Israel is involved in the turmoil, and we are too close to rapidly moving events to discern any clear pattern of this principle, but we may be sure it will emerge eventually. This has a voice to us as individuals, for we are exhorted to pray for the peace of Jerusalem, and those who in this and other ways show their love for the nation from which our Saviour sprang are promised a reward (Psa 122:6).
2. "I will curse him that curseth thee". Although we are giving separate consideration to this, both blessing and cursing are bracketed together here and in the two passages quoted above (27:29; Num 24:9).

The idea of God cursing offends the sensibilities of those who confine their conception of curse to the petulant imprecation of some malevolent person, such as Shimei who cursed king David (2 Sam 16:5). In the case of God it is the pronouncement of righteous retribution based on His just displeasure. Examples are given in Deut 27:13-26.

There does not appear to be any specific instance of this principle in the experience of Abraham. God's rebuke of Pharaoh and Abimelech can hardly be regarded as examples because their actions were not motivated by malevolence toward Abraham. As with blessing, the principle emerges more clearly in the attitude of nations to Israel, but usually in the slow processes of history. However, at the climax of this present age when Christ returns in power and glory it will be dramatically illustrated by Christ's blessing on those who had succoured Israel in her age-end troubles and the pronouncement of a curse on those who had been indifferent to her plight (Matt 25:36-46).

3. "In thee shall all families of the earth be blessed". This does not mean every separate household-group but all the nations of the world as is made clear in 18:18 and 22:18. As mentioned earlier, Abraham's life must have left its impression on others for the glory of God, but obviously this promise looks forward to the distant future; he did not live to see it fulfilled, but he died relying on it in faith (Heb 11:13). Accordingly the angel's message from heaven on Mount Moriah replaces "in thee" with "in thy seed", and "all families" with "all nations". That this goes beyond his immediate descendants is clear from the fact that the angel here speaks of his seed being as the stars of heaven and as the sand which is on the seashore (22:17, 18). As the promise is later repeated to Isaac in the same terms, it is clear that the seed is the nation of Israel (26:4; Rom 9:7).

As the acorn to the mighty oak so is this promise pregnant with the great scheme of OT prophecy; it is hoped therefore that the reader will agree that its wide implications should be considered. Volumes have been written on this tremendous theme, but no more will be attempted here than an outline of what we see to be the purposes of God summed up in these few words to Abraham, whilst respecting those who may sincerely see difficulties.

Israel A Kingdom Of Priests

It was God's intention that the nation of Israel which sprang from Abraham should be "a kingdom of priests and a holy nation" through whom the blessing of God would be mediated to the nations of the world (Exod 19:6). Sadly Israel came to think of their privileges as evidences of being God's favourites, an attitude of mind which came to regard religious observations as satisfying His requirements. An exclusive spirit developed which mistook isolation for separation, and the Jews despised those to whom they should have been a blessing, even referring to them as Gentile dogs. The result was that the name of God was blasphemed among the Gentiles because, while Jews boasted in having God's Law committed to them, they dishonoured that very Law by their transgressions of it (Rom 2:23-24).

They grudged the Gentiles any blessing, and whilst they would not go into the kingdom of heaven in the sense of genuinely submitting to the rule of God, they would prevent others entering in. The extremes to which the Pharisees in general went may be seen from the awful denunciations of the Saviour in the woes pronounced on them by the Saviour in Matt 23. This was solemnly illustrated when the Jews were infuriated at the very idea of despised Gentiles being admitted to blessing (Acts 22:21-23). This surely is a warning voice to the church, which in this age supersedes Israel as God's witness to the world, that we should despise no man but by all means endeavour to save some.

Christ The Seed

At this point it will be appropriate to notice how Paul saw the promised "seed" to be preeminently Christ, through whom the blessing of Abraham comes on the Gentiles (Gal 3:14-16). In this connection it is remarkable that Simeon in blessing God described the child Jesus as "a light to lighten the Gentiles and the glory of thy people Israel". Seeing that in the same passage Simeon is said to have been waiting for the consolation of Israel we would have expected that he would have given Israel priority, but speaking by the Holy Spirit upon him he was guided to place the illumination of the Gentiles first (Luke 2:25-32). Surely this is an intimation, no doubt obscure at the time, of the later revealed mystery that blindness in part has happened to Israel until the fulness of the Gentiles be come in (Rom 11:25). Cp. Paul in Acts 26:23. There will be occasion to go into this more fully after considering Christ as the fulfilment of the promise to Abraham.

Christ a Blessing to Israel, but Rejected

At Pentecost Peter declared to the "men of Israel" that God had sent Jesus to bless them (Acts 3:26), but this was linked with turning from their iniquities, which is a prelude to any blessing. The blessing would have been welcome if it had been in the form of deliverance from the political yoke of the Roman Empire, but the greater blessing of deliverance from the bondage of sin made no appeal. So although Christ came unto His own (i.e. His own things, that which pertained to Him) His own (i.e. His own people, the Jews) did not receive Him, although there were happy individual exceptions who believed on Him and so became children of God (John 1:11, 12). On occasions He was greeted with superficial enthusiasm which reached its climax when He rode into Jerusalem and was greeted by excited crowds chanting, "Hosanna to the Son of David. Blessed is he that cometh in the name of the Lord" (Matt 21:9). The enthusiasm soon evaporated, and the Lord was decisively rejected and delivered up to crucifixion. Although Peter declared the enormity of their guilt in unmistakable terms, he nevertheless recognised that it was done in ignorance: "And now brethren I wot that through ignorance ye did it, as also your rulers". Was he thinking of the Saviour's plea on the cross, "Father forgive them for they know not what they do" and so was emboldened to affirm that God was ready to answer that plea by offering to bring in times of refreshing by sending Jesus to them again? Once more the promise is conditional, "Repent ye therefore and be converted that your sins may be blotted out" (Acts 3:12-21). Though it is happily true that many thousands of Jews in Jerusalem did respond, the majority rejected the gospel preached by the apostles, and before long Stephen had to denounce the leaders as stiffnecked and resisting the Holy Spirit. For this he was stoned to death.

Like them, their fellow-Jews scattered over the Roman Empire, rejected the claims of Christ when the gospel was brought to them, as for example at Antioch in Pisidia where Paul had to say, "It was necessary that the word of God should first have been spoken to you, but seeing you put it from you and judge yourselves unworthy of eternal life, lo we turn to the Gentiles" (Acts 13:46).

Christ The Channel Of Blessing To All Believers

The offer of the gospel implicit in the promise of blessing in Abraham was now thrown open to the world at large, as Paul's words to the Gentile believers in Galatia testify: "Christ hath redeemed us from the curse of the law ... that the blessing of Abraham might come on the Gentiles through Jesus Christ" (Gal 3:13, 14).

Now the believing Jew ceases to be a Jew and the Gentile believer ceases to be a Gentile: "For ye are all the children of God by faith in Christ ... There is neither Jew nor Greek ... for ye are all one in Christ Jesus" (Gal 3:28).

In Eph 2 speaking of former Jews and Gentiles it is said, "He (Christ) is our peace who hath made both one ... that he might reconcile both unto God in one body by the cross". Cp. 1:22, 23 concerning the church which is His body.

In this Church age the blessings of the gospel are open to all who are prepared to yield to Christ as Lord and Saviour, and God endows such with every spiritual blessing in Christ Jesus. The distinctive place which Israel occupied has been forfeited, and now "there is no difference between the Jew and the Greek for the same Lord over all is rich unto all that call upon him" (Rom 10:12).

Nevertheless, in the following chapter it is plainly indicated that the eclipse of Israel is not permanent: "God has not cast away his people which he foreknew" (v. 2). The seeming contradiction in v. 15, "the casting away of them", is due to two different Greek words being translated similarly in English. The first (apōtheō) means to cast away in the sense of abandoning them, which God has *not* done; nevertheless they *have* been cast away (apobolē) in the sense of being put aside. This is only for the time being. Blindness in part has happened to Israel but only until the fulness of the Gentiles has come in, i.e. until God's present purpose in visiting the Gentiles to take out of them a people for His name has been completed. Then the ruins of Israel will be rebuilt. See Acts 15:13-18; Rom 11:25.

Israel's Future

Despite the foregoing some maintain that there is no future for Israel as a special people for God, which is tantamount to saying that the numerous explicit and glowing prophecies of future blessing and glory for Israel will never be fulfilled. When we consider how godly Jews, generation after generation, and often in the darkest days, cherished hopes based on the entrancing prospects portrayed by prophet after prophet, the very thought that all such hopes based on solemn promises of God will prove a delusion is enough to fill us with horror. In view of the Saviour's repeated assurances that the Scriptures must be fulfilled, how can we dare to write off these prophecies as virtually meaningless? See, for example Matt 5:17-18; John 10:35.

Some who could not bring themselves to accept that and yet fight shy of a literal interpretation take refuge in an attempt to spiritualise these promises and see them fulfilled in the Church. Since the Church has been blessed with every spiritual blessing in Christ Jesus there is nothing strange in the spiritual blessings of Israel being enjoyed by the Church. But the claim that this satisfies the prophecies poses more problems than it solves. There is a preponderance of very specific elements in the prophecies quite inapplicable to anything short of Israel as a renewed nation settled in the land that God reserved for them. To go into this in detail would require a volume; instead we ask two questions based on passages in Luke's Gospel. How are we to see fulfilled in the Church the angel's promise to Mary concerning the Saviour, "The Lord God shall give him the throne of his father David and he shall reign over the house of Jacob for ever and ever"? Again —in what conceivable sense can the ministry of the apostles in the church be regarded as fulfilling the Lord's promise to them that they should "sit on thrones judging the twelve tribes of Israel" (Luke 1:32, 33; 22:30)?

No, although we have seen that in the present age believing Jews and believing Gentiles are reconciled unto God in one body, Paul's language is quite different when dealing with the purposes of God with the nation of Israel, for in Rom 11 he emphasises the distinction between Jew and Gentile as such: "When the fulness of the Gentiles has come in, all Israel shall be saved, as it is written, There shall come out of Sion the Deliverer and shall turn away ungodliness from Jacob" (v. 26).

The Return Of Christ For Israel

Quite distinct from the return of Christ for the Church, there are clear promises that He will return for Israel. To the promise already quoted we may add the words of Christ when sorrowfully he announced to Jerusalem that their house (once the House of God —the Temple) was left unto them desolate, yet added, "Ye shall not see me henceforth until ye shall say, Blessed is he that cometh in the name of the Lord". This will be a genuine welcome to Christ as the result of a great work of the Spirit, in contrast to the superficial enthusiasm of the excited multitudes when they chanted these words which would soon be superseded by the cry for His crucifixion (Matt 21:9; 23:39).

Before we turn our thoughts to the blessing to be brought to Israel, and the blessing to flow to others through them, it would be well to look briefly at the first effect on the nations by the return of Christ in power and glory. He will execute judgment on the godless as grass is mowed by the scythe of the reaper. It is a common sight in the country at hay harvest time to see luscious grass cut down so close to the ground that very little is left, and the uninitiated would think that considerable time would have to elapse before the grass could grow again sufficiently to provide pasture for cattle. Yet with gentle showers of rain the grass soon flourishes again.

The Nations Blessed

So it will be with the nations. This is the idea behind the beautiful image in Psa 72: "He shall come down like rain upon the mown grass: as showers that water the earth. In his days shall the righteous flourish and abundance of peace so long as the moon endureth". "His name shall endure for ever ... men shall be blessed in him; all nations shall call him blessed" (Psa 72:6, 7, 17). Then will be fulfilled the promise to Abraham: "in thy seed shall all nations of the earth be blessed". Initially through Christ as "the seed" and then, when Israel has been judged and the believing remnant renewed by the regenerating Spirit of God to form a spiritual, though literal, nation, through it the blessing brought by Christ will flow to the nations of the world.

Israel A Blessing To The Nations

The student will find pleasure in a close study of Hosea 14:4-9, but it must suffice now to notice that God promises to the true Israel, "I will heal their backsliding ... I will be as the

dew unto Israel", a delightful symbol of the gentle refreshing
of the Holy Spirit. Then as the head of the nations (Deut
28:12, 13) Israel will be in their midst, in the central place, and
reflecting the influence of their gracious Messiah will be "as
dew from the LORD, as the showers upon the grass" (Micah
5:7). So "It shall come to pass in the last days (RV latter days)
that the mountain of the LORD's house shall be established in
the top (marg. at the head) of the mountains ... and all nations
shall flow unto it. And many people shall say ... let us go to the
house of the God of Jacob; and he will teach us of his ways and
we will walk in his paths" (Isa 2:2-3). Is it any wonder that the
appearance of the God of glory to Abraham has been likened
to the bursting of a spring from a great reservoir hidden in the
depths of the everlasting hills, growing into a mighty river
winding its way through the changing scenes of history to the
end of time and eventually flowing into the boundless ocean
of eternity?

Sharing Abraham's Privileges

Is it possible to see in our lives anything bearing some
correspondence to God's self-revelation to Abraham?

1. Seeing the glory. The conversion of those whose up-
bringing has been against a Christian background usually
conforms to a broadly similar pattern, with the result that the
true wonder of the experience is often lost sight of. Some in
after years learn to look back on it with growing wonder as
more and more of the tremendous issues involved grip their
souls, athough it may safely be said that none of us will ever
realise its full significance until we stand around the throne of
God:

> When I stand before the throne
> Dressed in a beauty not my own,
> When I see thee as thou art
> Love Thee with unsinning heart,
> Then, Lord, shall I fully know,
> Not till then how much I owe.
> R. Murray M'Cheyne

In this connection it will be found very rewarding to make
careful comparisons between the Gospel accounts of the

Transfiguration with Peter's reflections more than 30 years later, showing how he had come to a deeper understanding and appreciation of that experience (2 Pet 1:16-21).

Whatever account we may have given of our conversion in terms of deciding to accept Christ, the fact is that just as God broke into the life of Abraham, so God took the initiative in breaking into our individual lives by His convicting and regenerating Spirit. The devil had blinded our minds. With what object? To prevent the light of the gospel of the glory of Christ, who is the image of God from dawning on us.

But the devil was circumvented; God, who commanded the light to shine out of primeval darkness, shone into our hearts, to give the light of the knowledge of the glory of God in the face of Jesus Christ (2 Cor 4:3-6).

Moreover, an on-going revelation can be enjoyed if the believer, with the eyes of the heart enlightened by the Spirit of God (Eph 1:18 RV), can share with David the experience of beholding the glory of the LORD in the sanctuary (Psa 63:2). Cp. Psa 27:4; 96:6.

The same theme occurs in 2 Cor 3:18, but expositors differ somewhat in their interpretation. To those who follow the AV, the mirror represents the Scriptures in which the enlightened believer may enjoy a reflected vision of the glory of Christ and in consequence is progressively changed into increasing moral likeness to Him by the Spirit of God. Those who accept the RV see the believer's Christ-like character as a mirror in which others see the glory of Christ reflected. This they feel is more in accord with the context, i.e. the glory shining in the face of Moses (v. 7). Even so, the point we have been making is unaffected because that shining was surely the reflection of the glory he had been allowed to see in the Mount. See Exod 34:4-6 and the notes on 33:18-19.

The believer who is enabled to enter into the full enjoyment of the privilege available to him in this respect, is not likely to feel deprived because his experience is not the exact parallel of Abraham's sight of the God of glory.

Paul, in 1 Cor 13:12, speaks of seeing in a glass dimly at present but hereafter face to face. Similarly John, after speaking of a partial revelation, looks forward to seeing Christ as He is. This complete revelation will effect an instantaneous and permanent transformation — we shall be like him. The believer to whom such a hope is a living reality will know its present effect in a process of purification (1 John

3:2, 3).

2. Hearing God's Call. But what shall be said about Abraham hearing the word of God calling him out of Ur and making such far reaching promises? Certainly this was in accord with the purposes of God in a vast realm, in contrast to our more limited niche in the purpose of God, but have we had no such experience as the call and promises of God?

Faith cometh by hearing and hearing by the word of God. But does this merely mean by hearing the Scripture quoted? Millions hear the Scriptures quoted without any effect upon heart and conscience whereas others are arrested and turn to God in repentance and to faith in the Lord Jesus. What is the difference? It is that the voice of God in His word was heard by the inner conscience, actually a more enduring experience than an audible voice.

Thus Paul could say of the Thessalonians, "our gospel came not unto you in word only but also in power and in the Holy Spirit". "When ye received the word of God which ye heard of us, ye received it not as the word of men but as it is in truth the word of God, which effectively worketh also in you that believe" (1 Thess 1:5; 2:13).

God's communication with Abraham was of a special character, but there is such a thing as a personal experience of God speaking to an individual through His Word in such a way that he feels justified in the assurance that he has had a promise from God for himself. David could say, "Remember thy word unto thy servant upon which thou hast caused me to hope; this is my comfort in my affliction for thy word has quickened me" (Psa 119:49-50).

It is not necessarily a flight of poetic fancy when a believer sings, "I heard the voice of Jesus say", or when the poet said:

Ages have past since at Thy word
Men marvelled as they heard.
And still our hearts within us burn
Whilst listening to Thy Word.
                    (Cf. Luke 4:22)

River And Ripple

Whilst we have thought of the outworking of God's age-spanning purpose through Abraham growing like a mighty river, most of us must feel in comparison that our lives can be little more than a stone dropped in to a small pond. Certainly it causes some ripples, but they gradually diminish until the movement is lost at the edge of the pond. There is this difference: anything accomplished in and through us by the Spirit of God is of eternal value.

But though causing only a ripple, the life of even the remotest believer must not be under-valued. When Paul, in a worshipful spirit, spoke of the immense privileges he enjoyed in the great work committed to him, he seems to have realised that many of his readers would be humble folk occupying a small sphere and likely to feel that they did not count. So he spoke of himself as less than the least of all saints, who had been granted grace for his task. Then later when speaking of those massive truths which apply to all believers without distinction (Eph 4:4-6) he went on to show that every individual life has its significance for "unto every one of us is given grace according to the measure of the gift of Christ" (Eph 3:7-11; 4:4-7).

Elisha is the prominent figure in the story of Naaman; the latter out of his experience with the prophet, became a witness to the true God in the influential sphere he occupied in his native Syria, yet the whole sequence of events was set in motion by the simple though courageous testimony of a slave girl who is not even named. There must be very few who have not come across cases where it can be seen in retrospect that humble and restricted lives have made impressions the ultimate results of which have exceeded anything that could have been expected at the time.

In a spiritual sense believers are of the seed of Abraham and they "walk in the steps of that faith of our father Abraham" (Rom 4:12, 16). In doing so we, too, shall not only be blessed but be made a blessing. Then none of us will have lived in vain, for what can the world offer comparable with the privilege of being at least a link in the chain of blessing to others?

Who can fail to be moved by the lines which enshrine sentiments expressed by the saintly Samuel Rutherford, minister of Anwoth, when in prison, awaiting death?

Fair Anwoth by the Solway
Thou still to me art dear,
E'en from the verge of heaven
I drop for thee a tear.

4

Yet if one soul from Anwoth
Meet me at God's right hand,
My heaven will be two heavens
In Immanuel's land.

Chapter IV
Entering Canaan

(Gen 12:4-9)

So Abraham Departed

Taking everything into consideration it could be argued that Abraham had been under an obligation to stay in Haran for Terah's sake, but, if so, it was an obligation he had incurred by failing to leave his kindred in the first place. However, the death of the old man set him free to resume his pilgrim path. Had he stayed on in Haran he would have jeopardised his whole future as a servant of God.

Our case is quite different; we are debtors to God, we owe Him everything; but we are not debtors to the flesh — we owe it nothing. It never did us any good, only evil, and we have not the slightest obligation to it. If we nevertheless "live after the flesh we shall die" —it will spell death to all that is best — but if through the Spirit (the only adequate power) we mortify (marg. make to die) the deeds of the body we shall live — live in the real worthwhile sense (Rom 8:12, 13). Otherwise the great privilege of acceptable service to God will be lost.

As The Lord Had Spoken

If this had been no more than the narrator's comment it would have been a generous touch, but when we remember that this was written by the inspiration of the Spirit it acquires a deeper charm, reflecting the Lord's pleasure in Abraham's response by connecting it with the original call, as if there had been no delay. Heb 11:8 has already been noticed in this connection.

When our short-comings are humbly acknowledged and rectified, God does not upbraid us as some foolish folk do when we confess we have made a mistake. He finds no pleasure in keeping alive the memory of our failures, although the recollection of them should humble us. He prefers to forgive and forget. He promises to remember our sins no more (this is more than forgetting) and not to forget (this is more than remembering) what has been done for His sake (Heb 6:10; 10:17). James tells us that if we discover our lack of wisdom and ask God to supply the lack He will give liberally without upbraiding. When the servant of Elisha expressed his contrition for his carelessness in losing the axe head, by which alone he could work effectively, the prophet did not chide him, but brought the axe head within his reach and bade him take it up again. Neither did the servant continue to lament his failure, but took the axe head gratefully and, we may hope, thereafter used it effectively (2 Kings 6:5-7).

Seventy-five Years Old

This is a useful note in that it enables us, by comparing it with other mentions of his age, to get some idea of how the many events of his life fitted into a time-scale; undoubtedly it was intended here to prompt other reflections. The length of time spent in Haran cannot be established, but however successful it may have been materially from a spiritual standpoint it was wasted. Precious time was lost and nearly half his life was gone (25:5). A happier thought is that he still had a hundred years left in which to serve God. He could not have known this, although he was later assured that he would live to a good old age (15:15). We are not given such guarantees for we do not know what a day may bring forth (Prov 27:1; Jas 4:14).

Even if we have cause to be humbled by wasted opportunities it is futile to lose more opportunities in fruitless repining:

Oh the years of sinning wasted
Could I but recall them now,
I would give them to my Saviour
To His will I'd gladly bow.

This may be a pious sentiment, but it is totally devoid of reality, firstly because past years are beyond recall, and secondly because if we are not now making the most of present privileges we would make no better use of restored opportunities.

Mistaken souls mourn over past failures and lament

pathetically that they cannot *feel* that the Lord has forgiven them; the truth is that they cannot forgive themselves. Unsuspected no doubt, this is only injured pride at having fallen from the pedestal they fondly imagined they were on. If we honestly confess not merely that we are sinners in a general sense, but the specific sins of which we have been made conscious, then God is both faithful and just to forgive us those sins (1 John 1:9). The promise says nothing about *feeling* forgiven; it assures us that we have been forgiven. The joy of forgiveness comes when we accept the glorious fact by faith and welcome being cleansed from all unrighteousness. Thus the ghosts of vain regret will haunt our souls no more.

Resolution

The recurrence of the word "departed" in v. 4 serves to emphasise Abraham's decision. It is the translation of a slightly different word, as though to carry the idea of resolution, more clearly brought out in v. 5.

It would also appear that Lot was beginning to show some initiative, for in contrast to 11:31, "Terah ... took Lot", we read that Lot "went" with his uncle, although the general impression remains that he was a somewhat pliable character, for almost immediately this is replaced by a statement that Abraham "took" him. Probably he was tempted to remain in Haran rather than be uprooted again but was not resolute enough to stand entirely on his own feet.

The idea of resolution is also brought out in the obviously intentional link between 11:31, "They went forth ... to go into the land of Canaan; and they came unto Haran and dwelt there", and 12:5, "they went forth to go into the land of Canaan; and into the land of Canaan they came". So despite all that had gone before they were at last where God intended Abraham to be. Nevertheless, although the aspect of human responsibility to yield the obedience of faith is thus recognised, it is interesting to note how the element of divine sovereignty is brought out in 15:7, "I am the Lord that brought thee out of Ur of the Chaldees to give thee this land to inherit it". Cf. Josh 24:3; Neh 9:7.

This is an encouragement to all who wish to enter into the enjoyment of their spiritual Canaan. Decision and resolution are needed on our part, but human weakness can rely on divine aid.

The above Scriptures do not say God brought Abraham out of Haran — it almost seems another oblique way of intimating that Haran is best forgotten.

Canaan's Typical Meaning

It may be appropriate here to point out that, despite what many hymns assert, Canaan does not typify heaven but rather the spiritual heritage the believer has in Christ, into the enjoyment of which he is urged to enter. Many of Abraham's experiences when in the land are utterly inconsistent with this false idea, but we need not go further than our present portion — the immediate mention of the presence of the abominable Canaanites in the land is enough to dispel this notion. Nor is Canaan different in the time of the Israelites; this, of course, is the background of the hymns in question. Israel had to fight its way into the inheritance and dispossess the resident tribes. In this there was sometimes defeat in consequence of sin; in fact they never succeeded in ridding the land entirely of their foes. A very curious picture of heaven by any standard!

No. Canaan, the inheritance of God's earthly people, serves better as a type of our spiritual inheritance in Christ. The book of Joshua which records Israel's entry into the promised land finds its spiritual counterpart in the Epistle to the Ephesians, where the believer is seen as having been blessed with every spiritual blessing. Doctrinally this epistle is a spiritual mountain from which the believer may survey his inheritance as Abraham was shown large stretches of Canaan from a vantage point (13:14), and just as he was told to walk through the length and breadth of it, so Paul prayed that his readers might come to know the breadth and length and depth and height of what is theirs in Christ. Possession of Canaan was resisted by foes of flesh and blood, but we wrestle not against flesh and blood but against evil spiritual forces intent on preventing our enjoyment of what God has bestowed upon us (Eph 1:3; 3:14-20; 6:12).

We have seen that it was by divine enabling that Abraham left Ur and entered Canaan. Similarly Paul indicates that the practical enjoyment of our inheritance depends on being "strengthened with might by his Spirit in the inner man", and then concludes with a doxology to the One who "is able to do exceeding abundantly above all that we ask or think, according to the power that worketh in us". Why then should our foes be allowed to withstand us?

The River Jordan: A Digression

The mistaken notion that Canaan is an illustration of heaven has led to such regrettable consequences that a digression from our main theme will, hopefully, be regarded as fully justified. Once accepted, this view of Canaan requires us to see the river Jordan, by which the Israelites entered Canaan, as representing death by which the believer enters heaven. So we are invited to sing such nonsense as Jordan's tide rolling over us, or having to ford death's cold sullen stream, in flagrant disregard of the fact that the bed of Jordan was crossed on dry ground. These and many such frightening metaphors make death a terrible bogey to many poorly-instructed souls, who ought to be enjoying the comfort to be derived from the NT's consistent use of totally different conceptions of death; it is even described as the believer's servant. Death is our servant to usher us into the Lord's presence (1 Cor 3:22). Indignation at the way in which many have been robbed of the peace they should enjoy must not be allowed to take up further space. We return to Abraham, and his first recorded experience in Canaan.

Sichem: Also Called Shechem And Sychar

Since the distance from Ur to Sichem is about 400 miles, it follows that the journey must have been in stages, occupying something like four weeks. He could have little imagined that the time would come that his grandson Jacob would drive his flocks and herds on the same journey; it is fairly safe to assume that if Jacob saw advantages in the route via Jabbok and across Jordan the same considerations would weigh with Abraham. But what of the incident which was to take place here, not two generations but near two thousand years later? When Abraham was given to foresee Christ's day all we know of the effect was that he was glad. No doubt his conceptions of the glory of the coming Christ were conditioned to some extent by the far-reaching implications of God's promises, but we can only conjecture what he actually anticipated. Would he have been astonished to learn that God's Anointed, weary with His journey, would sit on the wall of a well (near the site of his first altar) and, talking kindly to a poor sinful Samaritan woman about worshipping God as Father, would lead her to recognise Him as the Saviour of the world, the Giver of eternal life (John 4)?

Equally as exhilarating as the microscopic examination of the minute detail of Scripture is the telescopic view, tracing over long stretches of time God's over all superintendence of events great and small. If angels now desire to look into these things to discern the manifold ("much varied, many sided") wisdom of God, surely one of the joys of heaven will be the restrospective view of the whole panorama of human history revealing how innumerable threads, even in the lives of individuals whether prominent or obscure, have been skilfully woven into God's grand and perfect design (1 Pet 1:12; Eph 3:10, 11).

Sichem: The Canaanites and the Altar

In Abraham's time Sichem was of considerable importance, but, of course, he would not have settled in the town but in the adjacent countryside. The "plain of Moreh" apparently means the "oak of Moreh", perhaps referring to a notable oak under which Abraham pitched his own tent, whilst no doubt other trees provided shade for his staff.

Here the Lord appeared to him for the first time since he left Ur, thereby expressing approval of his entry into the land, and encouraging him when he probably felt uneasy in his new environment. The apparently incidental remark that the "Canaanite was then in the land" has an ominous undertone in light of what is revealed about these people (13:6; 24:3; Deut 20:17, 18; Psa 106:38).

That the same God who had appeared to him in Ur should also appear to him in Sichem would have greater significance for him than we might at first suppose. We must remember that this was an early stage in his walk with God, and that he lived in an age which might be called the dawn of a new phase in revelation. As the inheritors of a revelation which developed through the centuries and culminated in the manifestation of God in Christ we are apt to forget that, in comparison, Abraham was only emerging from the night of paganism. He had much to learn about God, and it is interesting to see how new truth was imparted (14:19; 15:1; 17:1; 18:25; 21:33). Nor must we forget that, although we have *available* to us the final revelation of God in Christ, we are far from a *full appreciation* of it. Happy are we if, in line with Col 1:10, we are "increasing in the knowledge of God" for we still know only "in part" (1 Cor 13:12).

Although *we* have no difficulty in believing it the all-pervading presence of God throughout the whole universe is not easy to understand; how much more difficult for one who had comparatively recently emerged from that darkness of idolatry with its notion of local gods. Despite his more privileged background, Jacob seems to have been surprised to discover that God was as near to him at Bethel as He was at his home in Beer-sheba (28:16). God's promise to "show" him the land might have prepared Abraham to accept the promise that God would be with him, but the visible confirmation of this must have been a great comfort to his developing faith.

Moreover, although it was possible for Abraham to have inferred an enlargement of the original promise to show him the land, he must have valued the specific declaration, "Unto thy seed will I give this land". The promise was further enlarged later.

Thereupon "he builded an altar unto the Lord who appeared unto him". The connection between the two gives the impression that the building of the altar was prompted by a deep sense of gratitude for God's gracious dealing with him. It was also an act of courage in identifying himself as a worshipper of Jehovah in the midst of a people given over to the worship of false gods, and who would not in any case be favourably disposed toward an unwelcome intruder. (Cf. Ezra 3:3.) This was the first altar that he built; although only three other altars are mentioned, no doubt he built several in different places. But he never built anything other than altars in all his long life.

Apart from his declaration to the king of Sodom and his charge to his servant (14:22; 24:7) there is no record of Abraham bearing verbal witness to God; this does not give us any grounds for saying he did not. But testimony is not necessarily verbal — Abraham's altar spoke for itself. Evidence of devotion and faithfulness to God can be most eloquent; contrariwise, no eloquence makes verbal testimony effective where this is lacking; indeed it may do more harm than good. Among those to whom Peter wrote, were believers who were surrounded by ill-disposed detractors; in these circumstances spoken testimony would have done little good.

They were nevertheless encouraged to hope that their good works would eventually make an impression which would cause their critics to glorify God on some future occasion. The apostle was but echoing the Saviour's words (1 Pet 2:12; Matt 5:11, 16).

Possibly his stay in Sichem was not prolonged — it is likely that he would wish to do some prospecting to better acquaint himself with the land of his adoption.

The Mountain Near Bethel

His next encampment was on a mountain about twenty miles further to the south, and so about ten miles north of Jerusalem. The particularity with which the situation is defined invites attention. It was between Bethel on the west and Hai on the east. The latter is the same place frequently referred to as Ai, especially in the Book of Joshua. The difference is simply due to the fact that here and in 13:3 our translators have indicated that the original has the definite article, meaning 'the heap'. Why they did not do so in other passages is not clear. We are now told that he pitched his tent, perhaps indicating that here a more permanent settlement was contemplated than at Sichem.

It does not need an ingenious mind to see spiritual significance in mountain experiences, but if a hint were needed it is found in the well known words, "And when he had sent the multitude away he went up into a mountain apart to pray" (Matt 14:23). After an exhausting day, thronged by importunate multitudes, the Saviour sought solitude with His Father, or as the hymn puts it, "Where Jesus knelt to share with Thee the silence of eternity interpreted by love". So a mountain carries the idea of communion with God, withdrawn from the distractions of the busy world below (which looks so much smaller when viewed from the height), enjoying a purer air and being able to see wider horizons. None of this needs interpretation to any thoughtful person.

This particular mountain afforded a splendid view of the surrounding country if, as we judge, it was the vantage point from which Lot later saw all the well-watered plain of Jordan, and Abraham was able to look north, south, east and west (13:10, 14).

Hai: The Heap

As mentioned, the name Hai means "the heap" which is suggestive of ruins. At some subsequent date it must have been rebuilt for it stood in the way of Israel's possession of their inheritance until Joshua destroyed it and "made it a heap for ever" (Josh 8:28). How suggestive of a world which has been ruined by sin but which vain man still strives to rebuild in independence of God, but his efforts are doomed to failure.

Bethel: The House Of God

Bethel, which is mentioned more frequently in Scripture than any other town except Jerusalem, means "the house of God". If Abraham looked toward the east, where the sun rises to usher in man's day (and incidentally in the direction in which his former home lay), he would see a heap of ruins. When he looked to the west, where the setting sun ends man's day, he would see the house of God. This beautifully illustrates the Christian's true attitude, turning his back on a world ruined by sin and looking beyond the sunset to his eternal home, enjoying the assurance of the psalmist that, after goodness and mercy have followed him all the days of his life, he will dwell in the house of the Lord for ever.

The Name Of The Lord (Jehovah)

In view of God's statement to Moses that He had not made Himself known to Abraham, Isaac and Jacob by the name Jehovah some have seen difficulty in Abraham building an altar unto the Lord, that is, to Jehovah. One explanation is that the name is introduced retrospectively, in effect saying that, although the God to whom Abraham erected the altar was in fact Jehovah, he did not understand this at the time. In some circumstances such an explanation would be acceptable, but it is hardly adequate to satisfy the statement that he "called on the name of the Lord". Then again in 15:2, 8 he is said to have addressed God as "Lord God" i.e. Adonai-Jehovah. May it not be that through the manifestation mentioned in v. 7 he had come to know that the God whom he had trusted was Jehovah, but without understanding what that name implied, whereas to Moses it revealed that God stood in a special covenant relationship with Israel. This would be a very important point when he was sent with a message of hope to the nation whose knowledge of God had become very dim (Exod 3:13, 14; 6:2-4).

Nevertheless the fact that whereas it is simply said that at Sichem he built an altar "unto the Lord" but that at Bethel he "called on the name of the Lord" does seem to imply that he appreciated this further step in the knowledge of God.

Toward The South

The word "still" ("going on still toward the south") seems to convey, at least, a faint hint that this is not what would have been expected. Certainly it was a move which placed Abraham in a very difficult situation and eventually led to one of the saddest experiences of his long life. We would have liked to pass over it as perhaps the chronicler would have done if he had been free to follow his own inclination. An author writing for fellow-Hebrews who were fanatically proud of their lineage would hardly have chosen to record this and other faults of their revered progenitor. If he were like most biographers he would have presented us with a character so near perfect as to discourage lesser mortals. But the Bible is different. Here we have an account given under the guiding constraint of the Spirit of truth.

This story, then, like all other Scriptures, was written "for our learning" (Rom 15:4) so we must ponder it and lay to heart such lessons as we can learn. This calls for a sympathetic spirit which will try to understand the problems Abraham had to tackle in the south and then the immense pressure of the agonising situation which confronted him in a foreign land. Who dare sit in judgment on a great man whom God called His friend?

From its position in the southern part of Canaan this area was known as the Negeb. Here vegetation was abundant during the rainy season, but in the summer it became almost desert except where a few wadis still ran, or where springs and wells made limited irrigation possible. It certainly seems strange to leave the more fertile north for such an unpromising region, but perhaps he was attracted by the lush but temporary pasture. However, the ensuing summer drought on this occasion was more severe than usual, for not only was there a famine but it is stressed that it was a grievous famine. It is easy to understand what a heavy burden of responsibility and anxiety this would impose upon a man with such large flocks and herds. The question naturally arises, "Why did he not return to the more fertile north?" Was he so conscious of his reputation as an expert that his pride would not allow him to retrace his steps lest it be seen by his herdsmen as an acknowledgement of having blundered? Would he rather put a brave face on it by going farther on into Egypt? If so, instead of saving face a much more serious humiliation awaited him. Of course, he could argue that Egypt often had such abundance that it could provide for others, although it was not exempt from famine as we well know from Joseph's story.

If only he had "enquired of the Lord" as David did when famine struck (2 Sam 21:1), although admittedly he was tardy about it. If only! What laments are associated with these two sad words. Cf. Isa 48:18. What tragedies Abraham would have averted if he had sought the Lord's will, for it becomes quite clear as the story unfolds that he would have been led to return north.

There are frequent assurances that God can unfailingly provide for His people when they are in the line of His will. The following passages are of particular interest in the context of famine:—

Psa 33:18, 19: "Those who fear the Lord and hope in His mercy will be kept alive in famine."

Psa 37:18, 19: "The upright shall be satisfied in days of famine."

Psa 37:3: Here is a promise particularly appropriate to Abram's situation at this time, "Trust in the Lord ... dwell in the land and verily thou shalt be fed".

Although these promises were not actually on record at this time we cannot doubt that the same principles would have applied to Abraham had he trusted God and stayed in the land to which he had been called.

In confirmation of this, there is the case of Naomi and her husband. Although they were well-placed ("full", Ruth 1:21) and could very well have survived the famine as their neighbours did, unnecessary panic drove them to forsake their heritage in Bethlehem (The House of Bread) and to emigrate to the country of Moab, with tragic results upon which there is no need to enlarge. News of how "the Lord had visited his people in giving them bread" (1:6) induced her to return home but bereft of her husband and sons, and herself destitute ("empty", 1:21). They would have been wiser to stay in the land to which they belonged, and so with Abraham.

Spiritual Famine

To be starved in body is a traumatic experience from which most of us have been mercifully preserved, but it is well to realise that there is such a serious condition as soul starvation. Amos 8:11 speaks of a famine, not of bread, but of hearing the word of the Lord. It is vital that we be fed with spiritual food, and each has a responsibility to find sustenance for himself in the Holy Scriptures, building up himself (how modern it sounds) on his most holy faith (Jude 20) and enjoying Jeremiah's experience, "Thy words were found and I did eat them; and thy word was unto me the joy and rejoicing of mine heart" (Jer 15:16). Nevertheless, a grave responsibility rests upon those called to be shepherds in the church, a great part of whose duty is to feed the flock of God. This is stressed in all three of the solemn charges given respectively by the Great Shepherd and two of His under-shepherds, Paul and Peter (John 21:15-17; Acts 20:28; 1 Pet 5:1, 2).

The Saviour in rejecting the devil's temptation to put physical needs first, quoted Deut 8:3, "Man doth not live by bread only, but by every word that proceedeth out of the mouth of the Lord ...". The clause "proceedeth out of the mouth of the Lord" is of great importance, and failure to give sufficient weight to the same qualification in Isa 55:11 has led to the false idea that glib quotation of Scripture is equivalent to a vital message from God. To help believers to an intelligent grasp of doctrine is a great service, and we cannot be too thankful for God-given teachers with the ability to make the truth plain. However, food for the mind is not always bread for the soul — a word from God is needed.

If young converts, who with their new life in Christ have a Spirit-imparted appetite, are not suitably nourished, they suffer from soul famine and may be tempted to turn to the world (of which Egypt is a type); there all they can secure is the poor fare with which the prodigal in the far country, away from his father's house, tried to satisfy his hunger — mere husks, food not suitable for the child of God (Luke 15:16).

Those expert in the care of sheep tell us that their charges are far less likely to stray, or suffer from ailments to which they are otherwise prone, if they are provided with abundant green pastures, containing a healthy variety of grasses. As someone has said, they can be tethered by their teeth.

Faith Fails

On drawing near to Egypt Abraham became prey again to earlier fears, in contrast to the courage he had shown when he boldly built an altar to the Lord in the midst of the Canaanites. Was this because he was losing the sense of God's presence and realising that he was out of the current of His will? It is always dangerous to embark on any course which robs us of the sense of the peace of God ruling in our hearts (Col 3:15). He reverts to a subterfuge which, as he confessed to Abimelech (20:13), he had suggested to his wife before they left Ur, namely that she should show him kindness by saying in every place to which they came, that she was his sister. What he had in mind becomes clear from our present passage. Sarai was a beautiful woman, and he assumed that wherever they were there would always be the risk that some rich and powerful man would want to take her into his household, and that if he knew that they were a married couple he would kill Abraham so as to remove any obstacle. The strange thing is that Abraham's proposal actually increased the risk of her abduction by removing whatever degree of protection her married status might afford; the evidence is that this was not inconsiderable.

But why should Abraham want to put the onus of the deception on Sarai instead of being ready himself to say that he was her brother? The probable answer will emerge.

In any case, it all seems so unnecessary. There is nothing to suggest that Sarai consented, rather the contrary. Again, no such situation as Abraham feared had arisen since they left Ur, not even among the Canaanites who, from what we know of them, would not have had many scruples. This was no doubt due to the protection of God; the fact remains that Abraham's fears were groundless. Did he suppose that the Egyptians would be more unscrupulous than other people? Allowance must be made for the fact that he may have been suffering from the anxiety and strain occasioned by the grievous famine which threatened disaster. Mental fatigue can make us prone to pessimism. But the major reason was undoubtedly that he was not enjoying his former fellowship with God and could no longer rely on His protection.

Self Preservation

Now emerges what Abraham had meant when he asked his wife to show him kindness by saying she was his sister. The unpleasant fact has to be faced — he was more concerned about his own skin than the honour of his wife. His fears have increased. He is now no longer thinking of *potential* danger, it has become certain: "they *will* kill me". He is therefore desperately anxious to secure the co-operation which Sarai had previously been unwilling to give, and so introduces the subject very carefully: "Behold now, I know that thou art a fair woman to look upon". "Now" belongs to "behold" not to "I know". There is no suggestion that he had ceased of late to be aware of Sarai's beauty and was only now beginning to realise it afresh! The expression "Behold now" is simply a request for a patient hearing. To pave the way for what he is coming to he refers to her attractiveness. This was no empty compliment. At this time Sarai would have been little more than 65 years of age (cf. 12:4; 17:17) which, seen in relation to her life-span of 127, would be the equivalent of about 35 to-day. She must have been an exceptionally beautiful woman, for not only did the Egyptians consider her "very fair" but even at 90 years of age she had retained her appeal (20:2). Feeling the danger in Egypt to be more real, his plea is more earnest: "I pray thee". He is resigned to losing her, but what concerns him is the peril to his own life: "they will kill me". "Say I pray thee that thou art my sister; that it may be well with me for thy sake; and my soul shall live because of thee".

The promises of God, upon which he had acted in leaving Ur, involved the preservation of his life, but his faith had been eclipsed and he was no longer enjoying the good of these promises, although they were as solid as ever. To resort to such an artifice was as unnecessary as it was dishonouring to God.

Lack of Foresight

No doubt he regarded his plan as evidence of being far-sighted, but it was in reality very short-sighted. Obviously he had not thought out the problem in any depth, but when men begin to contrive, their minds become too clouded to see clearly all the complications in which they may involve themselves. This has been the downfall of many crafty criminals. If Abraham's vision had been unclouded he would have realised that he was heading for a precipice and might have turned back before it was too late, despite the problems such a retreat would bring if conditions had not improved in the Negeb.

We suspect that womanly instinct enabled Sarai to see that her husband was weaving a tangled web from which he would have difficulty in extricating himself. She would not be party to a device which could lead only to complications. If he was bent on his scheme she saw no alternative to accepting the unspeakable humiliation, but he must take the responsibility for saying he was her brother. The most she would do was to keep silent on the point for his sake. It begins to become clear why he had hoped that she would comply — if he said it, and the deception was later discovered, he might have to face the wrath of the man he had deceived. However, that could not be helped now — he would have to take the risk.

In Egypt

Having arrived in Egypt matters first of all turned out much as he had expected, except for an alarming complication he had not dreamed of — he found himself dangerously involved with no less a person than the mighty and despotic Pharoah.

The Egyptians in general were impressed with Sarai. "They beheld the woman that she was very fair", but none of the rank and file posed any threat. But it did not end there. Abraham was evidently of sufficient consequence to be in touch with the princes of Pharaoh, several of whom would have been quite likely to attempt to take Sarai had they not been deterred by the dread of incurring the king's jealousy. Instead they hoped to curry favour by bringing her to his notice, and he, as supreme ruler, exercised what he considered to be his right by taking her into his household — or, to put it more bluntly, adding her to his harem.

Pharaoh's Gifts

If Abraham had been simply one of the many immigrants the king would probably have paid scant regard to him, but regarding him as a man of some importance he entreated him well. The extent of the largesse he lavished on him reflects the satisfaction he felt in securing what he regarded as a great

5

prize, but perhaps with the additional purpose of putting Abraham under an obligation to create no difficulties. He was affluent enough not to need such additions to his wealth, and it must have been humiliating to receive what was in effect a bribe. However, he could not risk the consequences of refusing it and thereby offending a haughty monarch.

With flocks and herds he was also given men servants and women servants, no doubt slaves with no choice in the matter, and at least some Egyptians among them. This off-hand disposal of men and women like so many chattels had an element of cruelty in consigning them to bondage to an alien with the possibility of eventual removal to a foreign land. Nevertheless, they probably found employment with Abraham preferable to slaving for their former master.

It may be seriously questioned whether these extra possessions brought any real benefit to Abraham.

Abraham's Agonising Plight

Now Abraham had to face the consequences of his ill-advised stratagem, the full seriousness of which he could not have taken into account when he decided upon it. Now that Sarai was taken there were only two courses open to him, either of which would place him in an intolerable situation.

Would he stay on in Egypt? Any sort of communication with Sarai in the palace was out of the question — she being completely cut off. Maybe Pharaoh would sooner or later tire of her charms, but in that case she would probably be relegated to some minor role in the large menage while some new favourite took her place. The likelihood of Pharaoh restoring her to Abraham was remote, but he could perhaps cherish the hope. Meanwhile his conscience tortured him as he thought of her enduring Pharaoh's unwelcome attention on the one hand, and the jealous spite of other concubines. Moreover, the risk of the truth leaking out was very real. Even if his retainers were not actually told what had happened they had drawn their own conlusions when the extravagant gifts from Pharaoh coincided with the disappearance of the mistress. Even if they loyally wished to keep the secret of the true relationship between Abraham and Sarai it was almost inevitable that an inadvertent remark when in contact with the Egyptians would arouse suspicion and start rumours floating around. Even if, owing to Pharaoh's regal isolation, rumours were unlikely to reach him, Abraham wondered whether his embarrassment had been obvious to Pharaoh and whether, linked with this, Sarai's puzzling silence might set him thinking. Added to the sense of isolation a guilty conscience imposes, was the realisation that his behaviour must have earned the contempt of his own people. What sort of existence would that be?

The only alternative was Canaan, but there his plight would be substantially the same, the only advantage being that he would be beyond reprisals if Pharaoh did learn the truth. This would be offset by the feeling that his abandonment of Sarai was now irrevocable. Many places in Canaan would bring sad reminders of happier days, and maybe the contempt of his followers might be deepened at his leaving Sarai to her fate in a distant land.

What an entrancing destiny God had set before him, even comparatively recently in Sichem; was all that ruined now, for ever? Only God's intervention saved both Abraham and Sarai from what would have been a living death.

Pharaoh Plagued

God's purpose was that Abraham should be a channel of blessing, but in Egypt he was the cause of Pharaoh and his household being visited with great plagues.

Did God speak to the king explaining the reason for these inflictions? If so, it is remarkable that nothing is said to this effect, whereas in the later but very similar case of Abimelech we are given a good deal of detail of God's communications with him. If we were intended to make an assumption it would seem more appropriate to invite it in the second case on the analogy of the first, rather than to base an assumption in the first case on the later incident. On the other hand, if God did not directly enlighten Pharaoh, how came he to connect the plagues with the presence of Sarai in his house? This seems to argue for an uneasy conscience; did he have more than a suspicion that she was Abraham's wife?

We have already considered reasons for thinking this could have been so. But if he had suspected the truth he was able to put on a very convincing air of injured and indignant innocence in reproving Abraham. The reference in Psa 105:14 to God rebuking kings for the sake of His people could perhaps be regarded as including Pharaoh, so on balance it is safer to conclude that Pharaoh was genuinely misled and was enlightened directly by God.

Pharaoh's Protest

Pharaoh's emphatic use of "thou" in each of his three scornful questions puts it beyond question that it was Abraham, and not Sarai, who had deceived him. He was too disgusted to wait for any excuses. How Abraham must have squirmed under the deserved rebuke and the peculiar sting in the repeated and contemptuous reference to "thy wife". It must have been a relief, albeit a humiliating one, to be summarily dismissed by one who had previously shown his anxiety to be on good terms with him. "Now therefore, behold thy wife, take her and go thy way". The overall impression is that if Pharaoh had known that Sarai was his wife, she would have been safe. There is no reason to suppose that Egypt's general standards were very high, but they were certainly better than Abraham had given them credit for. It emerges quite clearly that if Abraham had been prepared to stand by the truth and leave the consequences with God this appalling situation would never have occurred. It is natural to suppose that Sarai's respect for and confidence in her husband was severely shaken, but these situations must not be judged by twentieth century norms (such as they are) but in the light of an age when people had to accept, as philosophically as possible, the harsh realities of ruthless, and often despotic, regimes.

Escorted Out Of The Country

Pharaoh's command to his men to escort Abraham and his wife and all that he had may have been to ensure that they left the country, but the fact that he was allowed to retain what had been given him and Pharaoh (the RV rendering) "brought him on the way" make one wonder whether a badly shaken man was anxious to placate a God who had shown by the plagues such an astonishing concern for Sarai's integrity and who might show further displeasure if the couple were treated badly.

How amazed he would have been if he could have been told that God's interest stemmed from the fact that, in His invincible purposes spanning the ages, Sarai was the destined ancestress of a twelve-tribed nation, which in generations to come, would play varied but decisive roles in the fortunes of his country, culminating in the overthrow of a subsequent Egyptian dynasty.

Who can calculate the dishonour to God when believers out of fellowship with Him are guilty of conduct to which many worldly men would not stoop? Pharaoh was no paragon, but he was justified in rebuking God's servant, just as rough heathen seamen were shown up to better advantage than Jonah when he was acting in disobedience to God's will. With what anguish Paul heard that Christians in Corinth tolerated immorality, which was "not so much as named among the Gentiles" (1 Cor 5:1). Cf. 1 Tim 5:8; 2 Sam 12:14.

"Wherefore let him that standeth take heed lest he fall" (1 Cor 10:12).

A Question of Relationships

No doubt Abraham had tried to salve his conscience on the grounds that Sarai was his sister in a sense, or not to put too fine a point on it, a half-sister. This is how he excused himself to Abimelech — Pharaoh seems to have been too impatient to wait for any extenuation of his deceit. That relationship had come about in a natural way, but it had been superseded by a closer and more sacred tie of his own choice, which nothing should have been allowed to break. At best it was only a half truth, but that can amount to a lie when it is intended to conceal the real position.

This has a bearing on the believer's relationship to Christ. The truth concerning him is that he is vitally united for time and eternity to his Lord and Saviour to whom he owes everything. If he forsakes the pilgrim path to go down to the spiritual Egypt (the world where his Saviour is still despised and rejected) he will not find it easy to own his true relationship to Christ lest it invite the scorn and ridicule of his fellows. There is the danger of being content with a half truth. There is usually no reproach in being a church member, or even being actively engaged in religious work — most men of the world will look patronisingly on this, even though it may strike them as odd. If a Christian is content to let unbelievers think that this is the whole truth, then he is virtually denying the real truth, that he belongs to Christ. A man of God like Timothy needed courage not to be ashamed of the testimony of Christ, but if we are flirting with the world it is almost impossible to be true to Him.

Chapter V
Out of Egypt

(Gen 13:1-18)

The sad statement in 12:10, "Abram went down into Egypt" finds its happy counterpart in 13:1, "Abram went up out of Egypt"; both are true not only in the geographical sense but spiritually as well. Had not God mercifully intervened, the Egyptian venture would have ended in disaster but now Abraham and Sarai were once more put on the path of blessing. In some circles great stress is put on the perseverance of saints, whilst little is said about the perseverance of God who patiently bears with His people and steadfastly pursues His purpose for their blessing. Paul was an outstanding example of endurance and could justly claim when addressing king Agrippa that he had continued right up to that very day, but he was careful to make it clear that it was because he had "obtained the help of God" (Acts 26:22). Cf. 2 Tim 4:18.

Once again we learn that failure need not be final; there are, however, cases where, for various reasons, God in discipline removes an offender (Acts 5:1-11; 1 Cor 11:30; 1 John 5:16).

Re-United

The six-fold occurrence of the word "wife" in 12:11-19 culminating in, "they sent him away, and his wife and all that he had" (v. 20), followed by the seemingly needless repetition of the phrase in 13:1, bring into sharp focus the wonderful fact that man and wife were now re-united; only a few days previously it had looked as if they would never see each other again. Such a complete deliverance was without question remarkable evidence of God's deep interest in them and must have so filled their hearts with gratitude that there would be no inclination to spoil their new joy in each other by fruitlessly raking up the unhappy past. It is more likely that light hearts made light feet as together they re-trod the trail that before had been a dismal and weary trek.

Lot went with them, but as it is not said that Abraham took him the conclusion is that this time it was entirely his own decision. As he was not involved in the recent scandal and so did not incur the wrath of Pharaoh, the likelihood is that he could have stayed on had he so wished. There is reason to think that this fertile land appealed to him but that on balance the advantages of remaining with his uncle outweighed the attractions of Egypt; but it was a fellowship soon to be disrupted. No doubt Pharaoh's gifts contributed to Abraham being "very rich in cattle, in silver, and in gold", but they were not an unmixed blessing.

The South

The king's men "sent him away" so it involved little choice on his part that he "went up" out of Egypt, but now we read that he "went on" (v. 3); he was glad enough to be out of Egypt and he intended to remedy his mistakes. He eventually reached the region where the grievous famine had induced him to resort to Egypt instead of returning to the more northerly parts of Canaan. It would be apparent to him now that this was where he had made a crucial mistake. If we are right in thinking that the humiliation of having to acknowledge this militated against retracing his steps, he must have felt keenly the greater humiliations he had incurred by the later consequences of his decision. How often foolish pride has induced a man to take further risks rather than acknowledge a mistake.

Step By Step Recovery

The unmistakable and close correspondence between the journey from Bethel to Egypt as recorded in 12:8-14 and the return journey set out in 13:1-4 compel thoughtful attention:

DOWN TO EGYPT
↓

"Pitched his tent"	"Where his tent had been"
"having Bethel on the west and Hai on the east"	"Between Bethel and Hai"
"There he builded an altar"	"The place of the altar which he had made there"
"Called upon the name of the Lord"	"Called on the name of the Lord"
"Journeyed, going on"	"Went on his journeys"
"Toward the south"	"From the south"
"Went down into Egypt".	"Went up out of Egypt".

↘ → → ↑

OUT OF EGYPT

It is thus forced upon our attention that his path had to be retraced step by step, and the plural "journeys" serves to emphasise the stages through which he passed. This illustrates the important spiritual principle that when a believer has been convicted of departure in heart from God, with its resultant mistakes and failures, and longs for the restoration of that fellowship he once enjoyed, he will need to return in heart to that point where he lost touch with God. If he has wandered far from God and has become entangled in evil he may find, in the spiritual sense as Abraham did in the physical sense, that the way back is long and painful although amply rewarded in the end. Abraham's recovery involved getting back to the very location, and there are cases which may necessitate a child of God returning to the actual place and service where he had been happy in the consciousness of being in the line of God's will. This is not to say that this must be his permanent place; as with Abraham, when matters have been put right he may find that God has a wider sphere for him.

On this point, the risen Lord's message to the church at Ephesus is full of significance. They had left their first love and were called upon to remember from whence they had fallen. To recall happier days is more effective than morbid occupation with failure. (The prodigal thought of his father's house, where he had enjoyed bread in plenty, rather than the husks.) Then, remembering those happier days they were given the opportunity to repent and "do the first works".

The two expressions, "where his tent had been *at the beginning*" and "unto the place of the altar which he had made there *at the first*", are curious seeing that his first base and altar in the land were at Shechem before he came to Bethel. These expressions seem intended to point to the beginning of that phase in his experience where he took the first steps on the long path which eventually led to distant Egypt. Now he was to begin afresh where he left off.

Back at Bethel

After a journey taking some weeks he was back on the mountain near Bethel. Had the altar he had built there some time ago suffered no damage during his long absence, or had he the humbling task of regathering the scattered stones to repair it? Whichever way it was, the grand fact is that once again "he called on the name of the Lord". Though on a bare mountain it was more splendid than all the grandeur of Egypt. There he was not his true self, but now we shall see the real Abraham as he was when in communion with his God.

In due course he left Bethel and we have no record of his returning to it, but when he left it was because God had another sphere for him.

A great deal of interest attaches to Bethel. It is mentioned more frequently in Scripture than any other place except Jerusalem, and it had a long and chequered history which cannot concern us now, but its associations with Abraham's grandson, Jacob, have lessons for us which are quite in keeping with our present study.

Jacob At Bethel

It would be worthwhile reading the two narratives connecting Jacob with Bethel to refresh the memory (28:10-19 and 34:30 to 35:10). On his way from Beer-Sheba to Haran the Lord God of Abraham and of his father Isaac appeared to him, applying to him the promises made to Abraham, and also, in effect, undertaking to be his friend, guard and guide.

The question arises how a holy God could thus deal in grace with a sinner fleeing from home to escape the consequences of his wrong-doing. The answer seems to lie in the particular place to which he was unwittingly divinely led when he lost his way in the approaching darkness of night. It was not where he had planned to spend the night for "he lighted on a certain place". That this spot had a special significance is stressed by six mentions of the word "place" in the phrases "a certain place", "that place", "this place". When it is remembered that "he took of the stones of that place" upon which to rest, and only on awaking in the morning discovered that he was at Bethel, "the place of the altar which Abraham had made there" (13:4), it seems not unreasonable to infer a meaningful link deserving further examination than we can embark on now.

Be that as it may, the point we wish to make is that when, long after, Jacob had made such a hash of things that he had lost control of his family and was tolerating their "strange gods" God told him to return to Bethel: "Arise, go up to Bethel and dwell there, and make there an altar unto God that appeared to thee when thou fleddest from the face of Esau". God was now able to discern in his servant qualities which enabled Him to call him Israel a prince with God. He had been given that name before (32:28), but had not lived up to it.

We thus have the same lesson suggested by Abraham's return to Bethel: that the way of recovery for a backsliding child of God is to get back to where he had once enjoyed the blessing of God.

Trouble Brewing

Again it is said that Lot went with Abraham, but here the word means that they kept together as they moved around the area with their respective flocks. Strange though it may seem, Abraham's new found peace was to be disturbed. When he returned to Bethel he did not come back to a situation which had remained unaltered. Formerly the presence of the Canaanite had not posed any problem, for there had been space enough to deploy his flocks without clashing with them, but, taking advantage of his absence, the Perizzite had moved in and occupied some of the available land. Abraham and Lot therefore found that the wide pastures formerly open to them were more restricted now; the problem was made more acute by the recent increases in their flocks and herds and "the land was not able to bear them". This led to strife between the two sets of herdsmen when they both wanted to graze the same area. It would not be altogether surprising if a factor contributing to this lack of discipline was a diminishing respect for the leader Abraham as a result of his behaviour in Egypt. Whilst Abraham's deliverance from Egypt was complete, things were not quite the same as they had been. So it is with us if we lose touch with the Lord and leave the ground we had possessed; it enables the devil to establish some sort of bridgehead in our lives which creates difficulties we might never otherwise have had. Even when forgiveness has been full and free and restoration real, it remains true that "whatsoever a man sows that shall he also reap". An extreme case is seen in the life of David. Although his penitence was deep and real, and although he was assured that the Lord had put away his sin, its repercussions could not be averted (2 Sam 12:7-14).

Riches Causing Strife

The strife between the herdsmen threatened to involve Abraham and Lot, much to the former's distress evidenced in his earnest appeal, "Let there be no strife I pray thee between me and thee". How different from the previous circumstances when he had said "I pray thee", to his wife (12:13).

It has often been the case that money or property has led to conflict between those who had hitherto been able to live together in harmony. It is remarkable that this led to trouble when Israel entered the land under Joshua; when the remnant returned from Babylon; and it posed the first threat to the early church's testimony and unity (Josh 7:1; Neh 5:1-13; Acts 5:3; 6:1). Peter's shock at Judas' betrayal of Jesus for thirty pieces of silver, followed by his unhappy experiences in the incidents just quoted, evidently gave him a thorough distaste for what he called "filthy lucre" (Acts 3:6; 8:20; 1 Pet 5:2). Of course, the trouble is not with money as such, but with the love of it which constrains some to get rich at all costs. God-given wealth can be used for God-glorifying purposes (1 Tim 6:10). See further remarks on 14:23.

Abraham's Prompt Action

In contrast to his behaviour in Egypt we now see the true Abraham in his prompt and resolute action linked with magnanimity. He could have adopted a dictatorial attitude in reminding Lot that not only was he the senior as his uncle, but the leader to whom Lot owed a great deal of his success; on those grounds he could have imposed his own solution upon Lot. Instead he based his appeal for peace on the ground that they were brethren. Nor was this an empty platitude, witness the lengths to which he was prepared to go when he "heard that his brother was taken captive" (14:14), and the earnestness of his intercession for Sodom, largely no doubt on account of Lot (19:29).

We cannot doubt that Abraham had been deeply distressed at the dishonour he had brought upon God in the eyes of the Egyptians and was now appalled at the damage which could be done to the testimony if the heathen Canaanite and Perizzite saw that those who professed to be worshippers of the one true God could not live in peace. This must be avoided at all costs even if the solution turned out to his disadvantage. He therefore waived his own right to choose and gave it to the younger man, content to leave the issue with God. Whichever Lot chose, whether left or right, Abraham would take the alternative.

Strife among the people of God quickly becomes known, and this has a devastating effect on their witness to the world. Realising this, the devil makes unity his target. Abraham was acting in the spirit of the exhortation to the Corinthians that they should be prepared to suffer wrong or even to be defrauded in preference to damage being done to the church's testimony (1 Cor 6:7). See also 1 Pet 2:19-20. For the same reason the Philippians were urged to "do all things without murmurings and disputings" that by first of all *shining* as lights in the world they would be effective in holding forth the word of life (Phil 2:14-16; cf. 2 Tim 2:24).

Without touching the debated question of where the blame lay, consider what must have been the wide repercussions of the lamentable contention between two such close friends as Paul and Barnabas. It must have badly shaken the comparatively young church at Antioch to whom these fine men had been such a help in shared service. Moreover, when Paul and Barnabas revisited separately some parts of the mission field where formerly they had worked together so harmoniously and successfully, each would undoubtedly be questioned about the absence of the other and the sorry story would have to be told, with effects which can easily be imagined. The course eventually adopted, Barnabas taking John Mark and Paul taking Silas, thereby covering more ground, could have been agreed upon amicably if there had been greater readiness to understand each other's point of view, and no harm would have been done.

Lot's Choice

It would have been to Lot's credit had he deferred to his uncle, but he gives the impression of readily seizing the opportunity: "He lifted up his eyes and beheld all the plain of Jordan". The first thing which attracted him was that "it was well watered everywhere"; perhaps he had unpleasant memories of the terrible drought in the south.

It so enchanted him that it struck him as being like "the garden of the Lord". This may be the Hebrew way of expressing what is superlative, but if we link Gen 2:8, "The Lord God planted a garden eastward in Eden", with Isa 51:3, "He will make her wilderness like Eden, and her desert like the garden of the Lord", it does seem possible that Lot called to mind the traditions which had been handed down of the ideal conditions in the earliest days of human history, before spoiled by sin. Rather incongruous with this image is the next comparison: "like the land of Egypt". That this was a commendation shows that he retained pleasant memories of that land.

Enchanted with the prospect, not so much for its beauty but its business potential — ideal for flocks and herds — he "chose him all the plain of Jordan, and journeyed east". We have already ventured to suggest that, in some cases at least, there is a typical significance in movements toward the east.

A Doomed Scene

Although the very pleasant and promising aspect of the plain of Jordan is given due prominence, the ominous rider is added, "before the Lord destroyed Sodom and Gomorrah". Deceived by present appearances, Lot little realised that he was looking on an area under impending judgment. What a different picture it presented to Abraham some time later: "behold the smoke of the country went up as the smoke of a furnace" (19:28).

Although the devil tried to tempt the Saviour with a far more glorious vision than the prospect which allured Lot, namely all the kingdoms of the world and the glory of them, he was not able to sustain that vision for more than a moment of time before the discerning eyes of Christ. Yet, alas, he succeeds in deceiving many with a mere fraction of this world's false and transitory glamour — he is really dangling before their eyes a tinsel toy.

James bluntly says that the one who makes himself a friend of the world constitutes himself an enemy of God (Jas 4:4), whilst John says that love of the world cannot co-exist with love for the Father (1 John 2:15). This need not be love for that aspect of the world depicted by the moral depravity of Sodom. There is the world of false religion represented by Babylon, and the cultured world of which Egypt is a type; any one of these can be a snare to the child of God. Although the Galatians were said to have been delivered from this present evil world, the word "evil" is omitted when it is said that Demas forsook Paul, having loved this present world. In the sense that the world is opposed to God it is bound to be evil, but Paul seems to wish to avoid implying that Demas was attracted by anthing sordid. If he had been ensnared in moral evil he would hardly have chosen to go to Thessalonica, which was probably his home town, where other Thessalonians such as Aristarchus and Secundus, his one time fellow-labourers, belonged. It is not at all unlikely that he returned to the fellowship of the church there, but the world in its fairer aspects was more attractive than self-sacrificial service for Christ.

Sinners Against The Lord

Lot could have been excused for his ignorance of the impending destruction of Sodom, but he surely knew at least something of the immoral conditions which were inviting that overthrow. If he was unaware of it when he parted from Abraham he could hardly have remained in ignorance when he settled near the city. The men of Sodom were not only wicked but sinners exceedingly, and not merely "before the Lord" but "against the Lord" (v. 13 RV). The most serious aspect of sin is that whether it is against others or even against one's self, sin is primarily against God whose creatures we all are (20:6; Lev 6:2). Joseph resisted temptation because yielding would have been sin not so much against his temptress and her husband but against God: "How can I do this great wickedness and sin against God?" (39:9). David had compounded his sin against Bath-sheba and her husband by murdering the latter by proxy in the hope of avoiding exposure. Although he became deeply convicted of the enormity of his sin and in genuine repentance confessed it, yet the overwhelming sense of the offence he had given God so overshadowed all else that he exclaimed, "Against thee, and thee only, have I sinned and done this great evil in thy sight" (Psa 51:4). Cf. Luke 15:18. Paul was astonished and dismayed to learn that his persecution of Christians was tantamount to persecuting Christ (Acts 9:4). This was a principle he never forgot, and it coloured a great deal of his thinking; witness his remonstrance with those who were thoughtlessly doing injury to the conscience of others: "when ye so sin against the brethren and wound their weak conscience ye sin against Christ" (1 Cor 8:12).

If Lot had not been so absorbed in business he might have realised that he was exposing his family to the evil influence of Sodom's way-of-life, the nature of which is revealed in ch. 19. The fertility of the plain of Jordan tended to make life easy and, human nature being what it is, idle hands soon found mischief to do. The comparison with Sodom suggested in Ezek 16:49 is illuminating. "Pride, fulness of bread and abundance of idleness" is a combination which has spelt the moral deterioration of many nations in the course of history, of which the collapse of the once mighty Roman Empire is an outstanding example.

Toward Sodom

Lot pitched his tent toward Sodom, no doubt telling himself that he would never allow himself to be involved in its life, but when he next comes before our attention he is living in the city and very much involved, from what he would possibly argue were the best of motives. Some of his family became entangled, and, although we can only conjecture how this came about, perhaps the experience of Jacob at Shalem suggests a possible answer. When *he* pitched his tent toward the city his daughter Dinah, who had probably lived a very sheltered life up to that time, was understandably curious to see how the daughters of the land lived. The outcome was disastrous (33:18-34:31). Lot's family had always lived a pastoral life except for the brief acquaintance with the more sophisticated style of Egypt. If they became dissatisfied with what, by contrast, seemed a primitive sort of life, they may have brought pressure to bear on their somewhat pliable father not to be so old-fashioned. If he was disturbed at moral conditions in Sodom, why not use his influence to improve matters? The validity of this argument would be put to the test before long.

Separation

The separation between Abraham and Lot is mentioned three times in vv. 9-14. It relieved Abraham of an encumbrance and brought him nearer to the fulfilment of God's original call. However, he did not consider that separation should mean washing his hands of his nephew, for whom he retained a proper affection. Attention has already been drawn to the fact that he remained interested in his welfare and was prepared to take action for his protection. True separation springs from heart separation to God, and separation from what is not of God follows as a natural consequence; many sincere souls have mistakenly restricted their potential for the blessing of others by the false idea that separation means isolation. No one has ever been so completely separated to God or so completely separated from sinners as our Lord, yet at the same time He was eminently approachable. His enemies scornfully referred to Him as a friend of publicans and sinners, a charge He would not have been in the least inclined to refute. He invited Himself to the house of the publican, Zacchaeus, because He knew He would be more than welcome, but He was ready also to accept invitations from other classes, even from self-righteous Pharisees, in the hope of being a blessing to them.

There is this difference; He was undefiled and could not be defiled, like the rays of the sun which can shine on the rubbish heap without losing their purity. We have to be cautious lest we expose ourselves to undue risks, and above all we need to be sure of the purity of our motives.

6

God's Choice For Abraham

The next communication from the Lord is distinctly linked with Abraham's separation from Lot, apparently inferring that this met with His approval, as in the somewhat similar situation in 12:7. "Abram said unto Lot" in v. 8 is replaced with "The Lord said unto Abram". What a difference!

Lot acted very promptly and eagerly, lifting up his eyes before deciding between left and right. Abraham, instead of having to carry out his intention of taking the alternative was invited by God to lift up his eyes, not merely to left and right but to encompass the whole of the horizon, seen evidently from the peak of the highest mountain in the area. Lot made his own choice, and it turned out to be a wretched one, but Abraham found that God had chosen for him. Happy are those who are willing to leave the disposition of their affairs to God, in the confidence of the psalmist, "He shall choose our inheritance for us" (Psa 47:4). This does not mean supine irresponsibility masquerading as dependence on God, which is often no more than a willingness to let others carry the burden, but rather a readiness to embrace God's plan in the conviction that His will is best.

It has been said of Abraham that:
1. he left all *for* God (11:31; 12:4; Heb 11:8, 15) and was rewarded by the promises of Gen 12:2-3;
2. he left all *with* God (13:9) and was rewarded by the extended promises of 13:14-17;
3. he found all *in* God (14:22-23) and was rewarded by, "I am ... thy exceeding great reward" (15:1);
4. he yielded all *to* God (22:16) and was rewarded by being called the friend of God (Jas 2:23).

Maybe this will not satisfy the critical analyst, but it may serve to stimulate a profitable line of thought.

In our present context (with 2. above in mind) it is plain that the original promises were extended: the land was to be his and his seed's "for ever", and in addition to his becoming a great nation, his seed was to be as the dust of the earth. This is not saying that the number of his descendants would equal the number of particles of dust in the earth, but that as the particles are too numerous to count, so would his descendants be. See remarks on the stars in 15:5.

The Length And Breadth Of The Land

He was encouraged to walk through the length and breadth of the land, and it may be concluded from this that he took many journeys of which we have no record. There are sufficient time gaps to allow for this.

Although the promise to give him the land (v. 15) is almost immediately repeated (v. 17) as if by way of emphasis, the fact remains, as Stephen declared in Acts 7:5, that he was not given any inheritance in it, no, not so much as to set his foot on. This is in strange contrast to the message Moses was authorised to give to the Israelites when encouraging them to take posssession of Canaan: "Every place whereon the soles of your feet shall tread shall be yours" (Deut 11:24; Josh 1:3; 14:9). Abraham set his foot on a great part of the land, but all that became his actual possession was a burial-plot for which he paid the market price (23:18).

As Stephen recognised, there is an apparent inconsistency here, but the explanation is full of encouragement for those who, after cherishing for long years what they believed to be God's promise to them, are approaching the end of life with the promise unfulfilled.

Abraham, and Isaac, and Jacob after him, did not live to see God's promises fulfilled. They saw them afar off, yet faith made them so real, and brought them so near that they could embrace them, and they were content to die in the confidence that one day all would come to pass. They looked into the remote future, but we are thinking of earnest souls who longed to see their prayers answered in their life time and have died disheartened. Others, though disappointed, have nevertheless died clinging to the conviction that God would honour their faith in His own good time. Their friends have lived to see it, and sometimes in a manner exceeding the expectations of the departed. Who can gauge how gratifying it must be to the heart of the Father when His children show something of the confidence shown by Jacob who "when he was a dying blessed both the sons of Joseph, and worshipped leaning on the top of his staff" (Heb 11:13, 21)?

Mamre In Hebron

Abraham then removed his tent and dwelt in Mamre which was in Hebron. The RV replaces "the plains of Mamre" with "the oaks of Mamre", which is generally accepted as correct. (The word used in v. 10 is quite different.) There were large groves of oaks, some of the trees quite massive in Abraham's time, and we can imagine him taking advantage of the shade for his tent and those of his retainers.

He would have travelled about 30 miles south from Bethel, but in circumstances very different from those in which he had left Bethel previously on that journey southward which turned out so disastrously. Now he had a warrant from God, and, moving in happy fellowship with God, one of his first acts on arriving at Mamre was to build an altar.

The Lord later visited him in Mamre in circumstances which left no doubt of His approval. What is morally wrong can never be right, but a course of action which may be a mistake at one time, as lacking the Lord's guidance, may on another occasion be appropriate as being in the line of His will. Compare 26:2 with 46:3, although different individuals were involved. See also 2 Sam 5:18-25, where the Lord gave David different directions for his course of action in two very similar sets of circumstances.

Hebron means "fellowship" and Mamre "firmness, vigour". Some see in this the twin ideas that Abraham was compensated for the loss of Lot's company by closer fellowship with God, and that he was therefore characterised by increased firmness and vigour, as for example in the incident related in the following chapter. Certainly in many instances the meanings of the place names seem to have some relevance to the associated scriptural narratives, but readers must judge for themselves how much weight to attach to the interpretations offered.

Chapter VI

Kings and Kings

(Gen 14:1-17)

Chedorlaomer's Campaigns

The political situation described in vv. 1-7 is quite in accord with what is known of the history of that period and the names of the four kings have been deciphered on tablets unearthed by archaeologists. Their territories were in the southern part of Mesopotamia, and Chedorlaomer seems to have been the most powerful of them; he has been called "the Napoleon of his day". His name probably means "Ravager of the West", i.e. of the countries west of Mesopotamia, which include Canaan. This passage shows how appropriate the name was.

Scripture ignores the great wars of antiquity except as they affect God's people, as in this case. Before Abraham had entered Canaan, Chedorlaomer had invaded the area and, having inflicted defeat on the various small kingdoms (including the five mentioned in v. 2), laid them under tribute which they paid for twelve years. Then in the thirteenth year, perhaps thinking that the conqueror was too far off to bother any more and growing weary of the burden of continuing to find the money to pay the exactions, they rashly risked rebellion.

Naturally it took some time for the news to reach their oppressor but when it did he formed an alliance with three neighbouring kings and embarked on an expedition of reprisal, arriving in Canaan the following year. They penetrated to the south of Canaan, punished the rebels there, and, turning back northwards, subdued the Amalekites and the Amorites. As the victorious armies approached the region of Sodom and Gomorrah, their kings Bera and Birsha joined with three other local kings evidently with the optimistic intention of repelling the invaders.

Sodom Confederacy Defeated

These five kings apparently argued that if they joined battle in the Vale of Siddim the slime pits there would hamper their foes and place them at a great disadvantage. In the event, the forces of Admah, Zeboiim and Bela were overthrown. The kings of Sodom and Gomorrah had no more stomach for the fight and took to ignominious flight. Perhaps their luxurious and decadent life-style had sapped their moral stamina. (See note on 13:10.)

In their headlong panic they stumbled on the very slime pits which they had hoped would prove their enemies' undoing. When we are told that "they fell there" it does not necessarily mean that they perished. It is possible, though unlikely, that they succeeded in extricating themselves, but the next statement, "they that remained fled to the mountains", does not sound as if they were among the survivors. The latter, no doubt, eventually made their way back to their homes when they felt it was safe to do so.

The Cities Pillaged

The conquerors now entered both Sodom and Gomorrah which, being unable to offer any resistance, may have escaped serious damage, but the houses were thoroughly ransacked: "They took all the goods ... and all their victuals".

Attention is now focussed on Sodom alone because the involvement of Lot is the important point. The inhabitants were taken captive (v. 16 "the people", v. 21 "the persons") but Lot is the first mentioned: "they took Lot, Abram's brother's son" (v. 12). Poor Lot, how often he was "taken" (11:31; 12:4; 13:1; 19:16). He was a pliable sort of character and seldom acted on his own initiative; when he did so it usually turned out disastrously (13:11; 19:20). V. 16 seems to refer to the women of his household. If, as 19:12 suggests, he had sons, they had possibly been recruited for the battle and were among those who escaped to the mountains and returned to their home later when it was safe.

The victorious kings now set off for distant Mesopotamia whence Lot years before had emigrated, and but for his uncle's prowess he would have been doomed to end his days there, not as a citizen but as a slave.

Abram The Hebrew

One who escaped made his way to report the capture of Lot to "Abram the Hebrew" whose camp was among the oaks in the territory of Mamre. Obviously the relationship, and Abraham's location, were known. Was this because uncle and nephew kept up communication, or because Lot, or some of his family, had boasted of the connection? This is not at all unlikely seeing that Abraham was of sufficient consequence to enhance their prestige. It is interesting to note that the patriarch was known to his neighbours as "the Hebrew". The LXX has "the crosser". It denotes one who has crossed a frontier as an immigrant to another land and so is committed to another way-of-life. (Compare the spiritual experience of a Christian. He has been "delivered from the power of darkness and translated into the kingdom of God's dear Son", Col 1:13.) The Jews did not use the word *Hebrews* among themselves but only when speaking to non-Jews (Exod 7:16; Jon 1:9; 2 Cor 11:22; Phil 3:5).

As an immigrant, and a wealthy one with a large establishment, he might have been regarded as an unwelcome intruder, but it says a lot for his character, tact and courtesy that he evidently established good relationships with the inhabitants of his adopted country, without concealing the fact that he was a worshipper of the Lord and not of any of their false gods. As soon as he settled in Mamre he did what he was accustomed to do, he "built there an altar unto the Lord" (13:18). Although his camp was in his territory, Mamre and his two brothers, Eschol and Aner, were willing to ally with him. No doubt they deemed it expedient and advantageous in view of the fact that Abraham's followers were numerous, including 318 men born in his house (not mercenaries), trained to afford protection against marauders. Obviously there is a great deal about Abraham which has not been disclosed in the record. Such an alliance with heathen people may strike us as strange in view of the warnings given to Israel and the separation urged on Christians, but we are dealing with a unique period in sacred history and we must learn not to judge an early situation by the light of later revelation. (Cf. remarks on ch. 16.) However, separation from evil should not degenerate into a frosty isolation from our fellow-men. Our Lord, the perfect example in all things, was "holy, harmless, undefiled, separate from sinners", but He was also "a friend of sinners" (Heb 7:26; Matt 11:19). Chedorlaomer and his confederates, in their triumphant march through the country, had not disturbed Abraham's life in Mamre and he did not involve himself in what did not concern him. But when he heard of his nephew's plight it was a different matter!

The Rescue Of Lot

However much Abraham may have been moved by the pathetic plight of his nephew, "brother", he would be well aware that any attempt at rescue would be fraught with very formidable difficulties and very real dangers. It was certainly not a task for an amateur; but he was no amateur. Although the record does not satisfy curiosity it is plain that he had good reasons for maintaining a small, but clearly efficient, private army, and the way in which he took command and acquitted himself on the field leaves no doubt about his capability.

Nevertheless, had he given way to a common human failing of shirking unpleasant responsibility he could have made a good excuse by arguing that Lot had only himself to blame. Had he not involved himself in Sodom he would not have been involved in its overthrow. On the other hand, it is not unlikely that he had the uneasy feeling that he was partly to blame for Lot's unhappy choice, for if he had not taken him to Egypt where he acquired a taste for luxury, he may not have been tempted by the fertile area which appealed to him "even as the garden of the Lord, like the land of Egypt" (13:10).

Significantly enough we talk of *making* excuses but we do not *make* reasons, and Abraham could have pleaded very good reasons for declining to embark on such a hazardous expedition. The apparently irrelevant details of the invaders' sweeping victories prior to the utter defeat of the Sodom confederacy (vv. 5-7) serve to underline the inadequacy, militarily speaking, of such forces as he could muster. The dangers of such a confrontation were self-evident, and the consequences to Abraham's household of a possible defeat would be disastrous. We cannot suppose that he did not take all this into account.

Furthermore he could have argued that it was now too late. By the time the escapee reached Hebron with his report Chedorlaomer and his allies were already on their way home. Abraham could not suddenly drop everything and start off in pursuit without any preparation — he would not be guilty of that folly. By the time he had completed the necessary dispositions for the affairs of his establishment in his absence, and made provision for his forces, the enemy would be farther away still. We know that in the event he had to cover a distance of over 150 miles before overtaking the foe at Dan.

With the encumbrance of their massive booty and their numerous prisoners that journey must have taken the enemy well over a week. Abraham, with camels, would be able to travel faster but would nevertheless take a few days.

However, none of these considerations weighed with Abraham against what he saw to be his paramount duty — to come to the aid of a brother in his hour of need. In effect he was willing to risk having to lay down his life. John tells us that "we ought to lay down our lives for the brethren" (1 John 3:16) but, of course, he quotes the greater example of One who fought a greater foe and paid a greater price for our deliverance.

It is apparent that Abraham's decision to take on this massive and perilous operation called for tremendous courage and resolution. Faith is not a supine dependence upon God which relieves us of all responsibility — it issues in appropriate action: by faith Abel offered; by faith Noah prepared an ark; by faith Abraham went out; by faith warriors subdued kingdoms (Heb 11). (Cf. Jas 2:18, "I will shew thee my faith by my works".) In this connection it is intriguing to recall the meanings given to the site of his camp: Mamre, firmness or vigour; Hebron, company or fellowship. The contrast with his lack of active faith, and consequent fear and duplicity when he was out of fellowship with God in Egypt, suggests lessons too obvious to call for comment.

The Three Brothers

In fairness to his allies it must be remembered that the difficulties and dangers mentioned were no less real for them, and the fact that they were willing to face them (without having the same personal motivation) says much for their loyalty to their respected neighbour. The value of the part they played was later recognised in the allocation of the spoils (v. 24), but the focussing of attention on Abraham (note the personal pronouns "he", "himself" and "his") indicates that he was the prime mover and that his leadership was accepted.

They were wise in this.

The Strategy

Abraham chose to swoop on the enemy's camp under cover of darkness when the greater part of the company would be sound asleep feeling secure from any attack. Moreover, by dividing his forces so that the attack came from more than one direction the confusion was increased. It was sound strategy to strike at the leaders —Chedorlaomer and the kings who were with him were slaughtered. Deprived of their main commanders the remainder fled in confusion and panic. Abraham was too good a strategist to give them any opportunity of regrouping; he pursued them for another 50 miles or so. It is likely that he first of all took some time to restore some order for the sake of the captives, otherwise he would have overtaken the fugitives in a shorter distance. Then he returned to Dan and reorganised everything for the long trek back home with all the captives safe and all the goods intact.

Rescuing Spiritual Captives

The NT use of the imagery of captivity in a spiritual sense invites us to look for some lessons from this story. The sight of the well-watered plain of Jordan had lured Lot into abandoning fellowship with Abraham and pitching his tent toward Sodom. It was in the nature of a compromise — always a dangerous step in the wrong direction. It was not long before he abandoned his tent-life (symbol of pilgrim character) for a permanent dwelling in the city. Unknowingly he fell into a trap and was eventually captured by the enemy. We are warned against loving the world and the things which are in the world (1 John 2:15). Like Christian in Bunyan's *Pilgrim's Progress*, if we trespass on the devil's ground we are likely to be caught. It is dangerous to flirt with the world (Jas 4:4). We read of those who having fallen into the snare of the devil were taken captive by him at his will, and of others who were led captive laden with sins (2 Tim 2:26; 3:6).

As already suggested, liberating Lot was no work for an amateur; neither is the restoring of a believer who has been captured by the devil a task for a novice (1 Tim 3:6). Lot did not knowingly risk being captured — he was overtaken, caught unawares. Similarly in Gal 6:1 Paul is not thinking of a person who deliberately goes into sin but rather of one who has been overtaken; sin has come up from behind and caught him unawares. His restoration calls for spiritual men experienced and equipped spiritually as Abraham was in the literal sense.

In the same strain, but using a different metaphor, Jude speaks of those who have fallen into a fire, not deliberately, but as a result of being snared by false teachers and led into sin. Those qualified to pull them out of the fire are those who are built up on their most holy faith, who pray in the Holy Spirit and keep themselves in the love of God; these thus have discernment enough to distinguish between those who are wilfully perverse and those who have need of compassion. They are to make a difference. Consider the blessedness of rescuing a soul.

How sweet 'twill be at evening
If you and I can say,
Good Shepherd we've been seeking
The sheep that went astray.
Jas 5:19-20; 1 John 5:16

As in Abraham's case there are dangers. The spiritual of Gal 6:1 are warned to act in a spirit of meekness, considering themselves lest they also be tempted, and likewise be overtaken by a subtle foe. Jude speaks of acting with fear. Those who play with fire can get burned. There have been sincere servants of Christ who through lack of caution have fallen into the very snare from which they ventured to rescue others. However, if the motive is right — the rescue of a brother — and the attitude that of prayerful caution, there is One who can keep us from falling (Jude 16-24).

The King Of Sodom's Dilemma

If Bera perished in the vale of Siddim as seems to be the case, then the king who went to meet Abraham was his successor. What an empty title was his; what a dismal inheritance — a ghost-city, houses empty save for a few bewildered and bereaved survivors of that disastrous battle. But the new king was not inclined to relinquish his long-cherished hopes of grandeur; if at all possible he would rebuild the shattered kingdom — despite the problems.

News of Abraham returning in triumph with all the property recovered and all the captives liberated had travelled ahead of the slow-moving columns. Sodom, well aware of a conqueror's rights, would realise that Abraham was equally aware of them. If the latter, from his position of strength, chose to assert his claims Sodom could do nothing but yield. Worse than that was the possibility that Abraham, emboldened by his remarkable victory and conscious of augmented strength, might contemplate setting up himself as the new ruler. His abhorrence of the corrupt regime might make the prospect of bringing about reforms attractive, especially in view of his proven concern for his nephew. Sodom may not have been very far out in his assessment of the situation.

Did The Devil Play A Part?

Would it be surprising if the devil thought the following line of argument whispered in Abraham's ear could be used to deflect him from the pilgrim path and so frustrate the purpose of God? The liberated captives were not likely to have much confidence in a regime whose ill-advised rebellion and rash attack on their overlords had resulted in such a debacle. Instead they would feel indebted to their deliverer whose intrepidity had been matched by sound judgment and superb generalship. Moreover the long trek home would have given them an opportunity to observe his splendid character and perhaps to glimpse a better kind of life. Might they not be better off if such a man, whose qualities of leadership had been recognised by his allies, were their king? (Think of the occasion when the multitude, having had their need miraculously met by Christ, enthusiastically decided that this was the sort of king they wanted, John 6:15.)

Let us consider the devil's tactics when he attempted to deflect Christ from the path His Father had laid down for Him. God had promised His Son that in due time he would give Him "the uttermost parts of the earth for a possession" (Psa 2:8). The devil showed Christ all the kingdoms of the world and suggested that there was a short-cut to His inheritance. When the Saviour rebutted him with the word of God, he took his cue and cunningly misused a promise in the Word to justify the next temptation, deceitfully omitting a vital qualifying phrase: "in all thy ways". (Cf. Luke 4:10-11 with Psa 91:11-12.)

God had recently promised Abraham: "all the land which thou seest to thee will I give it" (13:15), later expanded to "all the land of Canaan for an everlasting possession" (17:8). Did the devil insinuate that now was a providential opportunity to take a short-cut in that direction by taking possession of Sodom as a first step? Of course, he would wish Abraham to forget the accompanying charge to the promise: "walk through the land in the length and breadth of it", that involved waiting God's own time, certainly not settling in Sodom.

It is impossible to say what course Abraham would have taken had not another king of a very different character forestalled the king of Sodom, and by his opportune and appropriate ministry given a new direction to Abraham's thoughts.

The deeply significant timing of Melchizedek's intervention certainly suggests that God had seen the need to save Abraham from some serious mistake.

Chapter VII
Melchizedek

(Gen 14:18-20)

Those three short verses offer much food for thought. It has been said that as a meteor bursts into view in the night sky, blazes brilliantly for a short while and then disappears, so Melchizedek broke into Abraham's experience suddenly and dramatically, dominated the scene in a brief episode, and then disappeared completely from Scripture; he re-appears in a brief but pregnant verse a thousand years later in Psa 110:4 and then disappears again, only to be brought before our notice at greater length in Heb 7 after another thousand years.

A Christophany?

The sudden unexplained appearance and disappearance, the absence of any information about his past history or future career, coupled with the wonderful revelation of God he imparted, and even more, perhaps, what is said in Heb 7:3, leaves many with the feeling that it was a Christophany, i.e. a pre-incarnation manifestation of Christ in human form. Consequently an air of mystery is allowed to cling to this admittedly remarkable figure. However, the narrative does not bear the marks of the several divine manifestations to Abraham, or of the many appearances of the Angel of the Lord, which were evidently Christophanies. (See Appendix A.) Although some expressions in Heb 7 (which will be considered later) are alleged to identify Melchizedek with Christ, that passage makes it clear that they are quite distinct.

The following treatment of the story is therefore based the more natural view that this man was an inhabitant of Canaan — albeit an illustrious one.

The Meaning Of Melchizedek

It was not a personal name but the combining of two Hebrew words meaning "king" and "righteousness", "being by interpretation King of righteousness" (Heb 7:2). It could mean that he was a righteous king in contrast to the unrighteousness rampant in Canaan, or that because he ruled in righteousness he earned the title. This amounts to the same thing. It is interesting to note a somewhat similar title Adoni-Zedek (Lord of Righteousness) claimed hundreds of years later by one of the Amorite kings, though he was far from righteous (Josh 10:1). The fact that this man was king in Jerusalem is interesting in view of what will be said about Salem.

King Of Salem

Melchizedek was king of Salem, which means king of peace. This raises three questions: (a) does this simply mean that his reign was peaceful? or (b) was Salem a city where he had his throne? and if so (c) was that city later known as Jerusalem (meaning "possession of peace")? There has been a great deal of learned but inconclusive discussion on these points. The reference to Jerusalem in Josh 10:1 already noted may have a bearing on this question. Moreover in Psa 76:2 Salem is linked with Zion and it has been suggested that Salem refers to the secular aspect of Jerusalem and Zion to its religious significance.

There is some attraction in the idea that Salem was a city which became Jerusalem, but those who wish to explore the matter more deeply will be able to consult a good Bible Dictionary or similar work. It has no significant bearing on the particular purpose of these pages, which is to learn as much as possible from God's dealings with Abraham.

Righteousness And Peace

It is most instructive to notice that Heb 7:2 draws attention to the order of titles in Gen 14: "first ... King of righteousness, and after that also king of Salem, which is, King of peace". This invites consideration of the very important principle, often seen in Scripture, that there can be no real peace unless it rests on the basis of righteousness. This is true in regard to

(a) man's relationship with God (b) nation with nation (c) individuals with their fellows, and (d) church fellowship.

a. Man And God

The Epistle to the Romans tackles the age-old question raised by Job: "How can a man be just with God?" (Job 9:2), and shows clearly that peace with God must be on the basis of His righteous claims being satisfied by the redemption accomplished by Christ; so that while God cannot be other than perfectly just or righteous He can at the same time justify (reckon righteous) the one who believes in Jesus. Notice the stress on righteousness in Rom 3:21-26. Only when the foundation of righteousness has been laid do we read of "peace with God through our Lord Jesus Christ" (5:1). Paradoxical though it may seem at first sight, the peace and security of the pardoned sinner do not rest on the love or on the mercy of God but upon His righteousness. The love of God is not mentioned until this foundation has been laid (5:5). Wonderful though this love is, the apostles did not mention it in the preaching of the gospel.

b. Nation And Nation

In international affairs peace usually means no more than absence of actual fighting, but real peace is that condition of things which is congenial to the One who is called the God of peace, in which we are free to live worthwhile and satisfying lives in fellowship with God and in harmony with others. The reason why there is no real peace in the world is that fallen man is unwilling, indeed unable, to do what is right in human affairs. There is much talk of human rights, but history is a sad tale of human wrongs. Individuals, and communities, do not treat each other as they ought. In greed for place, or possession, or power, the strong over-ride the weak. There have been statesmen who have seen the wrong of it all, and it would be ungenerous not to applaud any palliation achieved, but human nature has not been changed. There will be no peace on earth until Christ takes the reins of government, "Behold a king shall reign in righteousness" (Isa 32:1). The result? "The work of righteousness shall be peace and the effect of righteousness quietness and assurance for ever" (v. 17); "He shall judge the people with righteousness — the mountains shall bring peace to the people" (Psa 72:2); "Mercy and truth have met together ... righteousness and peace have kissed each other" (Psa 85:10).

c. The Christian In Society

Few Christians are in a position to exert any influence on international or national affairs but each Christian has a responsibility in his proper sphere in the community. We are told to "live peaceably with all men", but for all his splendid idealism Paul is also very practical and he qualifies his exhortation in two ways:

1. "if it be possible", realising that some contentious people cannot be appeased,
2. "as much as lieth in you", that is to say, we can only do our best.

d. Our Responsibility In The Church

It should be quite different with fellow-believers who share a common life in Christ as children of one Father. The absence of the above qualifications will be noticed in the exhortation to the church at Thessalonica. "Be at peace among yourselves" (1 Thess 5:13). Nevertheless if there is to be true peace in the church there must be righteousness; conditions must be as God would have them. "The kingdom of God is not meat and drink but righteousness and peace and joy in the Holy Ghost ... He that in these things serveth Christ is acceptable to God and approved of men" (Rom 14:17-18). Such people our Lord pronounced blessed: "Blessed are the peacemakers for they shall be called the children (RV sons) of God", i.e. those who resemble their Father. This is more than patching up quarrels which seldom achieves lasting success, but rather "following after those things which make for peace" — i.e. which help to bring about that spiritual atmosphere in which an ungrieved Holy Spirit can exert His gracious influence unhindered (Rom 14:17-19. Cf. Jas 3:17-18).

Kingship And Priesthood

Under the Levitical system priesthood and kingship were quite separate orders, the first pertaining to the tribe of Levi and the other to the tribe of Judah. The two offices were never combined in one person. King Uzziah paid dearly for his presumption in daring to usurp the priest's prerogative (2 Chron 26:16-21). Even our Lord who sprang out of Judah could not have been a priest of the Aaronic order (Heb 7:13-14; 8:4).

It is true that in the equipping and functioning of the Aaronic priesthood we can see beautiful illustrations of Christ's priestly work. Because of this it has been said that His

7

priestly ministry is after the *pattern* of Aaron, but this must not be allowed to obscure the important fact that His priesthood is after the *order* of Melchizedek.

It is a signal honour bestowed on Melchizedek that holding both offices of king and priest he is the only one privileged to be a type of Christ as a "priest upon his throne" (Zech 6:13).

A Kingdom Of Priests

God's will is that under Christ, His people should be a kingdom of priests now, a "holy priesthood" Godward in worship and intercession, and "a royal priesthood" manward in testimony to the world (1 Pet 2:5, 9), as they will also be in a future age (Rev 1:6; 5:9-10). Is there a suggestion in Heb 7:3 ("abideth a priest continually") that Melchizedek did not cease to be a priest at death and that he will be among that holy and royal priesthood?

Timing

Sodom no doubt planned to intervene at the time and place best suited to his purpose; we do not know what the result would have been had his timing succeeded. In the event Melchizedek's timing was superior and he forestalled Sodom. This simple statement leaves unanswered several interesting questions; they are worth asking if only to stimulate thought and help us to set the scene in a real life situation. How did he come to interest himself in Abraham? Had there been any earlier but unrecorded contacts? He seems to have brought to Abraham a fresh concept of God which argues against an earlier meeting. How did he become aware of Abraham's bold venture against the four kings? What prompted him to intervene? Did he foresee Abraham's success and the possible undesirable outcome of such success and so wanted to guard against this? How could he have timed his movements so skilfully?

Or are all these questions beside the point? Was it rather the case of a man walking so closely with God that he could be divinely prompted, enlightened and guided independently of any human agency. We have met individuals with Simeon-like character (Luke 2:25-27) whose movements at times have evidently been divinely guided in remarkable ways beyond coincidence. (But there is good reason to be cautious of those who glibly claim that the Lord had told them to do this or that, and to say this and that. What they proceed to do and say usually reveals to the spiritually discerning that their claim was mistaken.) Think of Elijah given an insight by the angel of the Lord into Ahaziah's condition and reprehensible consultation with the false god of Ekram (2 Kings 1:1-4). Later his successor Elisha was enabled to acquaint the king of Israel with the secret plans of his enemy and so saved Israel from defeat (2 Kings 6:8-12). So why could not the Priest of the Most High God be supernaturally enlightened of Abraham's circumstances, Sodom's scheme, and so be guided that he intervened at the crucial moment?

Be that as it may, Abraham owed Melchizedek a great debt; what shall we say of the debt we owe to our great High Priest, at the throne of grace? Omniscient and omnipotent, knowing all our circumstances, our weaknesses, our temptations and all the plots of the evil one, He is able to "save to the uttermost all who come to God by him" (Heb 7:24-25). Elijah's knowledge of Ahaziah is as nothing in comparison. With what delight Nathaniel, despite his earlier scepticism, learned that Christ was acquainted with his yearnings and problems (John 1:45-51). Moreover as Syria's plans were an open book to Elisha so in a much more wonderful way the machinations of Satan are as clear as noonday to our heavenly Elisha. He knew what was happening in the realm of the unseen as Satan was scheming to bring about Peter's downfall, and He took action to frustrate those tactics as Melchizedek frustrated Sodom (Luke 22:31-32). We shall never know while here below how often we have been saved from Satan's snares. What revelations await us when we review our lives in the light of the throne!

Bread and Wine

Because Melchizedek was a priest some see a sacramental significance in the provision of bread and wine, even to the extent of linking it with the Lord's supper. Surely this is fanciful. Is it not simpler to see it as a gracious act in refreshing the weary warrior and establishing a relaxed attitude of fellowship? Will it be thought fanciful, however, to see in the bread ("which strengtheneth man's heart", Psa 104:15) a reminder of the spiritual strength to resist the tempter imparted by the bread of God's Word? "I have written

unto you young men because ye are strong, and the word of
God abideth in you and ye have overcome the wicked one" (1
John 2:14). In the temptation, after saying, "It is written, Man
shall not live by bread alone, but by every word that
proceedeth out of the mouth of God", our Lord showed that it
was by the word of God He defeated the tempter: "Get thee
behind me Satan for it is written ..." (Matt 4:3-10). The wine
("that maketh glad the heart of man", Psa 104:15) typifies the
joy imparted by the Holy Spirit: "Ye ... received the word in
much affliction with joy of the Holy Ghost" (1 Thess 1:6);
"The joy of the Lord is your strength" (Neh 8:10). Certainly
our divine Melchizedek ministers strength to us by this
spiritual bread and wine.

Priest Of The Most High God

Abraham had spent his whole life in the midst of pagan
nations whose false gods were regarded as being more or less
local and inoperative outside their sphere. God's promise to
"show" him the land to which he was called helped Abraham
to realise that his God was not so restricted. Nevertheless it
must have been a welcome assurance to him when the Lord
appeared to him on his arrival in Canaan. It is significant that
his first altar was to "the Lord who appeared to him" (12:7).
From a spiritual standpoint his life was a lonely one, the only
like-minded believers being in his own camp, and they were
probably few. It must therefore have been a great thrill to him
to find amid the spiritual and moral degradation of the
Canaanites a priest of the Most High God, and even a
believing community, for a priest implies that there were
those whom he represented before God. This is one of several
indications we have that through the ages of time God has had
His witnesses in earth's darkest corners, even if among the
relatively small population in the awful days before the Flood
(when humanity sank to perhaps the lowest level it has ever
reached) that witness was confined to the family of Noah. The
case of Jethro, the priest of Midian with whom the fugitive
Moses found shelter, comes to mind. It is not unlikely that Job
and his God-fearing friends lived in patriarchal times.

It is a subject of fascinating interest, but the OT does not
provide a record of the Spirit of God's movements among the
nations during those ages. Such a record would require more
volumes than most of us would have time to read. The OT is

principally concerned with the origins and history of His chosen people Israel.

Abraham himself had once been a worshipper of false gods (Josh 24:2, 14), and he was now surrounded by the Canaanites who had various false gods of their own (Psa 106:34-38). He was to learn from Melchizedek that the God whose call he had obeyed was the Most High God — the uppermost God — none higher than He. As Psa 95:3 puts it, "The Lord is a great God and a great king above all gods". Growing experimental knowledge of God is the essence of spiritual progress, and we shall see that Abraham appropriated for himself, and benefited from, this further concept of God. Paul recognising that the Colossians had known the grace of God prayed that they might be filled with the knowledge of His will, and increase in the knowledge of God Himself (Col 1:6-10). As for himself he counted all he had sacrificed as nothing compared with the excellence of a growing acquaintance with Christ (Phil 3:8). Christ Himself said that to know the only true God and Jesus Christ whom He had sent was eternal life (John 17:3).

Priestly Blessing

It was in his office as priest of the Most High God that Melchizedek blessed Abraham. To a limited extent the patriarchs filled a priest-like role in their own households and sometimes in relation to others. Abraham prayed for Sodom, (18:25ff) and for Abimelech, although in that case he is called a prophet (20:7). Jacob blessed Pharaoh (thereby showing himself superior to Pharaoh) and later his sons, with prophetic vision and foresight. Cf. Job and his household (Job 1:5).

This is not the case of patriarchal blessing between equals but the exercise of a prerogative which marked Melchizedek as greater than Abraham (Heb 7:7); if he was greater than Abraham then he must have been great indeed: "Consider how great this man was" (Heb 7:4). It is tempting to wonder whether his blessing anticipated, in spirit at least, that beautiful and well known form of blessing defined for the guidance of Aaron and his sons (Num 6:23-26).

The blessing implied God's approval of a courageous expedition and at the same time saved Abraham from any temptation to be proud of his prowess, by declaring that the

Most High God had delivered his enemies into his hand. It is interesting that Lot's enemies were regarded as his also, because he was ready to identify himself with the cause of his nephew whom he regarded as his brother (13:8). David so identified himself with the cause of God that he reckoned God's enemies to be his (Psa 139:21-22) and amazingly God identifies Himself with His people and reckons their enemies to be His (Zech 2:8).

As Abraham waged war against the invading kings so the Church is called to wage war against the powers of evil. Abraham had to use physical weapons against the physical foe, but our weapons are spiritual yet "mighty through God to the pulling down of strongholds" (2 Cor 10:3-5). Like Abraham, "We are not sufficient of ourselves to think anything of ourselves"; happy are we if we can truthfully add "our sufficiency is of God" (2 Cor 3:5).

Possessor Of Heaven And Earth

The blessing pronounced was in the name of the Most High God but with this addition: "possessor of heaven and earth". This was probably a new development in Abraham's conception of God, and the sequel shows that he took a firm grasp of this revelation and entered into the good of it. With our ready access to instruction in theology there is the danger of being satisfied with increasing knowledge about God without being sufficiently concerned with the need of growing acquaintance with God. It is well to remember that all belongs to God: "Every beast of the forest is mine and the cattle on a thousand hills ... The world is mine and the fulness thereof" (Psa 50:10-12). This fact should not only save the child of God from anxiety as to his heavenly Father's ability to supply his need but it should also influence his ideas of ownership. Certainly our lawfully-acquired property is ours in the sense that God gives us the right to own it and to choose what use we make of it, although, alas! the right is often wrongly used. Peter recognised that Ananias had the right to decide what to do with his wealth — his offence was in being deceitful (Acts 5:4). Paul does not say it is wrong to be rich, although he warns of the dangers of riches, especially when a person is determined to get rich. Nevertheless we can properly enjoy what God had entrusted to us and at the same time be desirous of being rich in good works by using our resources for the benefit of the needy (1 Tim 6:10-17). Money in itself is not evil, it is the love of money which is the root of all (kinds of) evil. There are many other roots of evil, but the love of money has led men into all kinds of evil to procure it (1 Tim 6:9-10 RV).

It is a safeguard to remember that all we have has been given us. Even in the matter of Christian service our talents and privileges are gifts from the risen Lord (Eph 4:7). Hence Paul says in this very connection, "What hast thou that thou didst not receive? Now if thou didst receive it why dost thou glory ...?" (1 Cor 4:7). To be so foolish as to take pride in any gift entrusted to us is one of the surest ways to destroy its usefulness. Are we proud of what we may think is our generosity in the practical support of the work of God? David can teach us a lesson here. When he had given so enthusiastically and lavishly to the construction of the temple he remembered that "all that is in the heavens and in the earth is thine ... all things come of thee and of thine own have we given thee" (1 Chron 29:3, 11, 14).

Tithes

"He (Abraham) gave him (Melchizedek) tithes (a tenth RV) of all" — i.e. of all the spoils. (A moment's thought as to what would be entailed in such a transaction will tell against the idea of Christophany). A tithe is not an act of generosity but a token that all belongs to God; He appreciates any sacrifice this may involve which is not usually very great. The instructions given in 1 Cor 16:1-2 have particular reference to the relief-fund the apostle and others were organising in Gentile churches on behalf of Jewish believers in Jerusalem who were suffering hardship. In this connection a study of the following passages would prove interesting and profitable: Acts 11:29; 24:17; Rom 15:26; 2 Cor 8:4; 9:1, 12; Gal 2:10. It will be noticed that the contributions to the fund were not determined on the basis of percentages but according to how a man had prospered and according as he purposes in his heart. Surely we may regard the same principles as applying to other contributions to the work of God, through various channels: "Not grudgingly or of necessity, for God loveth a cheerful giver". Although percentages are not the guide, it has been calculated that if every professing Christian gave one tenth of his income to Christian work the total would be sufficient to support adequately all that is being attempted world-wide. Of course, many Christians give much more than ten percent. On the other hand, it is possible for a person to give away what should have been used to discharge his proper responsibilities to his own dependants. Let such "learn first to show piety at home". "If any provide not for his own ... he hath denied the faith and is worse than an infidel (an unbeliever RV)" (1 Tim 5:4, 8).

When giving involves some personal sacrifice it is precious to God as the Saviour's wonderful commendation of the poor widow testifies. In His eyes she had given more than all the other offerers, although the temple treasurer may have thought the two mites an irritating entry in his cash book.

However, not to try the readers' patience too much we return to Abraham's tithe. Apart from the acknowledgement of God's rights it showed that having recovered Sodom's property Abraham (a) had a right to allocate the spoils, and (b) acknowledged Melchizedek's superiority as the one who could rightly receive tithes from him, as pointed out in Heb 7.

It may be worthwhile to consider before leaving the subject the form in which the tithe was paid. Presumably it would have been possible to assess the total value of the booty and to pay an appropriate weight of silver, as Abraham paid for the site of Sarah's burial (23:16). However, Heb 7:4 gives the impression that actual goods were transferred; if so, Melchizedek could not have transported such a load to Salem without adequate assistance. He almost certainly arrived on the scene with a retinue; we cannot suppose that a king had travelled alone. What a wonderful occasion it must have been for Abraham to enjoy, if only for a short time, fellowship with a company of like-minded men owning allegiance to God's king and priest. It must have remained a treasured memory. Do we so treasure our privileges (1 John 1:3-7)?

Melchizedek now makes his exit from Abraham's life; not so our great High Priest. We shall never be deprived of His ministry who "continueth ever ... able to save them to the uttermost that come unto God by him" (Heb 7:24-25; cf. 10:12, 14; 13:8).

The King Of Sodom's Proposal

Melchizedek's mission accomplished, he departed, and the king of Sodom appears on the scene hoping to negotiate a favourable settlement with Abraham. He had contrived to meet in the king's dale, perhaps thinking there might be some subtle psychological advantage in being on his own ground. It is too much to hope that he will be able to secure both goods and people. With industry and determination he can in due course replace the captured goods, but there is no possibility of establishing any kind of kingdom unless he has the personnel.

Knowing full well the victors' rights, he nevertheless puts on a brazen face, and assuming the air of a benefactor distributing largess with a liberal hand says, "Give me the persons and take the goods to thyself". Quite evidently he sees that Abraham is the man who matters and he ignores the others. Maybe, too, he thought this strange unworldly man would be what is called a "soft touch" compared with his associates. Probably he had tried to assess the possible reactions of Abraham and how best to respond to them, but the patriarch's reply completely took the wind out of his sails.

Abraham's Attitude

Abraham had embraced Melchizedek's fresh revelation of God as the Most High God, Possessor of heaven and earth, and it must have been a great thrill to realise that this was the same Lord (Jehovah) who had appeared to him and to whom he had built an altar when he had entered Canaan. So he linked the name Jehovah with these new titles (see v. 22).

He had foreseen a meeting with the king of Sodom, and whatever his earlier intentions had been, he solemnly resolved in the light of this new revelation that, seeing his God was the Possessor of heaven and earth and so fully capable of giving His servant what was good in His sight, he would take nothing from Sodom. He is a wise Christian who firmly settles his moral standards in the light of God's word before he has to face tests. Daniel purposed in his heart what he would do when he would have to take a stand (Dan 1:8).

Having allowed Sodom to say his piece this great man stands forward and with quiet dignity, perhaps again suiting the action to his word, announced the decision made previous to the encounter — "I have lift up my hand (i.e. in token of a solemn oath Exod 6:8 RV, Dan 12:7) unto the Lord, possessor of heaven and earth that I will not take from a thread to a shoe latchet". His reason for this was: "Lest thou shouldest say, I have made Abraham rich". Even so, there would have been no truth in such a claim, as any acquainted with the circumstances would know, but Abraham would not give Sodom even the chance of making such a claim. It would not be honouring to his God to allow even the slightest appearance of being indebted to such a man. It is not unlikely that he had been grieved by hearing some such whisper from some of his retainers when he came out of Egypt enriched by Pharaoh, and he was not going to risk a repetition.

A Reservation

Although acting in faith he renounced all claim to any of the spoils of war, yet he calmly showed his authority to dispose of it by reserving the rights of his three colleagues whom Sodom had chosen to ignore. He did not impose on them what was right for himself, an important principle for Christians to observe. Paul upheld the right of believers who had the faith to free themselves of legalistic prohibitions, but he warned them against any attempt to coerce others who lacked the same faith. "Hast thou faith? Have it to thyself before God" (Rom 14:22). Perhaps this is where a mistake was made with regard to Lot in the first place. He had not heard the call of God, and had not the word of God on which true faith is based, so went out on the strength of Abraham's faith (Rom 10:17).

The Effect On Sodom

No doubt the king congratulated himself on coming out of it so well — he kept all the personnel with the unexpected bonus of a quarter of the goods. Had all the recent events been a voice to him? From what is revealed in the Scriptures of God's providential dealing with the nations, the original defeat fourteen years before should have been a warning to the godless regime. That warning having been unheeded a severer blow had fallen on them, a louder voice calling for repentance. We might have thought that the magnanimity which made his re-establishment possible, and Abraham's powerful witness to the reality of the Most High God would have made him a humbler and wiser man. Alas he went his way with an unchanged heart, hardened by the deceitfulness of sin (Heb 3:13). The life of the city went from bad to worse

(18:20) until the mercy and forbearance of God were exhausted and the final blow fell resulting in its complete destruction to prevent the moral pollution infecting a wider circle.

Lot's Decision

It might have been thought that Lot, at least, would see the significance of all that had happened, and, impressed by his uncle's noble testimony, would repent of his folly by resuming a pastoral life in fellowship with his uncle. Trying to restore something like normal life in the ransacked city could not have been a very attractive prospect. He had found that the wickedness of his fellow-citizens had been a constant vexation to him (2 Pet 2:7) so why put up with it again? Ah, a more modern way-of-life in contrast to a pastoral set-up in tents had altered Lot's outlook and, in addition, his family had put down roots in the city and made their friends there as we learn later.

No doubt, too, there would be added prestige for him; his rescue had been the motivation for his uncle's magnificent expedition which had saved Sodom in the bargain. But worldliness gains a strange grip, and by not learning the lesson his capture might have taught him he resumed his role in Sodom, narrowly escaped its final overthrow, and ended his days in unutterable disgrace.

Chapter VIII

Cast Down

(Gen 15:1-21)

The Problem Of Depression

To the thoughtful this remarkable chapter offers invaluable insights into the fluctuating moods of doubt and fear, with occasional flashes of elation, which can perplex and distress believers under stress, but which they are reluctant to confess to others either because of the risk of being regarded as unspiritual or because like Asaph they are too conscientious to run the risk of unsettling the faith of others (Psa 73:15).

The way in which the Lord dealt with Abraham may yield guidance not only to such sufferers but to concerned friends who genuinely wish to be a help. Often victims of depression are at a loss to explain their moods, and when they think they have found the reason it can be the wrong one. On the other hand, those who aspire to be amateur psychologists may be cautioned not to rush too readily into the delicate task of helping burdened souls, for more harm than good can be done. The problem calls for mature and experienced Christians.

In this matter, as in others, Abraham's case is an extreme example, perhaps designedly to embrace in principle our lesser trials and put them in perspective. As we shall see in his case there was a combination of causes which falls to the lot of very few. It is important to remember that we are looking into a case of temporary depression; persisting fear and anxiety call for expert advice, although love and patience can never do any harm.

The Background

"After these things" leads us to consider what follows against the background of the recent events: Abraham's dramatic victory over the four kings, his rescue of Lot, his exhilarating encounter with the priest of the Most High God, and his consequent admirable rejection of Sodom's proposal.

This combination no doubt lifted him up on the crest of a wave of success (always a dangerous time), but as so often happens a reaction set in and the taxing days of exhausting physical effort, with the accompanying risks and tensions, were now taking their toll and he was sinking into a trough of depression. One element was fear.

Fear Hath Torment

We know from the later mention of the stars that it was night time, but the worn-out warrior was too unsettled to rest. If he had retired to the interior of his large tent he could not have been "brought forth abroad" without disturbing the other occupants, so we conclude he was sitting by the tent-door, brooding as he looked out on the now-silent camp where his tired followers were asleep. The oppressive quiet and loneliness of night when others are peacefully slumbering adds to the distress of burdened minds.

That he was afraid we know from the Lord's words, "Fear not, Abram"; this would have been pointless if he had not been afraid. How strange this seems in a man who a few days before had been the soul of courage in the face of formidable odds. Of what was he afraid? Since it must have some connection with recent events it needs no great effort of imagination to suggest the answer. Melchizedek had ascribed the victory to the Lord delivering Abraham's enemies into his hand, and we might have thought that this would have imparted a settled sense of security, but such is human nature that the comfort of earlier assurance can evaporate under depression. In this frame of mind he was quite likely to feel that perhaps after all success had been due quite naturally to the element of surprise in falling on an unsuspecting foe at night, and from different directions. Was he fearing that the scattered troops having been able to re-group were now on the march again resolved to avenge a humiliating defeat, his little army hopelessly outnumbered?

Considering that their leaders had been slain and their forces routed this fear was, of course, quite illogical, to say nothing of the fact that the God who had delivered him then could do so again. But who is rational when a prey to strong emotions whether of fear, envy, hate or desire? It is important to remember that the mere fact that a fear is groundless does not make it any the less real to the victim. Argument is of little use in these circumstances. Fear has torment but the love of God, where enjoyed, can cast it out (1 John 4:18).

Effects Of Disappointment

Our sympathy for Abraham must be all the greater when we realise that added to his fear was a keen disappointment suffered by an affectionate heart. The whole object of that splendid venture had been the rescue of his loved nephew. And what had been the result of all that effort and risk? Instead of learning the lesson and resuming a pastoral life with its blessings, Lot had simply returned to the ransacked Sodom to rebuild life there. Abraham may have felt that bond-service in Mesopotamia would be preferable to involvement again in that sink of iniquity. In that sense all had been in vain, and the only result, so it seemed, was that he was now exposed to possible revenge from those who had previously been content to leave him in peace.

Other Examples

Body, mind and soul inter-act in very subtle ways, and Abraham is far from being the only example of depression owing to physical and mental strains aggravated by disappointment. The point is so important that we will look at another case. That spiritual giant, Elijah, made a noble stand on Mount Carmel, exposing himself to considerable peril in a bid to turn the nation back to God. It was a long and exhausting day, but his life-style had made him a man of splendid physique who toward the end of the day could run in front of Ahab's chariot all the way to the gates of Jezreel. However, when the almost inevitable reaction set in he gave way to panic and fled from the empty threat of an evil queen whose wrath he had previously scorned. It was an empty threat, because if she had been determined to take the risk of killing a now popular figure she would not have given him a day's notice of her intention. It was bluff in the hope that he would flee the country and cease to be a thorn in her side, whilst at the same time being discredited as a coward. After a long and arduous journey he was alone in the wilderness tired and hungry. Like Abraham he was also a disappointed man. What on Mount

Carmel had seemed to be a marvellous revival of the nation's spiritual life proved to be very superficial, and in his dejection he imagined he was the only one who was faithful to God. He felt resentful against God's people, and feeling himself to be a failure lay down under the shade of a juniper tree and requested to die. He was badly in need of meat and drink and sleep, and when God had made provision for this he was able to take a two hundred mile journey to the Mount of God. There were years of service left to him, and when he had had the satisfaction of training a worthy successor, although of a very different disposition, he was honoured by being taken to heaven and, centuries later, by accompanying Moses to meet the Son of God on the Mount of Transfiguration. In a day still future he will be the herald of a movement of God which will usher in, not a superficial revival, but a new age of glory for Israel. Such are the ways of God whose purpose is not always clear to His servants when circumscribed by the limitations of frail human nature.

If the reader realises the relevance of all this for disheartened souls he may not be too impatient to consider one of the experiences of David. Though God had wonderfully delivered him from many perils since his youth he nevertheless fell a prey to fear and dejection after being hunted like a partridge by a jealous and impetuous king who had made several ineffectual attempts on his life. Losing confidence in the call of God, implied in his anointing by Samuel, he now felt convinced that he would one day perish at the hand of Saul. Then, quite illogically, he argued that by fleeing to Gath he would escape out of Saul's hand. We would have thought that when Gath came into his mind he would have been reminded of the giant of Gath who terrorised the armies of Israel but whom he slew with a sling in the name of the Lord, when he was but a youth. Fear is very short-sighted.

There is not the slightest intention to criticise these great men of God but rather to reinforce the lesson that even the most devoted and courageous hearts have passed through dark experiences, not suspecting that their moods were explicable on very natural grounds (1 Kings 18:17; 19:14; 1 Sam 26:20; 27:1).

Let us beware of feeling so indispensable that we have an uncomfortable feeling of guilt if we are not always busy. If any doubt the need of relaxation and refreshment let them consider the Saviour's gracious command to His disciples

when there had been many coming and going so that they had
not had sufficient leisure to eat in peace: "Come ye yourselves
apart into a desert place and rest awhile". Not "Go", but
"Come". There is a world of difference (Mark 6:31).

I Am Thy Shield

To return to Abraham. Sheer physical exhaustion caused
him to fall into a sleep so deep that the Lord had to penetrate
his consciousness by speaking in a vision — the only such
occasion in his life so far as we know. He was normally very
susceptible to the voice of God. Instead of chiding him for his
lack of faith, as many would have done, the Lord knowing that
he was not being his true self approached him sympathetically
by the kindly use of his name, not saying simply, "Fear not",
but "Fear not Abram" — a gentle touch recorded on only one
other critical occasion (22:1). With perfect understanding of
His servant's frame (Psa 103:14) He did not reason him out of
his fears, nor did He offer the platitudinous "Don't worry" so
often blithely given by friends, well-meaning but quite unable
to give any help in throwing off anxiety or to suggest any
practical alternative. Instead of going into reasons why an
enemy attack was out of the question the Lord gave him good
and solid grounds for not being afraid: "Fear not Abram: I am
thy shield". Notice the present tense; I am thy shield not
merely if and when the need should arise but now and always.
Cf. "My grace is sufficient for thee" (2 Cor 12:9).

God was saying in effect, "Before an enemy can penetrate
to you he must be able to penetrate me". Abraham was not
being asked to bolster up his faith by reliance upon some
doctrine, however precious, but upon a present fact — the
protection of the Almighty. No wonder those who trust God
can be assured that "no weapon that is formed against thee
shall prosper" (Isa 54:17). God Himself is the shield. This is
delightfully personal — doctrine can seem very academic
when one's condition is not in accord with it. The importance
of the enjoyment, in these conditions, of personal relationship
is perfectly obvious by the recurring pronouns in the
Saviour's invitation to those who are weary and heavy laden:
"Come unto me" (Matt 11:28-30).

Paul exhorts us to take the shield of faith wherewith to
quench all the fiery darts of the devil (Eph 6:16). This is not
the small round shield used to stop a single arrow but the large

shield a Roman soldier used to protect his whole body from a rain of missiles; thus Paul says "quench all the fiery darts of the wicked (one)". Some take this to mean that our faith is the shield, but, if this is the case, experience shows that it is a shield which can easily be pierced. Abraham's faith failed to protect him from fear in Egypt and again in Gerah in similar circumstances. Does it not rather mean the shield of which faith avails itself — God Himself. This is abundantly clear from the numerous references in the Psalms to God being His people's shield (Heb. *magen*). Interestingly enough both words in Psa 91:4 refer to two smaller types of shield — the buckler and the target (Heb. *tsinnah* and *socherah*).

The hundreds of exhortations to "fear not" or "be not afraid" testify to the universal prevalence of this debilitating and crippling emotion — it is one of the devil's favourite weapons and is difficult to throw off. However, when the Lord commands He can enable those who are willing to obey.

Thy Exceeding Great Reward

The Lord went further than the assurance that He was Abraham's shield; He added, "and thy exceeding great reward". Again this was very personal: "I" and "thy". This was not a promise of material gain; the reward as the shield was God Himself. He is the reward, the great reward, the exceeding great reward. This accords with the very clear Scriptural principle that the greatest spiritual enrichment and felicity is to be found in God Himself. It is very refreshing to trace the numerous references to gladness, joy and rejoicing which run like a refrain through the Psalms and to notice the many subjects which were causes for delight. However, the ultimate was God Himself. The writer of Psa 43 speaks of approach to God — he mentions God's light and truth, His holy hill and His tabernacles, of going to God's altar — but the ultimate is "unto God my exceeding joy" (cf. "Exceeding great reward"). Or listen to Asaph: "Whom have I in heaven but thee ... God ... my portion for ever" (Psa 73:26). What, according to Prov 2:1-5, is the grand reward of such earnest diligence as receiving, hiding, inclining, applying, crying, seeking and searching? Here it is: "Then shalt thou ... find the knowledge of God". When at his conversion the glory of Christ was revealed to Paul he set out on a life of service reckoning that all else was loss for the excellency of the knowledge of Christ Jesus as his Lord.

As he was drawing to the close of that devoted life, having now been stripped of everything for the Master's sake, he had not changed his mind: "for whom I have suffered the loss of all things and do count them but dung that I may win Christ ... I press toward the mark for the prize of the high calling of God in Christ Jesus" (Phil 3:7-14). The highest of all authorities said in speaking to His Father, "This is life eternal, that they might know thee, the only true God, and Jesus Christ whom thou hast sent" (John 17:3).

What Wilt Thou Give Me?

So unsettled was Abraham's mind that he seemed to ignore the assurance that God was his shield and took up instead the question of reward, although in his weariness and apathy he missed the real significance of it and assumed that God had some material gift in mind. We can sense an almost petulant tone in his response, "O Lord God (Adonai Jehovah) what wilt thou give me seeing I go (hence) childless? (v. 2 RV). It is as if he is saying that he is sufficiently provided for with material things, and that whilst no doubt as the Possessor of heaven and earth God could give him anything, what is there in all the world that would compensate for the bitter disappointment of having to leave this world childless. "I have set my heart on a posterity ever since you made promise to me when at your call I left Ur many years ago to become a stranger in this alien land. Now it is too late, I shall leave this world childless and a steward of mine is going to inherit all I possess". (The fact that he did not contemplate making Lot his heir is an indication of how disappointed he was with Lot.) He feels disillusioned as if God had let him down. He almost reproaches God for trying to retract His promise and for trying to buy him off with material things as a sort of poor consolation prize. Again v.3 opens like v.2, "And Abram said", almost as though Abraham had paused momentarily in a disgruntled fashion nursing his grievance and then had taken up the same complaint in almost the same words. How true this is of us when we are in a complaining mood.

He was speaking in bitterness of spirit in terms not appropriate to the reverence due to God, but again the Lord made gracious allowance for His distressed servant and bore patiently with him instead of rebuking him. With other

Scriptural examples in mind we almost venture to think that God would prefer us to say what we feel. After all if there is resentment in our hearts He knows it and efforts to mask it by uttering pious platitudes do not deceive Him.

One example is the case of Moses who, after reluctantly obeying God by going to Pharaoh, found that it had only resulted in the people's plight being made worse, and they not unnaturally vented their anger on him. Moses returned to the Lord to complain and ended up with, "Neither hast thou delivered thy people at all". Certainly God had given him fair warning to expect this in the early stages, but forgetting this he spoke out in the bitterness of his heart. Here again the Lord's reply shows that He understood his disappointment and reassured him. We must not, however, forget that when years after in a fit of anger he spoke unadvisedly in calling God's people rebels he had to pay a severe penalty.

Jeremiah in a later day obeyed God in going to the people with an unpopular message. When he was made a reproach and a derision for his pains, he complained that God had deceived him and regretted that he had allowed himself to be taken in. However, Jeremiah quickly recovered and rejoiced that the Lord was with him (Jer 20:7-11).

Lack of proper reverence must never be condoned, but the point of the foregoing remarks is that if there is bitterness in our hearts it is better to acknowledge it rather than let it smoulder beneath the surface, building up tension. The Lord understands the stresses which explain it, but He is always right in all His ways, and they are happy who can trust His wisdom, love and power when it is difficult to understand His dealings.

Under The Stars

Abraham had emerged from his deep sleep and the words, "and behold the word of the Lord came unto him", suggest that he could now be spoken to directly instead of in a vision. He was very emphatically assured that his steward would not be his heir — he should have a child of his own. Despite this emphatic assurance Abraham was not in a receptive mood, and the Lord knew that a gloomy shadowy camp was not a helpful environment for a despondent soul. The expression "brought him forth abroad" seems to convey a hint that some degree of gentle coercion was necessary to overcome his lethargy. Earlier when he had separated from Lot he had been invited to look north, south, east and west (13:14); now he is told to "look toward heaven". This is a very healthy attitude, in the spiritual sense of "looking not at the things which are seen but at the things which are not seen, for the things which are seen are temporal but the things which are not seen are eternal" (2 Cor 4:18). However, the literal act of looking toward heaven aids this attitude of mind, and we may with advantage follow our Master's example more often (John 17:1). Under a star-lit sky, with its suggestion of ageless infinity, not only is God's glory declared but man's seeming insignificance is felt. Pondering the untold ages during which these vast heavenly bodies have followed their appointed orbits through immeasurable space in obedience to their Creator's word impresses us with the brevity of human history — hardly more than a tick of the celestial clock. But it was not man's insignificance which struck David; it was rather the wonder of God's interest, in that He was mindful of man (Psa 8:3-4; 19:1-2).

The city dweller, deprived of the full glory of this splendid spectacle by the glare of street-lighting and some degree of pollution in the atmosphere, would be well advised to make a deliberate effort periodically to be alone on a clear moonless night in some quiet spot where he can gaze meditatively on what can be an awe-inspiring sight. If earth enjoyed this display only once every hundred years, the media world-wide would devote a good deal of space well in advance to the impending event and those whose life span fell between two such occasions would be objects of commiseration. Because it is so regularly available many never take advantage of it to their great loss.

Numbering The Stars

Abraham had often stood beneath the stars which in that latitude shine with a brilliance not seen in other parts, so he would not need to have his attention drawn to this splendid sight. Indeed he was challenged with the impossibility of numbering them. Remembering that it is only such stars as are visible to the unaided eye which were in question, it is clear that the impossibility did not lie in the visible stars being without number. Actually ancient astrologers, better placed than Abraham then was, did attempt to number the visible stars and arrived at an approximate number somewhat in excess of two thousand, but in the nature of the case they could not be exact. The practical difficulties in accounting for every star in a revolving hemisphere, with varying conditions in different parts of the sky, make it impossible. It is now thought that on a very clear night the stars visible to unaided average sight must be about three thousand.

The Lord was not telling Abraham that his posterity would equal the visible stars in number — that would be no great wonder. What was meant was that his descendants would be too numerous to count accurately. That this was the point is clear from the fact that Moses used the same comparison when the number of the children of Israel was already far in excess of the visible stars (Deut 1:10). David used the same figure of speech when the people were even more numerous; by this time it had probably become a sort of idiom (1 Chron 27:23). Nevertheless it is remarkable that Scripture did anticipate modern discovery in recognising that actually stars are literally beyond number, for Isa 40:26 says that the Holy One calls them all by name "by greatness of his might". Cf. Psa 147:4-5.

The knowledgeable who lived when there was no suspicion of the existence of innumerable invisible stars must have wondered how calling a few thousand by name could be cited as evidence of God's greatness. We now know that even the numbering of such billions would take thousands of years in the normal way, to say nothing about having a different name for each. We are quite confident that, as in the past, Scripture has often been shown to be wiser than its critics, so statements questioned to-day will yet be proved correct.

It would be a pity to pass on without noting that in the last quoted passage, Psa 147:4-5, the same mighty God is first of all spoken of as the Healer of the broken-hearted and the One who binds up wounds, as if this takes precedence. Cf. Luke 4:18.

The two references to the Lord speaking to Abraham in the one verse (v. 5) may be an indication that he was given a moment for the sight to sink in before the announcement was made, "So shall thy seed be".

Dust – Stars – Sand

He had already been given such a promise but with the dust

of the earth as a comparison. This use of an earthly and then of a heavenly figure has been taken to intimate a natural and a spiritual posterity, Rom 4:16 and Gal 3:29 being cited in support. Whilst admitting the idea that Abraham in the natural sense is the father of many nations and in the spiritual sense father of believers, it is a mistake to see Israel in the one and the Church in the other. The comparison of the stars with Israel is often made in the national sense without implying a distinction between the natural and the spiritual. The further figure in 22:17, "the sand on the sea shore", has been taken to signify the other nations which sprang from Abraham, but this figure is also applied to Israel (Isa 48:19). So while these studies accept a distinct element of typology in the Scriptures, we prefer to see these three figures taken from earth and sky and sea simply as different ways of emphasising the point.

Our interest in this chapter is more concerned with what may be learnt from God's deaings with him in his fluctuating moods.

He Believed In The Lord

Abraham seems to have been mentally refreshed by gazing on the stars — certainly his response to the promise, "So shall thy seed be", was in striking contrast to his recent doubt, having regard to the querulous scepticism he then showed. "He believed in (LXX into) the Lord" is a tremendous statement especially in his peculiar situation at this time. Its importance is underlined by the comment, so wonderfully anticipative of vital NT doctrine, "and it was counted unto him for righteousness"; it put him in a right relation with God as faith in Him and therefore in His word always does. This is much more than acknowledging a promise as something abstract and isolated, it is heart-reliance on the promise because of complete trust in the Promiser. Think of the use Paul made of this statement in his masterly treatment of the great doctrine of justification by faith and not by works. It is one of the many incidental evidences of the divine inspiration of Scripture that the seeds of such a vital doctrine should have been embedded in it at such an early stage of revelation (Rom 4:3; Gal 3:6). However, in the record of numerous OT worthies in Heb 11 faith is always linked with its practical outworkings, although only one example of the many effects of faith is chosen in each case, with but two exceptions. Faith is attributed to Moses in connection with two of his consequent decisions and with three in the case of Abraham. Remarkably enough the very important incident we are now considering is not mentioned; it was a matter of inward faith known only to God. What is mentioned is the outstanding evidence of Abraham's faith when years later he offered up Isaac.

Justified By Works

When James took up a similar line of thought he made a statement which has been a difficulty to many: "Abraham was justified by works". He has been understood as contradicting Paul but they are not in conflict with each other. Rather they are united in conflict against error, not confronting each other, but standing back to back defending the truth against attacks from opposite directions. James accepts the statement in Gen 15 that "Abraham believed in God and it was counted to him for righteousness", but he says that this Scripture was "fulfilled" when some twenty years later he offered his son. It was then that he was "justified by works" — the fact that he was ready to offer Isaac in the confidence that God would raise him from the dead demonstrated clearly the reality of his faith.

The explanation that he was justified by faith in the eyes of God who alone could see faith and was later justified by works in the eyes of men who could not see faith, looks in the right direction but it is not altogether satisfactory. It is not likely that many would feel that Abraham was justified in offering his son for a burnt-offering. Moreover, James cites the case of Rahab as another example of being justified by works when she collaborated with the spies. None of her fellow-citizens would see it in that light even if the Israelites did (Jas 2:21-25).

The difficulty arises partly from a tendency to force the meaning of a word (in this case the word "justified") into a rigid mould regardless of the context. When, for example, the Saviour said, "Wisdom is justified of (by) her children" (Matt 11:19) He meant that though His critics failed to understand the will of God and misinterpreted His care for sinners, the wisdom of God was vindicated by the beneficial results it produced. In the cases of Abraham and Rahab, the validity of their claim to believe in God was vindicated by their readiness to act on their conviction.

A Deeper Gloom

Perhaps nothing could better illustrate the vagaries of human nature than the disclosure here that the blessedness of revived faith can so soon be swamped by the misery of doubt again. The extent to which a disturbed soul can become involved in a conflict of emotions, swinging like a pendulum between hope and despair, is amazing. The writer of Psa 42 speaks of the joy he once had in going to the house of God and joining in praise with those who kept holy-day. Then he chides himself for being cast down, and then exhorts himself to hope in God in the confidence that he will soon be praising God again for His help. The words are hardly out of his mouth before he has to acknowledge that his soul is cast down again. He says that God's waves and billows have gone over him. Then confidence that the Lord will command his loving-kindness is followed by a pained enquiry as to why God has forgotten him. The Psalm ends with a renewed confession that his soul is cast down and again he encourages himself to hope in God.

Of course Abraham was weary in mind and body after so much sleeplessness and anxiety. But no night lasts for ever. With the coming of dawn the stars began to wane and finally faded from sight as the landscape gradually came into view. As he looked over the land across which he had travelled in various directions, God reminded him that just as He had brought him out of the gloom of the camp so He had brought him out of the darkness of idolatry in Ur to give him the land of Canaan. This was virtually the repetition of former promises, far less wonderful than the promise that his seed would be as the dust of the earth and as the stars of heaven. Yet the very man who had a few moments before risen to the heights of faith in that great matter fell a prey to doubt on this lesser issue. After walking through the length and breadth of it he could not call a single plot his own.

Asking For A Sign

"Whereby shall I know?" was in effect asking for some sign to bolster up his flagging faith. Again we have the unusual form of address as in v. 2, "O Lord God (Adonai Jehovah)", as if he were impatiently remonstrating with God.

Looking for a sign was not normally regarded as commendable, especially when springing from unbelief (Matt 12:39). Yet on occasions signs were granted, as with Moses and Gideon, when it was not so much lack of faith in God's power but lack of confidence in their own ability to carry out His purposes. If we do not have such inner conflicts it may be because we do not venture all for God as these men did.

In this instance God was prepared to encourage Abraham by a sign which must have exceeded his expectations. Although the purpose of the command to take three animals and two birds was not stated, Abraham would have no difficulty in understanding what was meant. It was an accepted practice that when two parties had entered into an important contract they would symbolically bind themselves to their mutual obligations by dividing the body of an animal and then both would walk between the pieces, the idea being that breaking their pledges would be no more possible than the two pieces coming together to become a living animal again (Jer 34:18-19). For God to propose doing this on such a large scale was a generous gesture which must have profoundly impressed Abraham as evidence that God was taking the matter very seriously indeed.

Typical Significance Of The Animals

The care in specifying three different animals, even as to their age, and naming two different birds convinces us that some special significance is to be sought. No such instructions would have been necessary had it been simply a question of the ratification of a covenant; Abraham could have seen to all the details without any directions. These creatures figure prominently in the Levitical offerings which set forth in type various aspects of the one great redeeming work of Christ. Have we not in the sacrifices of these animals, and in the fact that Abraham himself was not called upon to pass between the pieces, a representation of the truth that God's covenant with Abraham (and indeed all of God's redemptive purposes) rest alone on the foundation of that great redeeming work? At three years these animals would be at the peak of their vitality and value, the better to typify the perfection and worth of the work of Christ. Whether Abraham had any inkling of this is impossible to say, but it is at least clear that OT saints understood more than they are sometimes credited with.

Abraham's Preparations

We may be sure that Abraham in his enthusiasm at the expectation of a visit from the Lord to participate in this unusually elaborate ritual would eagerly begin preparations with the first light of dawn. The expense involved, though considerable, would not be a consideration to a wealthy cattle-owner. However, a moment's thought will make it clear that the preparations would involve a lot of time-consuming work. It is not to be supposed that he carried all this out personally; he must have employed the help of some of his staff (cf. 18:7).

The Lord's Arrival Awaited

There would be intense interest in the camp because these unusually elaborate arrangements would signify the expected arrival of some notable personage who had entered into some covenant of considerable importance (cf. 21:27).

Human nature being what it is it would not be at all surprising if mingled with Abraham's appreciation of the privilege that God was going to bestow on him would be some satisfaction at the prestige this would confer on him in the eyes of his establishment. He stood reverently in expectation of the Lord's arrival so that they could pass between the pieces together before the eyes of astonished witnesses. Abraham had to face bitter and humiliating disappointment. The only arrivals were loathsome birds of prey which, picking up the scent, descended on the carcases; this to Abraham was desecration. He drove them off, but these persistent vultures returned again and again; Abraham, hoping against hope that the expected visitor would arrive, drove them off each time. If some of his loyal staff had sufficient grace to sympathise with their master in this embarrassing situation it is to be feared that others must have found the spectacle amusing although they would be careful to conceal it. (If we accept that the animals sacrificed had some typical significance, then we can liken the vultures to the agents of the devil who attack the truth with regard to the redeeming work of Christ. A near parallel is found in the parable of the sower, Matt 13:4, 19.)

The Sun Going Down

The weary day was now drawing to a close; the sun was

setting with tropical speed and it would soon be dark; the vultures had retired to their nests and the servants to their tents. Still the Lord had not come. It was too late now to hope for His arrival. Dejected and bitterly disappointed he simply lay down where he was, none daring to disturb him and fell into a deep sleep. Even whilst the body was unconscious his soul was the prey of terrible emotions which could only be described as "a horror of great darkness". Undoubtedly he felt that he had been badly let down by the God with whom he had sought to walk and whom he had sought to please by obedience. It seemed cruel to raise his expectations so high and then to humiliate him before those who would be familiar with his devotion to God. He must have felt that God having forsaken him, the foundation on which he had built all his most cherished hopes had collapsed in ruins.

To feel forsaken of God is the darkest experience that a child of God can know. No child of God can actually be forsaken. The assurance of Psa 37:28, "The Lord forsaketh not his saints", is re-enforced by His own words, "I will never leave thee nor forsake thee" (Heb 13:5). Some however have felt forsaken and have left their mental and spiritual travail on record. As we have already noticed, the fact that one's anxieties are groundless makes no difference to their intensity for the sufferer.

Asaph's spirit was "overwhelmed" when he was tempted to think that he had been cast off and that God's mercy had "clean gone forever, and that His promise had failed for evermore". Happily he realised that this was not actually the case but that his feeings were due to his infirmity. He seems to have been a man subject to melancholy moods, and it must be recognised that temperament enters into the experience of Christians, if not into true Christian-experience. He wisely resolved to dwell rather on the revelation of God's ways as seen more clearly in the sanctuary which, perhaps in his pre-occupation with his religious duties, he had neglected of late (Psa 77:3-13; 73:16-17).

A Smoking Furnace And A Burning Lamp

As the sun was setting Abraham received a lengthy message from God which we will consider later. For the moment let us notice that evidently this message stirred Abraham into consciousness. By this time the sun had gone down and it was dark. Instinctively he looked toward the carcases, and to his intense surprise he saw a smoking-furnace and a burning-lamp passing between the pieces. From v. 18 we learn that in this way God made a covenant with Abraham which extended the promise to a far wider area than before. The point to notice particularly is that these symbols passed between the pieces whilst Abraham reclined in rest. He had no part in the covenant ritual, indicating that the fulfilment of the promises did not depend on him but on God — they were in God's safe-keeping alone. Did it occur to Abraham that God had chosen to act in this way to emphasise this fact?

Afflictions are made even more difficult to understand when they arise from seeking to do what one believes to be the will of God. When Joseph had taken a difficult journey at the age of seventeen to enquire after his brothers' welfare they cruelly sold him into slavery for twenty pieces of silver, ignoring his anguish (Gen 37:14, 28; 42:21). In Egypt the master he had served faithfully and efficiently threw him into prison on the false accusation of one whose solicitation to evil he had rejected. For part of the time his feet were put in iron fetters — but, worse than that, the iron entered his soul (Psa 105:18). He felt the bitterness of being apparently forgotten of God whose law he had honoured: "The word of God tried him". His faith was put to the test with a view to refining his character. But this was only "until that his word came" when God began to fulfil His promise and he could then see how God had been working out His purpose on a grand scale (Gen 45:4-8; Psa 105:17-22).

But there are mysteries which will never be explained until we see life in the light of the rainbow-encircled throne. Then, if not now, we shall be able to say in the words of Anne Cousin's hymn:

With mercy and with judgment
My web of time He wove;
And aye the dews of sorrow
Were lustred with His love.
I'll bless the hand that guided,
I'll bless the heart that planned,
When throned where glory dwelleth
In Immanuel's land.

The message, which stirred Abraham from his coma-like sleep, more or less explained in advance the meaning of the furnace and the lamp; both were active, smoking and burning, for the purposes of God are never dormant. The meaning of the smoking-furnace is made quite clear by three Scriptures which speak of Egypt as "a furnace of iron" in its affliction of the children of Israel (Deut 4:20; 1 Kings 8:51; Jer 11:4). In addition, Isa 48:10 speaks of God having chosen His people "in the furnace of affliction", which ties up with v. 13 of our chapter: "they shall afflict them four hundred years".

Abraham was told his seed would be strangers "in a land that is not theirs". How like their progenitor, who was a stranger in Canaan, a land which was not then his. How would he have felt if he had known that the land in question was Egypt where he had been humiliated by Pharaoh for his duplicity? Moreover as he came out of Egypt with great substance so would they, and in much the same way. Pharaoh was glad to get rid of Abraham who had been a cause of trouble, and it is clear that the Egyptians were at last glad to see the back of the Israelites, although it was in response to their demands that they loaded them with riches. The AV's use of the word "borrow" in Exod 3:21, 22; 11:2, 3; 12:35, 36 gives the impression that the Israelites asked for a loan of the Egyptians' riches with the implication that the loan would somehow be repaid. Even if such a highly improbable promise could have been made the circumstances were such that no Egyptian would have given it a moment's credence.

The RV rightly translates the Hebrew word (*shaal*) by "ask", which is in accord with the use of the word in numerous places. The Israelites with some definiteness asked for the riches, and no doubt their one-time oppressors were ready to pay the price to get rid of a people whose God had brought such disasters on the land. "Lend" in the AV of 12:36 naturally follows from its translation of the word *shaal* by "borrow". Again the form of the word makes it difficult to translate by one word in English so the RV has resorted to a clause: "they let them have what they asked". In each of the three passages quoted above the willingness of the Egyptians to comply with the demands is attributed to the Lord. There was nothing unjust in this. The Israelites by their forced labour under inhuman conditions had contributed enormously to Egypt's prosperity which explains why Pharaoh was so reluctant to free them. The wealth they took with them had been earned many times over.

The burning-lamp signified that through all their tribulations there would shine a light of the certain hope that one day Israel's sovereignty would be a reality. So in Psa 132:17, 18 God says that He will make the horn (symbol of power) of David to bud and that He has ordained a lamp for His anointed ... and that his crown will flourish. Later, despite the sin of Abijam, king of Judah, the Lord for David's sake gave him a lamp in Jerusalem to set up his son after him (1 Kings 15:4). In a day yet future the salvation of Israel will be "as a lamp that burneth" (Isa 62:1). Cf. 1 Kings 11:36; 2 Kings 8:19; in both instances "light" means "lamp" (see margins).

The message to Abraham also gives some examples of God's over-ruling in the destiny of nations. After God's forbearance of Egypt's long oppression of His people He would judge them with a great overthrow. The waiting period served to refine Israel in the furnace of affliction (Isa 48:10), whilst at the same time God was showing forbearance to the Amorites whose increasing iniquities would ultimately make divine intervention imperative. That judgment would fall on them through the agency of the triumphant Israelites as they took possession of the land God had promised them: "in the fourth generation they shall come hither again".

God could even look ahead down the long avenue of centuries and define the ultimate extent of Israel's kingdom — a vast area stretching from the river of Egypt to the great river Euphrates. There were times in the reigns of David and Solomon when their authority extended nearly that far, but the complete fulfilment awaits Israel's eventual establishment as the head of the nations under the millennial reign of great David's greater Son (2 Sam 8:3-8; 1 Chron 18:3; 1 Kings 4:21; 2 Chron 9:26). When the Most High divided to nations their inheritance their boundaries were settled to fit in with God's plans for his chosen people (Deut 32:8; Acts 17:26).

In these unsettled days it is a strength of faith to be reminded that God keeps His hand on the helm of history. How it enhances our conception of God's knowledge and wisdom when we think of the profound complexity of interacting human forces, with all their confusing cross-currents, and wide-ranging implications for the future, unpredictable by us, but clearly foreseen and provided for by God. We can only look back into history and see how man's ways in past generations have borne fruit in later generations. Nations, no less than individuals, reap what they sow for good or ill (Gal 6:7). Nebuchadnezzar learnt in the hard way that the Most High rules in the kingdoms of men (Dan 4:17, 25, 32).

A Peaceful End

Abraham's knowledge of God was growing. He had learnt that the God of glory who called him out of Ur was the Most High, Possessor of heaven and earth. Now he was given to understand that his God could foresee how nations would develop during coming centuries and (to speak after the manner of men) make His plans accordingly. This must have made a deep impression on him, but what brought God nearer to him was the more personal message. He need not be disturbed with great issues utterly beyond him; he could leave those with God. But the same God was interested in him. Instead of shortly passing away childless there was ample time for God's promises to be fulfilled. He would live to "a good old age" — it turned out that he had something like another ninety years pilgrimage — and he would die in peace. In the event, as we shall see, his end was even brighter than that.

Our little lives can bear no comparison with the immense significance of his, but we can take comfort and encouragement in knowing that they are at least essential threads being woven into the grand over-all design of Him "who works all things after the counsel of his own will" (Eph 1:11; 2 Tim 1:9).

Without doubt Abraham now faced the coming day in a better mood. Obviously the carcases would have to be cleared away with the help of some of his men. Naturally he would tell them what had happened in the night; and he may have feared that those sceptically inclined would think that he had mistaken a vivid dream for reality. But with his former dignity restored and a new insight into God's plans he would speak with a firm note of assurance that carried conviction.

Chapter IX
Domestic Triangle

(Gen 16:1-16)

Sarai's Barrenness

It was apparent, even in Ur, that Sarai was barren so the condition had been a long trial to her. In our society infertility is usually viewed with sympathy, but in those times it was an unfair reproach which women felt keenly. When Rachel eventually bore Joseph she said, "God hath taken away my reproach" (30:23) — words which were echoed by Elizabeth in the same situation nearly two thousand years later (Luke 1:25). It is the same in some parts of the world even today.

Now at last Sarai had come to the conclusion that her condition was irreversible — all hope was gone. Was she now reconciled to the fact or in a complaining mood as Naomi was in another situation: "The Almighty hath dealt very bitterly with me" (Ruth 1:20)? Or was she simply, as later became a habit of mind with the Hebrews, attributing everything to the direct action of God? She can hardly have been ignorant of God's promise to Abraham, but perhaps reflecting more deeply it now dawned on her that the promise had not specifically named her as mother, and so she turned her thoughts to an alternative.

Ancient Standards

In judging the propriety of suggesting that her husband take her handmaid we must face the fact that it was in no way contrary to accepted conventions and no one would have been in the least scandalised. Those who invest OT worthies with a Christian halo find it hard to accept that concubinage was practised even in the establishment of a man like Abraham but 25:1-6 makes it quite clear that such was the case. It is important that Christians in their study of the OT, and indeed in their contacts with people today, should appreciate the

128

immense strength of long established traditions. Although the utmost reverence and caution are called for when venturing to comment on the ways of God, it does seem that God in His complete understanding of fallen human nature graciously takes this into account. After all, if God granted His blessing only where conditions matched the divine ideal, who of the children of Adam could hope to be blessed?

Social Reform

Societies are not changed in a day, and attempts to superimpose a new life-style by force cannot effect a genuine change and only breed other evils. Modern history has shown that when primitive people have had a western style civilisation forced on them the change has only been a veneer, and when western influence has been removed the resurgence of a repressed pagan culture has had disastrous effects.

The convicting and regenerating work of the Holy Spirit can effect a rapid transformation in an individual, and there have been revivals where a whole community has been temporarily affected, as in the remarkable case of Nineveh (Jonah 3), and in more modern, if less dramatic, examples. Nevertheless, where there have been lasting improvements in the ethical and social structure of a nation they have been brought about by a gradual process. Had the apostles campaigned for the immediate abolition of slavery such a disastrous reaction would have been provoked that the cause of the gospel would have suffered immeasurable damage. Their wise approach in instructing Christian masters and Christian slaves averted the danger while attaining more success, at least in the church. Nevertheless slavery has never been completely abolished in the world.

How much more difficult it would have been to break hoary tradition in the early ages of human history when the population was smaller and life went on much the same from generation to generation. Indeed in some parts of the East today the way-of-life has not greatly changed from patriarchal times.

Hypocrisy

Hypocrisy is loathsome, as the terrible denunciations of the Saviour testify in the seven awful woes of Matt 23:13-25, but

9

we must not be too ready to apply the dreadful epithet to a person simply because we can see the inconsistency of his conduct. It may not be clear to him. Abraham had a perfectly clear conscience in the matter of concubinage as no doubt Christian slave-owners had in the time of the apostles when slave ownership was a way-of-life. More modern times furnish examples. Surely no one would question the integrity and sincerity of John Newton, the converted slave trader, later a devoted minister and writer of some beautiful hymns, perhaps the best known and loved being:

> Amazing grace, how sweet the sound
> That saved a wretch like me.

For a while after his conversion he continued in the slave trade, actually holding services for the benefit of the slaves, until he saw the incongruity of it all. Let us quote from a letter he wrote in retrospect: "I am sure that had I thought of the slave trade then as I have thought of it since, no consideration would have induced me to continue. Though my religious views were not very clear, my conscience was tender and I dared not displease God by acting against the light of my mind ... I would have been overwhelmed in distress and terror if I had known or suspected that I was acting wrongly." When he was convicted about it, he played a vital role in a twenty-year fight to get slavery abolished by law.

Of course, we are obliged to cherish and uphold Christian standards, but if we wish to provide the maximum help to our fellows we must try to understand the strength of tradition, even in religious matters. This is merely touching the fringe of a wide subject which servants of Christ should consider but which it would not be appropriate to enlarge on here. We must return to our subject — the unfolding of God's purposes in the life of Abraham.

Sarai's Proposal

Concubinage was an accepted way-of-life, and Sarai would not offend anyone's idea of propriety by giving her slave girl to her husband. Rachel was acting quite acceptably in taking the same course in a similar situation (30:1-6).

Usually the children of concubines were regarded within the menage as their own (25:6), but in the special case of a wife surrendering her own maid she became a sort of second wife: "She gave her to her husband to be his wife" (v. 3). In such a case the child would then be regarded as belonging to the mistress: "It may be that I may obtain children by her" (v. 2). From the mention of "children" it would appear that Sarai even contemplated a continuing relationship.

On the one hand there is no indication that Abraham had any enthusiasm for the idea, on the other there is no indication that he consulted God. Instead he weakly yielded to his wife's wishes. In the similar case of Rachel there was no problem with her maid in that Bilhah's children were readily recognised as belonging to her mistress. Hagar was a different character — proud, headstrong and probably embittered at being involuntarily removed from her native Egypt as a present from Pharaoh to foreigners. We shall see indications that her heart was still in Egypt.

Probably her relationship with Sarai was not at any time a happy one and when she realised that she was pregnant she brazenly showed her contempt for her barren mistress, who felt all the more humiliated at her failure to produce an heir for Abraham. It does not need much imagination to see how galling the whole situation was to Sarai and how destructive of domestic harmony, especially when we bear in mind that they were not living in a modern house but within the closer confines of a tent, although a tent owned by the head of an establishment like Abraham would be as large as a marquee if much more crudely designed.

Carnal Means To A Spiritual End

Sarai must be given credit for the well-meant motives which prompted her. She can even be admired for taking a course which must have been distasteful to her in what she regarded as the interests of her husband, to whom she seems to have been devoted. But even the best intentions in seeking to assist God's purposes by our own devices invite disaster. Paul speaks about having "no confidence in the flesh" (Phil 3:3). It was God's purpose that Jacob should be the privileged son, "the elder shall serve the younger" (25:23). He is to be commended for setting a high value on the birthright and thus on being a channel for the blessing promised to Abraham's posterity, but yielding to his bent for scheming and trickery he dishonoured God and brought upon himself and the family no end of trouble. He would have been wiser to leave the matter to God's hand.

Perhaps Sarai should by this time have known Hagar well enough to foresee the likely reaction of her temperament, but when we leave the path of faith and act in our own fancied wisdom we become very short-sighted. It must have been very exasperating for Abraham when she tried to put the blame on him for agreeing to her proposal! But, how true this is to human nature. When our bungling has humiliated us we are prone to look for a scape-goat. One of the first consequences of the Fall was that the woman blamed the serpent, and the man blamed the woman, and even tried to put part of the blame on God because He had given Eve to him! "It was your fault" — how often we are tempted to say this. James warns us against trying to shift the blame for our failings (Jas 1:13-14). Having seen the unfortunate consequences of following his wife's first suggestion, it was further weakness on his part to leave the solution of the problem to her: "Do to her as it pleaseth thee" (v. 6). Do we detect a weary desire to wash his hands of the whole affair? It certainly showed little feeling for the unfortunate girl to allow a vengeful woman a free-hand in the treatment of her. When Sarai "dealt harshly with her" it only made an already uncomfortable position even more unpleasant. How tangled matters become when, failing to learn from our own lack of wisdom, we try to remedy one mistake by blundering into another.

Influence Of Wives

It would be unfortunate if the foregoing remarks encouraged prejudice to dwell on other instances where wives have influenced their husbands in the wrong direction. It is a common mistake to draw sweeping general conclusions from particular cases. Have husbands always been founts of wisdom? After all Abraham's proposal before they left Ur that Sarai should pose as his sister, was indefensible, and yet he repeated the mistake after having seen the folly of it in Egypt (20:13). "A prudent wife is from the Lord" (Prov 19:14). Who can fail to admire the sound common-sense way in which Manoah's wife allayed his fears (Jud 13:22-23), or the wisdom of Abigail which could have saved Nabal but for his stubbornness and folly (1 Sam 25:18-38)? How much better for Pilate if cowardice had not closed his ears to his wife's urgent warning (Matt 27:19). Returning to Sarai, let it be remembered that Peter cites her as an example to Christian women in her attitude to her husband and also, by implication, commends her courage. This is not difficult to understand when we ponder what was involved in her venturing from Ur and in following the chequered pilgrim-life in Canaan. Peter takes a balanced view in exhorting husbands to honour their wives (1 Pet 3:7). Observe the same balance more strikingly set out in Eph 5:24-25. Where husbands live up to their responsibilities wives are not likely to fail in their response. The spiritual fellowship Peter envisaged reminds us of the beautiful partnership of Aquila and Priscilla in their home-based service for Christ (Acts 18:26).

The Angel Of The Lord

It is not unlikely that Sarai quickly realised from Hagar's attitude that the expected child would never be regarded as hers, and in her chagrin took advantage of Abraham's indifference to make the girl's life a misery. She "dealt harshly with her". If her purpose was to drive the girl away, she succeeded, but only temporarily, for before long she was back home to be a thorn in her mistress' side. The consequences of our mistakes usually recur. The fugitive made her way toward Shur on the caravan-route to Egypt, which suggests that she rashly hoped to make her way to her home-land; she landed up in a wilderness. Many think a wilderness is the equivalent of a sandy desert, resulting in some strange ideas about Israel's forty years in the wilderness. It means an uninhabited and therefore uncultivated area where nature is left to grow wild and where nomad shepherds grazed their flocks from time to time. Having left camp clandestinely it is not likely that she had been able to take many necessities, but providentially she lighted on a fountain, or spring, which would have encouraged edible growth. From the fact that in v. 14 the word *well* is also used we gather that at some time temporary inhabitants had opened up the spring. It was here that the angel of the Lord found her.

Genesis being a book of beginnings, it is inevitable that many scriptural words and topics occur there for the first time, and there is a tendency to read too much into a first occurrence. Nevertheless, in many places the so-called "law of first mention" (i.e. where a matter is mentioned for the first time something of significance is indicated) finds a good deal of justification. May we not draw comfort from the fact that the first recorded appearance of the angel of the Lord should not be to some notable as Enoch or Noah, or even to Abraham, but to a misused slave girl for whom nobody cared? It was not a question of standing, or privilege, but of need: "The Lord hath heard thy affliction". Is not the same lesson taught by the gracious act of the risen Lord appearing first, not to an apostle, but to a grief-stricken woman (Mark 16:9)?

Who then is the angel of the Lord? There are a vast number of angels but the angel of the Lord is not among them. He stands alone. His identity is looked at in more detail in Appendix A; in the present context it will suffice to notice that clearly a divine Person is referred to, for no creature could say "I will multiply thy seed". Yet in v. 13 it is said that it was the Lord who spake to her. Hagar realised this for she named Him, "Thou God seest me" (El-roi, "God of seeing"). Hagar did not regard this as a cause for terror, but rather for comfort (cf. 21:17). Bearing in mind the dread which many had when the angel of the Lord appeared to them, it is noteworthy that Hagar shows no sign of alarm, and it is pleasant to think that His gracious attitude put her at ease. However, her next words, "Have I also (even RV) here looked after him that seeth me", seem to indicate that she was grateful for having survived the experience. Is it fanciful to see here some indication that she had learned something of God from her master?

The angel's two questions were not seeking information. As often with the Saviour's questions His purpose was to evoke an appropriate response: "Whence comest thou?" and "Whither goest thou?". They brought home to Hagar the folly of a lonely and unprotected girl leaving the security of the camp for the perils of the wilderness, and the hopelessness of attempting to reach distant Egypt. The fact that she replied only to the first question suggests that her plight had already begun to make her repent of her impetuosity.

Hagar's Return

Obedient to the angel, she swallowed her pride and returned to her mistress; whether she was able to submit with grace must remain doubtful. Submission is difficult to human pride, but when it springs from genuine submission to the will of God it can never be degrading nor unfruitful

The angel's prediction as to the multitude of her offspring had ominous implications for the future — Ishmael's nature would be as untameable as a wild ass (v. 12 RV, and cf. Job 39:5-8); his hand against every man's hand would provoke retaliation. How this has been fulfilled through the centuries up to the present time in the constant friction between the descendants of Isaac and Ishmael is a matter of common knowledge. The promise that her seed would not be numbered for multitude has an obvious connection with the promise to Abraham, but with the significant omission of being a blessing; later it was said that he personally would be blessed, probably in the sense of having a great posterity (17:20).

How much of all this Hagar disclosed to Abraham and Sarai we do not know, but that she related some of her experience is clear from the fact that Abraham acted on the angel's instructions to Hagar when he named the child Ishmael ("God heareth").

Silent Years

Abraham was now eighty-six years of age (v. 16), so eleven years had elapsed since he left Haran at the age of seventy-five. As this fairly long period is covered in five short chapters there must be a number of time-gaps in the narrative in which incidents must have occurred which would have been interesting to us, but the purpose of Scripture is to instruct not to interest (Rom 15:4). Since no mention is made of such gaps, it is safe to conclude that nothing occurred essential to our instruction in the development of God's work in Abraham. There must be similar gaps in the later chapters to which the same applies.

Between the end of ch. 16 and the opening of ch. 17 there is a gap longer than the whole of the period of eleven years covered by the five chapters just mentioned. Moreover, in this case the text deliberately draws attention to it by noting in the last verse of ch. 16 that Abraham was eighty-six and in the next verse that he was ninety-nine, the chapter divisions being no part of the original text. Can we regard this as an invitation to look more closely into the matter in case any light can be thrown on this period?

Were They Happy Years?

First of all let us consider whether the situation described in ch. 16 helps us to judge what were the prospects of a happy outcome.

If on cooler reflection Sarai began to feel uneasy about her share in the fugitive's fate, the girl's return could have eased her conscience but this would be over-shadowed by further exasperation. Whether Hagar boasted of her wonderful experience or not, we have seen that at the very least she related some of it. The mere fact that this troublesome girl had been specially privileged with a unique, divine visitation was not likely to sweeten her mistress' jealous temper. So the outlook for harmony was not good. Now let us see whether future chapters throw back any light on these silent years.

Sarai's original hope was that Hagar's child should be regarded as hers (16:2). Indeed she contemplated the continuance of the relationship bringing her children. Far from matters turning out like this the attentive reader will notice that all the indications point the other way. Eight times Ishmael is called Abraham's son (16:15 (twice); 17:23, 25, 26; 21:11; 25:9, 12). Four times (once by God) he is called Hagar's son (21:9, 10 (twice), 13) but never once Sarai's son. That this is significant will be seen from the contrast in the otherwise similar case of Rachel and her bondwoman. Of Bilhah's first child she said, "God ... hath given me a son" (30:6) and it was Rachel's prerogative to give him his name, as also she did with Bilhah's second child. That this was all quite amicable is clear from the fact that she calls Bilhah "her sister". Contrast this with Sarai's repeated and scornful reference to "this bondwoman" (21:10). Leah likewise had the naming of the children she acquired through her handmaid, Zilpah (30:9-13). So Sarai was disappointed in her early hopes.

Ishmael's Character

What can we learn about Ishmael? If as the adage goes, "the child is father to the man", then he showed as he grew up some early signs of becoming untameable and aggressive. (See the earlier note on v. 12.) This is just what we find. Sarah could not have been very pleased at the teenager being present at the weaning party of his half-brother, Isaac — it was a "great feast" (21:8). Here he was daringly insolent in openly mocking the child, and he ruined, for Sarah at least, what should have been a joyous celebration. She was not unnaturally furious as v. 10 shows: "Cast out this bond-woman and her son". This daring exhibition of arrogance on such an occasion surely suggests that his predicted character had been developing through his childhood. This does not say much for his mother's influence on him; it rather looks as if she had not taken much pains to instil respect and to make the situation more agreeable to the mistress. She probably still resented Sarai because of the treatment she had earlier received.

Abraham's Affection For Ishmael

Nor was this all! Despite Ishmael's waywardness there seems to have been a certain amount of charm about him. Mischievousness can sometimes be diverting. At any rate he had obviously won a place in Abraham's heart. It was an auspicious occasion when the Lord appeared to Abraham as the Almighty God (17:1), and we will not anticipate treatment of the impressive revelation given, involving the changing of his name to Abraham (father of many nations) and Sarai's name to Sarah (Princess). Yet even in the very midst of this wonderful experience Abraham was anxious that Ishmael should not be overshadowed, "O, that Ishmael might live before thee". This was not a prayer that Ishmael be allowed to live — that was guaranteed by the angel in the wilderness (16:11-12). He was praying that Ishmael may live under God's benign eye — "live before thee". This is made clear by God's response — "I have heard thee. Behold I have blessed him" (17:18-20).

Furthermore, when Sarah insisted on the expulsion of Hagar and Ishmael, Abraham, though not indifferent about Hagar as in 16:6 ("Let it not be grievous because of the lad and because of thy bondwoman" — note the order!), found the proposal more than grievous — very grievous. Why? "Because of his son" (21:11-12). This marked change in attitudes toward Hagar and her child could not have been helpful to that harmony we like to see between husband and wife. All this is by way of looking back on the thirteen years. It is unthinkable that the whole period was a time of unrelieved tensions —life would have been intolerable.

Keturah

There is one more aspect of the matter to be considered. Chapter 25:1-6 must be considered a sort of appendix inserted out of chronological order as being no very essential part of the story as a whole, but added, as we would say, "to keep the record straight". For reasons we will go into at the proper time this passage really belongs more or less to the thirteen-year period we have been considering.

In that period Abraham took a woman named Keturah and she became a (secondary) wife as Sarai had originally intended Hagar to be. She bore six children, and we may hope that this turned out more happily. There were also concubines who had children; we know nothing about them except that, suitably endowed, they were eventually sent away to other parts, evidently quite amicably.

So, although the unfortunate expedient with Hagar caused so much unhappiness, we may hope that there were other features which brought welcome relief from tension.

The Challenge To Us

How down to earth all this is! The worthies of old were not recluses withdrawn from real life who lived instead in the rarified atmosphere of enraptured mystic contemplation, while leaving others to take responsibility. Abraham was a man of formidable spiritual stature, but he had to tackle the very practical day-to-day problems of the management and future planning of a large enterprise while playing his proper role in a delicate domestic situation. As Paul said of himself and his companions, and as James said of the great prophet Elijah, they were men of "like passions with us" (Acts 14:15; Jas 5:17). They were of the same common clay as ourselves and with faults and failings common to us all. This is comforting to us but not an excuse to be complacent about our failures — rather a warning against them. Let us remember what they became by the grace of God. Jacob the supplanter became a Prince with God. Abraham the one-time idolater won through and became the Friend of God. Let this challenge us to follow, not their faults, but their faith (Heb 13:7).

Chapter X

A Fifth Appearance: The Almighty God

(Gen 17:1-27)

After the birth of Ishmael nothing is recorded until thirteen years later the Lord appeared to Abraham for the fifth time, when he was 99 years of age. (There were, of course, other occasions when God communicated with him without a visible manifestation.)

His increasing knowledge of God is now taken a stage further by the revelation that He is the Almighty God, or as some prefer to translate the Hebrew, *El Shaddai*, the All-Sufficient God. Although the question may be of academic interest, for practical purposes both translations amount to the same thing, for if God is almighty then obviously He is all-sufficient; conversely if He is all-sufficient then He must necessarily be almighty.

To minds conditioned by the possession of a completed revelation and by modern conceptions of the vast universe, Melchizedek's description of God as the "possessor of heaven and earth" is practically equivalent to almightiness, but it must not be assumed that this would necessarily be apparent to Abraham. It must be constantly borne in mind that the light of revelation only gradually dispelled the darkness of ingrained pagan ideas. It would hardly have been necessary for God to announce Himself as the Almighty if this was already well understood. Certainly the appropriateness of this particular view of God is seen in the link between the promise of v. 16 and the question in 18:14, "Is anything too hard for the Lord?"

Omnipotence

The limitless power of God is of such importance that the devotion of some space to the subject seems amply justified.

Living in a material world we are apt to think of power in terms of physical force, but the way in which God's power is

139

exercised is quite different. Nevertheless Scripture does allow for our limitations by speaking of God measuring the heavens by the span of His hand, or weighing the mountains in scales, whilst at the same time warning us that such comparisons are inadequate (Isa 40:12, 25). There are many such examples, such as Psa 8:3; Isa 52:10.

Job tried to describe God's power in creation, perhaps most remarkably of all, by declaring that He "hangeth the earth upon nothing". Then after citing other mighty works of God he says that comparing what we can appreciate with the real extent of His power is like comparing a whisper with the peal of thunder (Job 26:7-14). This concept is even more impressive, and certainly more elegant, than the comment of an astronomer that in the recesses of space such mighty energy is released as would crush our planet as easily as a steam-hammer could crush an egg-shell. The stupendous discoveries which have been made in this realm cannot but excite the deep interest of Christians, but despite all the physicists are able to tell us, science cannot solve what to them are two impenetrable mysteries — how the universe originated and what is its ultimate purpose. The Christian who accepts the absolute authority of Scripture is at a great advantage. The solution of the first mystery lies open on its first page: "God said ... and it was so" (Gen 1:3, 6, 9, 11, 14). Here too is the secret of the mode in which almighty power operates. All that is in God's mind is potential — He has only to utter His word on any matter and it thereupon becomes actual. David understood this: "By the word of the Lord were the heavens made; and all the host of them by the breath of his mouth ... He spake and it was done" (Psa 33:6, 9). In the following verse he explains the continuing cohesion of the universe: "He commanded and it stood fast". In this he was anticipating Heb 1:3, where we learn how all things are upheld — it is by the word of Christ's power. Col 1:17 puts it this way: "By him all things consist (hold together)". If we wish to learn the purpose of it all, the previous verse will tell us: "All things were created by him, and for him". The mystery (secret) of God's will is "that in the dispensation of the fulness of times he might gather together in one all things in Christ" (Eph 1:9, 10).

Understandably such statements are meaningless to the scientist, as such, but they are pregnant with significance to the child of God by faith. It is not that faith runs contrary to reason — it travels with reason as far as reason can go, but when it fails faith will take the believer farther. "Through faith we understand that the worlds were framed by the word of God" (Heb 11:3). Then follows a statement on which science has thrown some light: "things which are seen were not made of things which do appear". To the scientist the invisible is energy in one form or another, to the Christian that energy is the mind of God expressed by His spoken word. Truly "the voice of the Lord is powerful" (Psa 29:4).

However, it is not only in what we call the material universe that the power of the word of God is manifest; it operates in the moral and spiritual realm. Thus it is that the gospel of Christ is the power of God unto salvation. This was proved by the Thessalonians, concerning whom Paul said, "the word of God which effectively worketh in you that believe" (Rom 1:16; 1 Thess 2:13). It is when we are confronted with such power that the awesome reality of free will emerges; the Almighty respects the right of choice which He has given to His responsible creatures: "I would ... ye would not" (Matt 23:37). Cf. John 5:40 in connection with 1 Tim 2:4.

What is of great comfort to the trusting soul is that reverential wonder at His limitless power does not make the Almighty remote. Abraham fell on his face in worshipful awe, but the Almighty "talked with him" (v. 3). Cf. v. 22. According to 2 Cor 6:18 it is the Lord Almighty who is willing to be a Father to us in enjoyed experience as His sons and daughters, so that we may find shelter under the shadow of the Almighty (Psa 91:1).

Walk Before Me

Abraham had earlier been assured that he could find shelter in God "Fear not Abram, I am thy shield" (15:1). Now the call is from the Almighty to *walk* before Him and to be perfect. "Perfect" means not absolute faultlessness but sincerity, genuineness, no pretence. Walking "before" God means living day by day in the consciousness that His eyes are upon us, all is naked and open, not in a threatening sense, but as the One to whom our inmost hearts are an open book. Abraham was not without his faults, but he could say with modesty and simple truth, when sending his eldest servant to find a bride for Isaac, "The Lord before whom I walk ... will prosper thy way" (24:40). The first effect on David was dismay when he was

made aware that God was not only fully acquainted with all
his actions and words but even with the thoughts beginning
to take shape in his mind; however, when it was brought
home to him that God's thoughts toward him were "precious
thoughts", he actually desired that God should search his
heart, his thoughts and his ways, and reveal to him anything
which was a grief to God, so that he may be led in the way
everlasting (Psa 139). This is more than walking before God, it
is walking with God, in companionship. The question in Amos
3:3, "Can two walk together except they be agreed?" does not
refer to oneness of mind, very desirable in itself, but rather to
the necessity of an appointment to meet a person with a
companionable walk in view. The story in Gen 3:1-9 allows us
to infer that before sin destroyed the relationship, the Lord
God had a standing appointment with our first parents to
meet them for a walk in the cool of the evening in the ideal
surroundings of Eden. In consequence of their disobedience
the voice of the Lord God, to which they had hitherto listened
happily, caused them to hide in fear. God's question, "Where
art thou?" was not prompted by the intention of retribution
but by disappointment at not finding them at the appointed
place. How beautiful to turn to the last book in the Bible and
read the Saviour's promise to the faithful, "They shall walk
with me in white", not in the ruined earthly Eden but among
the trees in the paradise of God, in the midst of which is the
eternal tree of life of which the overcomer may eat. See Rev
3:4 compared with 2:7 and Gen 3:24. That walk will be where
no shade nor stain can enter, but let us remember that Enoch
and Noah proved that it is possible to have a foretaste of that
privilege in walking with God here below though surrounded
by moral corruption (Gen 5:24; 6:9).

The Covenant Extended

As we have noticed already, Abraham fell on his face when
God talked with him. In both v. 9 and v. 15 it is additionally
said, "God said unto Abraham". Whether these words indicate
that there were three separate communications with an
interval between each, or simply that there were three stages
in the one communication, is not clear, but we are left with the
impression that it was one appearance. In that case it would
seem that Abraham did not remain prostrate, for v. 17 says he
fell on his face again when God spoke about Sarai. On the

whole it seems that it was a fairly long but companionable interview opening with "God talked with him" and closing with "He left off talking with him" (v. 22).

The first actual mention of a covenant with Abraham is in 15:13 following the impressive ritual sacrifice of three animals and two birds. There it simply refers to the extent of the territory promised to his seed, but here in ch. 17 there are no fewer than eight mentions of the covenant, linked with four references to the convenant of circumcision. The latter must be kept distinct from the basic covenant of which it is but a token. Circumcision will be considered later, but now we notice not only how the convenant in ch. 15 is extended but how the extensions even bring out elements not included in the far-reaching promises made to Abraham before the word covenant was used.

Adequate treatment of what may be termed the Abrahamic Covenant and its relation to other covenants cannot be attempted here but the following may stimulate further enquiry into this wide subject:

1. Abraham will be the father of many nations (cf. 12:2 "a great nation", i.e. Israel). Other nations would be principally descendants of Ishmael and Keturah (25:1-4); they were not in view then, but see v. 16. The tense in v. 5, "Have I made thee" prompts the comment in Rom 4:17, "God ... calleth those things which be not as though they were". The same may be said of the past tense "glorified" in Rom 8:30. Cf. remarks in the paragraph headed "omnipotence" on the effect of God uttering His mind.

2. In token of this his name was changed from Abram to Abraham, which means father of a multitude. See remarks on v. 15.

3. Kings are mentioned for the first time (cf. v. 16).

4. The covenant is everlasting (vv. 7, 13, 19). Cf. v. 8 and 13:15, "for ever". The Hebrew word *olam* essentially means "age-lasting", but is often the equivalent of "eternal". In this sense it is applied to God in 21:33, whereas in Exod 40:15 it clearly means age-lasting, for not only is the subject the now defunct Aaronic priesthood, but the word is explained by "throughout their generations". See Psa 105:6-8 where Abraham is referred to as the Lord's servant; it is said of God, "He hath remembered his covenant for ever, the word which he commanded to a thousand generations".

5. God will be the God of Abraham and his seed, (vv. 7, 8).
   This may strike us as obvious, but to Abraham it could
   have been a new thought that there would be a special
   relationship between God and himself, and the nation
   which would spring from him. Once he overcame his
   doubts this would mean a great deal to him. The individual
   believer to-day may well be thrilled at being able to claim a
   personal link with God. Think of Paul's "my God" in Phil
   4:19, and the many occurrences of the phrase in the
   Psalms, of which Psa 43:4 is a beautiful example. Who can
   forget Ruth's noble vow, "Thy people shall be my people,
   and thy God my God", or the words of Boaz to her, "A full
   reward be given thee of the Lord God of Israel under
   whose wing thou art come to trust" (Ruth 1:16; 2:12)?
   True to his promise, God is frequently called "the God of
   Abraham, of Isaac and of Jacob", and most wonderful of all
   is the statement in Heb 11:16 that He is not ashamed to be
   called their God. If we feel that, strictly speaking, we
   cannot appropriate that particular Scripture to ourselves,
   we can rejoice in the equally amazing statement that
   Christ is not ashamed to call us brethren (Heb 2:11. Cf.
   John 20:17).

6. The covenant will also be established with Isaac and his
   seed (cf. Rom 9:7).

   It would be inexcusable not to draw attention to a
   feature for which this chapter is remarkable, i.e. the large
   number of subjects which are stressed by repetition.

   (a) Fourteen times God says "I will", the object clearly
       being to impress on Abraham the divine determina-
       tion.
   (b) The phrase "my covenant between me and thee"
       occurs four times (vv. 2, 7, 10, 11) besides "my
       covenant is with thee" (v. 4). Was it because God, who
       understood so well His servant's state of mind, knew
       that unusual assurance was called for?
   (c) Three times the covenant is said to be "everlasting"
       (vv. 7, 13, 19). Cf. 13:15. See (4) above.
   (d) Nations are mentioned in three successive verses, in
       two of which they are described as many (vv. 4, 5, 6).
   (e) Twice God promises to be the God of Abraham and his
       seed (vv. 7, 8), and twice He affirms that the covenant
       will be established with Isaac (vv. 19-21; cf. Rom 9:7).
   (f) The promptness of Abraham's obedience in the matter

of circumcision is stressed by "the self same day" (vv. 23, 26) and the thoroughness of his obedience by the linkage between four occurrences of "born in thy house and bought with money" (vv. 12, 13, 23, 27). Cf. 14:14; 15:3. When thought is given to what was involved it not only highlights Abraham's obedience, but casts a side-light on his possession of slaves by purchase, and on the almost absolute nature of his authority over his large establishment, so that compliance with the rite was total.

The Significance Of Circumcision

Circumcision in itself, simply as a religious rite, accomplishes nothing (1 Cor 7:19; Gal 5:6; 6:15). Its purpose was to keep in perpetual memory the covenant between God and Abraham and his posterity, their God-given right to the land, the special relationship with God and the attendant obligation to God. However, as can so easily happen, what was intended as a token (v. 11), a sign, a seal (Rom 4:11), was given a prominence which defeated its object and became more important than what it was intended to signify. This tendency came to a head in apostolic days when zealous and fanatical Judaizers posed a threat to the universality of the gospel, by insisting that even Gentiles must submit to the rite in order to be saved. Paul's impassioned letter to the churches in Galatia reveals how serious that threat was. It has been said that if they had succeeded, Judaism, instead of simply being the cradle of Christianity, would have become its coffin.

Attention is drawn to the spiritual counterpart of circumcision in Rom 2:29; Phil 3:3 and Col 2:11, but it is important to bear in mind that the OT indicates the moral and spiritual implications of the ordinance, by linking it with ears circumcised to listen to God's word, lips circumcised to speak aright and hearts circumcised to love and obey the Lord (Exod 6:12, 30; Deut 10:12-16; 30:6; Jer 4:4; 6:10; 9:26). Stephen undoubtedly had such Scriptures in mind when he denounced those who, though laying stress on the physical rite, were so stiffnecked and uncircumcised in heart and ears that, far from heeding the word of God, they resisted the Holy Spirit as their ancestors had done, and went to the length of betraying and murdering the Son of God (Acts 7:51-53). The Lord did not criticise the Pharisees for being meticulous in tithing even insignificant items like mint but for neglecting the weightier matters of justice, mercy and faith (Matt 23:23).

Sarai's Name Changed

Husband and wife had their names changed on the same day, and unlike Jacob (32:28; 35:10) they were never again referred to by their former names.

The new name Sarah is literally "princess" as in 1 Kings 11:3; Lam 1:1. The word is translated "lady" in Jud 5:29; Est 1:18; and "queen" in Isa 49:23. Abraham's immediate adoption of the new name for his wife, in the thoughts of his heart, is a delightful touch, and it is pleasant to think that he felt some elation at God bestowing on her such a title of honour. She was further honoured by the promise that though she had so long endured the reproach of barrenness she would now not only be the mother of nations but also that kings of people would issue from her. Again, as so frequently in this chapter, the Lord conveys emphatic assurance by repetition: "I will bless her — yea I will bless her" (v. 16); "I will ... give thee a son also of her" (v. 16); "Sarah thy wife shall bear thee a son, indeed" (v. 19).

Though it is beyond question that it was God's intention from the first that she should be the mother of Abraham's promised son, this is, in fact, the first time it is definitely stated, which may be the reason why fourteen years earlier she had proposed that Abraham should take Hagar. How different was the Lord's gracious and honouring double use of the title "thy wife" (vv. 15, 19), from the scornful tone of Pharaoh when he twice used the same term in reproaching Abraham.

Abraham's Laugh

Whether Abraham's laugh was from delight or incredulity is difficult to decide. Incredulity seems inconsistent with the reverence shown by falling on his face for the second time, but in a state of excitement the human heart can be moved by fluctuating and even conflicting emotions almost at one and the same time. "Who against hope believed in hope" (Rom 4:18) aptly describes such a condition and calls to mind the curious but true-to-life confession of the tearful and distraught father, "Lord I believe; help thou mine unbelief"

(Mark 9:24. Cf. Gen 15:6-8). When years before Abraham had learned that God was the possessor of heaven and earth he immediately entered into the good of such a revelation, and in the strength of it decisively rejected Sodom's bribe (14:19-23). If on this present occasion he had been able to rest in the conviction that the same God was the Almighty (v. 1), surely he would not have wavered as he evidently did.

Ishmael

His mention of the advanced age of both of them (the only instance of a woman's age being given in Scripture) makes it evident that Abraham saw insuperable difficulties; his plea to God, "Oh that Ishmael might live before thee", certainly sounds as if he could not feel sure of any other heir, and the Lord's emphatic response confirms this. The request does not imply that Abraham had fears for Ishmael's survival; he is rather asking for God's blessing on Ishmael. This is plain from the Lord's reply, "As for Ishmael, I have heard thee: Behold I have blessed him" (v. 20).

At one time Abraham in despondency thought that his eldest servant would be his heir, but the Lord on that occasion assured him that the servant would not be his heir; his heir would be a child of his own (15:4). But Sarah was not mentioned as the one who would be the mother as is now made very plain (v. 16). Abraham's plea for Ishmael obviously shows that he is thinking that Ishmael will have to be the heir, for the Lord says, "Nay, Sarah thy wife shall bear thee a son indeed" (v. 19 RV). The name of that son is given, and it is declared that God's covenant will be established with him and not with Ishmael.

The angel of the Lord had told the fugitive Hagar that her son would be the progenitor of an innumerable multitude; but she had probably thought it expedient for obvious reasons to keep this from her master and mistress. Now, however, Abraham is told that Ishmael would beget twelve princes and that his descendants would become a great nation. The great nation promised at the beginning, before Ishmael was envisaged (12:2), referred to Israel; the great nation now mentioned refers to what became the Arabs. The tragic results of the hostility of the Arabs to the Jews with its consequences for world peace raises the question how far the history of the world has been changed as a result of Abraham listening to his wife's proposal.

Strong In Faith

The foregoing considerations lead us to enquire at what point it became true of Abraham, according to Rom 4:18-21, that "being not weak in faith ... he staggered (wavered) not at the promise of God through unbelief; but was strong in faith". Vv. 18, 19 refer to our present chapter, Gen 17:5, 17, whereas v. 22 looks back to Gen 15:6. It appears that Paul is not so much seeking to pin-point a particular occasion but is looking at the promises and Abraham's reactions in a general way, and stressing the settled conviction to which Abraham ultimately came, despite the previous changing moods in face of the formidable difficulties which challenged his faith. All things considered we incline to the view that God's final assertion before he left off talking with Abraham, "My covenant will I establish with Isaac, which Sarah shall bear unto thee at this set time of the year", enabled Abraham unwaveringly to cast aside all doubt and rest confidently in God's promises. This is in keeping with the fact that, despite the magnitude of the task, he immediately set about giving effect to the commandment concerning circumcision, accepting it as a token of the covenant. The Lord signally honoured him by the unique visit described in such detail in the passage which immediately follows.

Chapter XI

The Sixth Appearance

(Gen 18:1-33)

Three Visitors

The events recorded in the previous chapter must have been very fresh in Abraham's memory, on account of the brief interval between them and this manifestation.

He was sitting in the door of his tent in the heat of the day, at which time a siesta is the accepted practice in hot countries; he was in all probability drowsing. Although the appearance of the Lord vaguely alerted him he did not immediately realise what was happening. Recovering from surprise is aptly conveyed by "he lift up his eyes ... and looked ... and lo ...". The sudden sight of three unknown men standing a little distance away ("over against him" RV), of whose approach he had been unaware, was certainly enough to surprise him. The experience of Gideon probably explains what had happened. In his case the angel of the Lord sat invisible under an oak before he appeared to Gideon (Jud 6:11-12). Abraham naturally supposed that they had penetrated into the centre of the camp undetected because the servants were also resting. As it was very unusual to travel in the noontide heat this could have aroused suspicion in some minds, but the spontaneous response of Abraham, despite his age (99) and the oppressive heat, was to run to greet them with the intention of playing the part of host.

If Heb 13:2 (entertaining angels unaware) looks back to this incident among others, it but confirms what in any case seems clear, that he did not at first grasp the fact that they were celestial visitors. Certainly he sensed that they were of unusual distinction, for although he himself was not without considerable prestige, he paid them a mark of respect beyond the proverbial courtesy of the oriental, by bowing toward the ground. This was not quite the same as falling on his face, as he did but a very short time before when God revealed

149

Himself as the Almighty (17:3, 7), but it was more marked
than when he bowed down to the people of Heth, though they
had acknowledged him as a mighty prince (23:6-12).

Abraham was quick to see that one of the three was pre-
eminent in dignity, and he first of all addressed him as "my
Lord" (i.e. *Adonai*) a title almost exclusively reserved for deity,
although occasionally used for persons of great distinction as,
for example, Joseph when he was "lord of the land" (42:30).
The phrasing of his hospitable invitation reflects his sense of
this person's superior standing: "If I have found favour in thy
sight, pass not away I pray thee from thy servant". His use of
the word "servant" was no empty platitude as he proved later
by standing in the attitude of a waiter. Having paid particular
respect to the most eminent of the three, he tactfully and
courteously included the other two by changing from singular
pronouns to plural, but using again the word "pray" and still
taking the place of servant.

Assuming that they had walked some distance he offered
them the customary feet-washing and proposed that they rest
under the tree whilst he prepared for their nourishment. His
description of the sumptuous meal he had in mind as "a
morsel" makes one wonder what he would regard as a feast. It
is interesting to notice that the two were allowed to associate
themselves with their superior in acknowledging Abraham's
offered hospitality; "they said, So do as thou hast said".

A Meal Prepared

The speed and eagerness, almost exuberance, with which
he competently coped with the task of lavishly providing for
three unexpected guests at an awkward hour, is impressive,
reminding us of his prompt and capable tackling of greater
problems, such as the crisis created by Lot's capture (14:14)
and the carrying out of the command regarding circumcision
on the same day it was given (17:26-27).

He first hastened into the tent to urge Sarah to act quickly,
making his specific wishes very clear, namely to take three
measures of fine meal, knead it and make cakes on the hearth.
Three measures of meal would make enough cakes to satisfy
the heartiest of appetites. Leaving her to carry on with that,
he now ran still disregarding the heat to the herd to select
with an expert eye a good and tender calf. Killing it was left to
a young man so that his own clothes should not be soiled

making it necessary to change before attending to the visitors. That done he hastened to dress it so that there should not be the slightest avoidable delay in setting out a repast of veal with butter and milk and cake. All this must have taken considerable time, but the guests showed no sign of impatience. Having set the food before them he stood by them deferentially, ready to serve at table.

Enquiry For Sarah

The meal over the three again acted in unison in enquiring for Sarah, as if they had expected her to put in an appearance. For some reason Abraham did not take the hint but simply stated the obvious —that she was in the tent. A question arises as to how far he had taken his wife into his confidence regarding the promise he had received from the Almighty that she should bear a son (17:19). Some explanation must have been given for her change of name and for the institution of circumcision, but even if she had been specifically told that the Almighty had pledged Himself to give Abraham a son by her, she remained sceptical.

A Message Intended For Sarah

"They said" (vv. 5, 9) is now replaced by "he said"; the speaker is obviously the Lord; no further remark by the other two is recorded. His words, which would not be appropriate for any mere creature to use, were simply a restatement of what had been said to Abraham only a very short time ago; they need not have been repeated for his sake. They were evidently intended for the ears of Sarah who, not having been invited to join her husband, was eaves-dropping behind the tent door. The introduction of the fresh word "certainly" was no doubt intended to convey assurance to her so as to overcome her unbelief, but the possibility of bearing a son was still incredible to her; not daring to betray her presence by laughing aloud she laughed within herself.

It is now stated that the speaker was the Lord, and although He still addressed Abraham, His words were intended for Sarah to make her fully aware that He had read her thoughts: "Wherefore did Sarah laugh?".

Without pursuing the point at that moment He went on to ask, "Is anything too hard for the Lord?" perhaps reminding her, if she had heard it from her husband, that He was the Almighty.

The fact that He had heard her inaudible laughter put her in awe of Him and prompted her impetuously and unthinkingly to deny the charge, thereby giving away her presence. Either she did not pause to reflect that One who could see into her mind must necessarily know that her denial was false or she clutched at the faint hope that the question was prompted only by a shrewd guess.

Now that she had come out into the open the Lord could address her directly: "Nay, but thou didst laugh". She must have felt abashed at the disapproving and authoritative tone in which this was said, but there is ground for thinking that this cryptic reply carried to Sarah the conviction that there was no more to be said — the matter was settled. From Heb 11:11 we learn that at some point she exercised faith, judging that the one who had promised could be relied upon to fulfil His promise. In the absence of any other pointer this seems to have been the most likely moment when unbelief gave way to faith.

The Ways Of God

Matters having been settled with regard to Sarah, the three rose up, looked significantly toward Sodom, and then proceeded in that direction. Abraham now knew their identity, but as God had dealt with him so graciously over the past 25 years, appearing to him at critical times and communing with him, he was not ill-at-ease though careful to show becoming reverence; he continued to play the part of good host, accompanying them for some distance on their way.

As they were going along, the Lord was considering (the Scripture uses concepts we can understand) taking Abraham into His confidence as to what was afoot. In this He was looking upon him as much more than a servant turned host, but as a friend, in line with Christ's words to His disciples, "Henceforth I call you not servants, for the servant knoweth not what his lord doeth, but I have called you friends, for all things that I have heard of the Father I have made known to you" (John 15:15). See 2 Chron 20:7, "thy friend"; Isa 41:8, "my friend".

The Lord had in mind that Abraham was to become a great

and mighty nation and that all the nations of the world would be blessed in him. The RV of v. 19, "I have known him, to the end that he may command his children", points to God's purpose in choosing him, but at this stage it is safe to say that God also knew him in the sense that, having tested and tried him, God was satisfied that, despite his shortcomings, he could be trusted to use his influence aright.

It was therefore important that he should understand the principles on which God acted so that he could lead others "to keep the way of the Lord, to do justice and judgment". Later God took the same line with Moses, the leader of Israel. He made known His *acts* to the children of Israel — they were quite obvious to the people but not properly understood by them. But He made known His *ways* to Moses that he might be intelligent in interpreting the divine will (Psa 103:7). We are not called to fill such responsible roles, but it is well to ponder such Scriptures as Col 1:9; Eph 5:17.

Sodom Under Investigation

The afternoon was wearing on and the time for parting company had come; a vantage point from which Sodom could be seen (19:27-28) was a very suitable spot; there the group stood together for a while. Abraham, with a delicate sense of what was fitting, showed every deference to the Lord in the presence of His ministers by standing at a respectful distance. The Lord now made known to him some parts of His ways by explaining the reason behind this journey in terms he could understand, although the inmost nature of the unseen spiritual realm cannot be fully expressed within the resources of human language (2 Cor 12:4). Human affairs are reviewed in what may be termed judicial sessions in the court of heaven, presided over by God, and decisions taken there are reflected in events on earth. See remarks on Job chapters 1-2 in connection with the sacrifice of Isaac (ch. 15).

At the time of Lot's entry into Sodom the men of Sodom were described as "wicked and sinners against the Lord exceedingly" (13:13). It might have been thought that they would have learned wisdom from the providential discipline of God in their defeat by the four kings, and from His mercy in their undeserved deliverance through the instrumentality of God's servant. Instead they had become worse, and reports now put before the court of heaven showed that their sin had become "very grievous" (cf. 19:13). As already noted justice and judgment are cardinal in God's ways and, although He is omniscient and so unerring in judgment, justice must be seen to be done by the reports being openly investigated before sentence is pronounced. He would therefore "Go down and see whether they have done altogether according to the cry of it, which is come unto me". When He adds, "I will know", it was meant in the judicial sense of assessing evidence.

The explanation having been given, the two men went toward Sodom leaving Abraham alone with the Lord. It would appear that although the Lord used the first person pronoun in speaking of the investigation, it was actually deputed to the two men — who were, of course, angels. Cf. 19:1, "two angels" with 19:10, "the men". We have already seen that they were allowed to be associated with the Lord both in accepting Abraham's offer of hospitality and in enquiring after Sarah; we now learn that angels may be allowed to co-operate with God in some matters, although not, of course, in what are the prerogatives of deity. In the next chapter we are given grounds for thinking that angels may be allowed some degree of discretion in the execution of their responsibilities. Does this imply that God is desirous, under conditions He sees to be appropriate, of fostering fellowship with His creatures not only for His own gracious satisfaction but with a view to developing their potential? It is worth considering how far there are analogies in the service God's people are invited to render.

Intercession For Sodom

It can hardly be doubted that Abraham knew sufficient about conditions in Sodom to anticipate that the investigations would more than justify divine retribution. Therefore when the angels had departed he drew near to the Lord with an intimacy he would not have thought it proper to show in the presence of the angels. Cf. Heb 10:22; Jas 4:8. He now turned intercessor; the city was the subject of his plea but he was thinking particularly of Lot (see 19:29) for whom he still had an affectionate concern. Although he was bitterly disappointed in him he still regarded him as a righteous man, as indeed basically he was (2 Pet 2:7).

There are some situations which call for courage and decisive action and others where prayer is our only resource.

When Lot fell prey to invaders Abraham acted with astonishing courage and resolution in accomplishing his rescue, but now he realised that there was no action he could take other than prayer. It may have occurred to him to rush to Sodom to warn Lot, only to realise that angels would be more competent to do this; if they failed to deliver Lot out of the city there was not the remotest likelihood that he would succeed.

The two things which stand out are Abraham's persistence in pleading with God, and God's amazing patience and willingness to yield to his entreaties. There must have been a realisation that divine justice could be tempered with mercy. He begged God not to be angry with him because he was very conscious of his temerity, being but dust and ashes. It is a good thing to remember that we are no more than that, whilst not forgetting that God pities us as a father pities his children: "He knows our frame and remembers we are but dust" (Psa 103:13-14).

Our familiarity with the truth that God will judge the world in righteousness (Acts 17:31) must not close our eyes to the fact that it was because of Abraham's robust spiritual development that he had by this time arrived at the conviction that the God about whom he had already learnt so much, was the judge of all the earth, and that He could be relied upon to do what was right. A person must be either incredibly wise, or else singularly obtuse, if life poses no agonising problems for him. If we have faith like Abraham we shall find refuge for mind and heart in the conviction that one day we shall be able to sing the Song of Moses and the Song of the Lamb: "Great and marvellous are thy works Lord God Almighty, just and true are thy ways thou king of saints" (Rev 15:3).

After making several merciful concessions to Abraham's importunity the Lord went so far as to say that He would not destroy the city if even ten righteous persons could be found there. At this point Abraham ceased to plead, and the Lord left communing with him and went His way. There have been various attempts to explain why Abraham did not go beyond ten. Did he again and again reduce the basis of his petition because his spirit, made sensitive by many years experience of God, discerned from the tone of the Lord's reply that there was no likelihood of the required number being found? When at last he had to conclude that there were not even ten righteous persons, was it borne in on him that Sodom was past praying for? There can be such cases both as regards communities and individuals. See Jer 15:1; Ezek 14:14, 20; 1 John 5:16.

On the other hand, it has been thought that he gave Lot's household credit for being righteous, and as they numbered at least ten (19:12-14) he was satisfied. The difficulty here is that if, as was most likely, he knew the true state of affairs in that family he would hardly have had any such confidence.

It is difficult to arrive at any conclusion, but he must have returned to the camp in a very uneasy frame of mind judging from the fact that he arose early next morning to return to the same spot to see what had happened (19:27-28).

Abraham's Prayer Examined

The contents of Abraham's prayer have been cited as indicating important elements:

Reverence — "stood yet" (v. 22),
Communion — "drew near" (v. 23),
Compassion — "spare the place" (v. 24),
Faith — "do right" (v. 25),
Humility — "dust and ashes" (v. 27),
Persistence — (vv. 50, 45, 40, 30, 20, 10),
Earnestness — "Let not the Lord be angry" (vv. 30, 32),
Based on:—
  (a) Revelation of God's mind (vv. 21-23. Cf. Dan 9:1-5);
  (b) God's character as Judge of all the earth (v. 25).

Chapter XII
The Destruction Of Sodom

(Gen 19:1-38)

Lot In The Gate

In the heat of noon Abraham had been sitting in his tent door, but now when afternoon was giving way to evening Lot was "sitting in the gate of Sodom". Other interesting parallels between the two episodes provide food for thought.

Walls encircling cities for protection necessarily have gates at intervals to allow of normal access, and these are obviously of strategic importance because an enemy gaining control of a gate could establish a bridgehead within the city from which to advance. This explains the phrase "possess the gate of thy enemies" (22:17; 24:60). They were therefore fitted with bars so that at night-fall, or on the approach of foes, they could be securely closed.

The vicinity of a gate was also a focal point for social intercourse, where the comings and goings provided a passing interest. For reasons which will be given later it can be safely taken for granted that Lot was certainly not sitting in the gate fraternising with his neighbours. Merchants saw in this opportunities for doing business, and townsmen wishing to negotiate with neighbours could reckon on seeing some of them there. Inevitably, in course of time, one gate assumed greater importance than the others and so became the recognised place for discussing matters of general interest affecting the town as such. In this way it became the site for the formal gatherings of elected city elders, for the regulation of municipal affairs, and the hearing of complaints and petitions. As early as the time of Abraham such features, if not established, were certainly developing (see 23:10-11). "Sitting in the gate" may well have been an official phrase indicating that a person had been elected to office, not unlike that of a modern city councillor.

If at first sight it seems unlikely that an immigrant would be

157

appointed, it must be remembered that corrupt men who cannot trust each other are often glad to have a man of integrity in whom they can have confidence, however much they may dislike him personally. He is certain to have acquired a good deal of prestige some years earlier as the nephew of a powerful and capable man, who for Lot's sake had overthrown Sodom's enemies and whose continued interest would be well worth cultivating in case his help should be valuable in the future.

Was Lot Pressurised?

How can we explain not only Lot's continuing residence there but his acceptance of public office in such a city? It most certainly was not because he was happy there. On the contrary Peter reveals that he was a very unhappy man whose righteous soul was daily vexed, worn down, with the wickedness he could not help witnessing and the vile speech to which it was impossible to close his ears. Weak in some ways as he was, a tribute must be paid to his maintenance of personal standards when, like Joseph in Egypt, he stood virtually alone without a like-minded friend, unless his wife and daughters had some sympathy with him. In such a situation it would have been all too easy for the sharp edge of his convictions to be blunted, restricted as he was to a society in which moral standards were looked upon as ludicrously outdated.

Our day has witnessed this process, when the steep decline in moral standards has induced some religious leaders to attempt to make Christianity more palatable to a permissive society by discovering that biblical ethics are much more accommodating than they were previously thought to be!

Even if, after years of urban life with its modern amenities, he had lost his taste for pastoral life he must surely, at times, have thought wistfully of the wholesome life he once knew in the fellowship of Abraham, who was content with tent life for more than a hundred years and whose end was immeasurably happier than poor Lot's fate. So why did he remain in Sodom?

Although we are glad to see redeeming features he was on the whole a pliable character and was probably inhibited by his family's disinclination to be uprooted and seek another home. At least two of his daughters and two sons had found their spouses there. To his credit he had succeeded in keeping his two youngest daughters uncontaminated but later events proved that they with their mother were loath to leave even when the city was under threat of destruction.

If in earlier years he had protested to his family about the wickedness of the city, what more likely than that they responded by saying that if he were so concerned, he should take the opportunity of serving on the city council where, instead of merely deploring the state of affairs, he could do something practical about it, to say nothing about enhancing the family's image.

This is more likely to be the explanation for his presence in the gate, than any desire for the company of his fellow-citizens.

The experience of many since who have hoped to wield a salutary influence in the political sphere has, we believe, proved generally frustrating and disappointing. The Scriptures do record cases where certain men such as Joseph and Daniel were called of God to high office for special reasons, although it is striking that Moses, who could have put his feet on the first steps to Pharaoh's throne, did not take Joseph's case as a precedent to follow. He could have argued that he would be able to do a great deal for his oppressed kinsmen if he had political power. The effectiveness of Lot's influence was soon to be put to the test. The man who had more influence on Sodom's fate walked with God at a distance from Sodom within whose walls he was probably never seen; he had influence where it really mattered — not in the council of Sodom but in the courts of heaven. Whilst making allowance for exceptional cases where God has been pleased to raise men to high office, the more scriptural role for the majority of believers is supplication for all men, including those in authority, that we may lead quiet and peaceable lives in all godliness and honesty (1 Tim 2:1-3).

Two Arrivals

The RV by inserting the definite article, "the two angels came", puts beyond doubt what is fairly obvious, i.e. that the two whose arrival is now mentioned were the same two angels, in human form, who had accompanied the Lord to Abraham's camp at mid-day. Although the narrative here concerns itself only with the two, it must not be supposed that they were the only persons approaching the gate. At that time

of day some who had been away on business and others who
had been working in the fields would be making their way in
before the gate was closed for the night. Then again, it would
not be uncommon for travellers to break their journey to seek
shelter for the night within the walls. In the ordinary way
such folk entering the city would not excite any exceptional
interest, but the impressive aspect and bearing of these two
arrested the attention of Lot and, as appears later, the
unpleasant interest of others. Lot's behaviour is quite in
accord with the supposition that he was there in his capacity
as a city elder, part of whose duty would be to give a welcome
to any auspicious visitors, and these were evidently worthy of
a special reception.

In quite different circumstances Abraham ran spontaneously
to greet his visitors but, as was more seemly in the present
case, "Lot seeing them rose up to meet them". Even allowing
for the elaborate courtesy of the East, the attention he paid
them testifies to their being obviously of considerable status,
for his reception of them was very similar to Abraham's,
although not quite so deferential at the first. For example he
did not, until much later, speak, as Abraham had done, of
finding favour in their sight, and whereas Abraham had
addressed his principal guest as "my Lord" (*Adonai*) Lot used a
form for both which was quite commonly used as a mark of
respect to superiors, "my lords". Nevertheless, as Abraham
did, he "prayed" them to accept his hospitality and spoke of
himself as their "servant". He, too, mentioned washing their
feet for comfort's sake, but his curious remark, "and ye shall
rise up early and go on your ways", was hardly calculated to
assure visitors that they were very welcome. This, of course,
was not his idea; either he had interpreted an air of urgency as
impatience with anything which might delay their departure
on the morrow, or maybe it was not unusual for travellers
who had been obliged to spend a night there to be anxious to
leave as soon as possible a city with such an unsavoury
reputation. He simply wished to assure them that they would
not be hindered as a result of accepting his invitation. How
little did he dream what that early hour would bring.

A Feast Prepared

Unlike the ready reception of Abraham's hospitality, the
angels, for some reason, demurred, expressing their intention

of spending the night in the open, which was not exceptional when the nights were warm. However, they yielded to his persuasion, made more pressing because Lot was well aware that they might be subjected to unwelcome attention in the street and, even at the best, sleeping out was unthinkable for persons of such distinction.

In view of the considerable lengths to which Abraham went it is fitting that some details were recorded of the substantial repast he laid before his guests; considering the better facilities available to Lot it suffices to say he provided a feast. Unleavened bread was provided in the place of cakes, but that can hardly be intended to have a spiritual significance; it more likely means that there was not sufficient time for leaven to ferment and cause the dough to rise before baking.

So far everything had gone smoothly, and it appears that the angels considerately did not intend to alarm Lot until he had some rest, for it is said that they were getting ready to lie down. But there was to be a violent interruption in contrast to the unruffled calm in which the earlier meal under the trees had been enjoyed.

Lot's House Attacked

The arrival in the city of two men of attractive appearance and their reception into Lot's house had not gone unnoticed by some of the men of Sodom. After they had stirred up general but unhealthy interest a mob gathered, some intent on perpetrating foul evil and others with prurient curiosity. The state of Sodom is reflected not only by the size of the rabble, "from every quarter", but by the presence of young and old and some of the more prominent citizens with the rank and file —the great and the small. Neither the old or the great set a good example to the younger generation, as has too often been the case since.

Lot had come a long way since his tent days; he lived in a detached house which the disorderly crowd encompassed demanding that his guests be delivered over to them. It is important to bear in mind that ugly lust is incensed by, and hates, beauty and purity to which it cannot aspire; a fiendish desire to destroy what it hates explains many of the atrocities which have been committed. This has such relevance for our day that Christians with some responsibility to understand the mentality of offenders should not shirk pondering the

11

illuminating use of the words "humble", "defile" and "force" in the following passages among others. They are translations of the same word *anah*: Gen 34:2; Deut 21:14; Jud 20:5; 2 Sam 13:13-32. The utterly unreasonable hatred of Amnon and his heartless treatment of his innocent and helpless victim, Tamar, though unpleasant reading, gives a penetrating insight into his so-called love. Not all cases are so despicable. Shechem behaved honourably in genuine efforts to rectify the position (34:1,4).

Lot's Courage

We have already noticed how this strange man, Lot, so weak in some ways, had shown quite surprising moral stamina in resisting over many years the debilitating tendency of surrounding depravity. Now it is pleasant to see that in a crisis he was capable of showing exceptional courage. He was brave enough to leave the shelter of the house, carefully shutting the door behind him for the safety of others, though cutting off his own retreat, to face this unruly gathering who were in an ugly mood, in the hope of reasoning with them. His claim to some sort of kinship with them ("my brethren" RV) to reinforce his appeal must have sprung from near desperation. The words must have stuck in his throat, for there is no sign that his abhorrence of their manner of life had recently abated and that he had been cultivating more brotherly relations with them. Is it possible that even in the tumult there flashed into his mind the honourable way in which his uncle had included him in a bond of genuine brotherhood (13:8; 14:14)?

He pleaded the well-recognised sanctity of hospitality which in the culture of that day would ordinarily have carried tremendous weight, but the clamourers were in no mood to listen to even the most potent of arguments. Sensing this, courage gave way to panic which drove Lot to make the monstrous proposal to protect his guests at the expense of his two virgin daughters. The fact that hitherto they had been protected from contamination with the evil amidst which they had been brought up, whilst in itself a credit to their home, made the suggestion even more revolting if that were possible. It is difficult to believe that even those among his contemporaries who held the strictest and strongest views on the sacredness of hospitality would on that account have excused a father for yielding up his daughters to such unmentionable degradation. It is hoped that the girls never learned how they might have been betrayed by the one in whose faithfulness they should have been able to repose the fullest confidence. The most determined effort to find some excuse for the poor man can do no more than admit that he must have been distraught with terror. The very thought of what might have happened if the infamous proposal had been accepted causes a shudder.

But even this intended distraction did not deter the men from pursuit of their particular evil purpose — they simply extended their vile threat to Lot himself and made a move to break into the house.

His description of their intention as "wickedness" was an irritating reminder of protests in the past, but the fruitlessness of his well-meant attempts to bring about some reform is sadly illustrated in their contemptuous description of him: "This one fellow came in to sojourn and he will needs be a judge". It sounds as if no one else had presumed to disapprove of their way-of-life.

Timely Intervention

The angels saved the situation by pulling Lot back into the house and smiting the men with blindness. As they wearied themselves groping around, colliding with each other in the confusion, fear of the unknown strangers' miraculous powers must have sobered them. The blindness was doubtless only temporary and as sight returned they made their way home afraid to risk further punishment from these extraordinary individuals.

If as suggested in ch. 18 definite evidence was required that the iniquity of Sodom was as heinous as reports claimed, there could now be no doubt that corruption had infected the whole community. After the previous references to conditions there (13:13; 18:20), the angels disclosed to Lot that instead of any improvements matters had got progressively worse: "the cry of them is waxen (has grown) great before the face of the Lord", and the destruction of the city had been decided upon judicially. Although from the human standpoint the catastrophe was brought about by terrestrial upheaval, the carrying out of the divine sentence was entrusted to the two angels wielding super-natural power to control the forces of nature.

Fleeing From The City

In view of the impending overthrow Lot was urged to get his whole family out of the place speedily. Once again he displayed some courage in venturing out in the dark night without any guarantee that evil men were not still abroad. He visited the homes of his sons-in-law, but nothing is said about his sons. He failed to impress them with the reality of the peril and his urgent advice went unheeded. It must have been agonising and mortifying to find that they would not take him seriously — they treated it as a joke. It is difficult to enter into his feelings of despair as he sadly made his way back home from his fruitless mission.

Morning had now come, and he was told to take his wife and two daughters out of the city. Looking back with our knowledge of the fiery avalanche which overwhelmed the whole area, his hesitation in leaving may seem strange; in his situation, as it was at that moment, his. lingering is understandable. To abandon, almost at a moment's notice we might say, all he had laboured to build up over at least twenty years was bad enough, but we can form but a poor conception of the agony of leaving to their fate his whole family-circle save his wife and two daughters. As he faced the horrific decision, did some demon whisper in his ear that the predicted inferno might not happen? Did the confident ridicule of his sons-in-law cause him momentarily to waver, wondering whether after all the danger was as real as represented, thinking what a fool he would look if the threatened destruction did not take place? It is all very well to say he had the word of the angels, but he did not put implicit trust in the angelic promise that he would be safe in Zoar. Cf. v. 21 with v. 30. There could have been a little delay in gathering together some easily portable valuables so that they would not be destitute in a new environment, but we venture to think that this would have been excused as a sensible thing to do. Even so, any avoidable delay was so dangerous that the angels laid hold of the four, each taking the hands of two and almost dragging them out. Apparently the angels accompanied the three escapees to the vicinity of Zoar which could not have been very far from Sodom as a comparison of v. 15 with v. 23 shows. Hitherto the angels had spoken and acted in unison, but the interesting fact now emerges that one of them was higher in rank for he became and remained the spokesman, "When they had brought them forth abroad he said, Escape for thy life ... to the mountain".

Where The Miraculous Is Unnecessary

Although by no means the most striking example, we have here an instance of what may be called the divine economy in the sparing use of the miraculous, in contrast to the extravagances of fables. They were not transported through the air by the waving of an angel's wand but had to trudge every step of the way. God cannot be expected to do for us what we can do for ourselves (Matt 14:19; John 11:39, 44). Only a miracle could multiply the five loaves and two small fishes, but the disciples had the formidable task of distributing the food to the huge company. Only divine power could raise Lazarus, but others could roll away the stone and remove the graveclothes.

Not So My Lord

Lot perceived the change for, although he acknowledged both, he addressed the speaker as "my Lord" and attributed to him the grace and mercy which had been shown, although the angel was but the mediator of the mercy of the Lord (v. 16). Yet how strangely inappropriate to use the expression "my Lord" and refer to himself as "thy servant" and at the same time reject the order to flee to the mountain. (Cf. Peter Acts 10:14). He did not say he would prefer not to escape to the mountain, but "I cannot". He had some undisclosed fear of the mountain which is difficult to understand seeing that in years gone by he had ample experience of mountain-life and proved it to be more secure than city life (14:12). He felt he would be safer in a litle city; he makes the point that Zoar was small, as if it was therefore likely to be less wicked than the larger cities and would therefore be exempt from the disaster. In this he was mistaken because the angel clearly implied that it was to be overthrown. This angel evidently had greater authority than his companion and, within that authority delegated by God, he was allowed a measure of discretion in the carrying out the Lord's commission, for not only did he accept Lot's plea but he gave his personal promise not to destroy the city.

He also inferred that he was to be the prime mover in the general destruction, and that he was unable to act until Lot was safe.

The fact that Zoar was saved for Lot's sake, through his prayer defective as that prayer was, tempts us to wonder what might have been the outcome if, like Abraham, he had powerfully interceded for Sodom. But, hypothetical questions do not take us very far. It is however salutary to ask ourselves whether we have played our part in line with the injunction of 1 Tim 2:1-5.

Those who wish to enquire further into the differing roles angels play in their service for God may find it useful to examine the implications of Eph 1:21; 3:10; Col 1:16 in conjunction with the special spheres of the two angelic beings who are named, Michael and Gabriel: Dan 10:13-21; 12:1; Rev 12:7; Dan 8:16; 9:21; Luke 1:19, 26. There is practical value in such a study; it enhances our appreciation of God's government and suggests challenging analogies between angelic service and the privileges believers can enjoy in their God-appointed spheres. For example, if Gabriel could say, "I ... stand in the presence of God" Elijah could say, "The Lord God ... before whom I stand" (1 Kings 17:1; 18:15).

The Fateful Day

The four, accompanied part way by the angels, left Sodom "when the morning arose", and Zoar not being far away they entered "as the sun was risen upon the earth". It was therefore early in the day when "the Lord rained upon Sodom and upon Gomorrah brimstone and fire from the Lord out of heaven".

Christ's words to His disciples in Luke 17:28-32 show that almost up to the very last, normal life had gone on, full of activity and progress: "they did eat, they drank, they sold, they planted, they builded". On this very morning they were preparing to resume their usual occupations in what they naturally thought would be another normal day, little dreaming of the catastrophe about to overtake them. The Saviour went on to say that this is how it will be in the day when the Son of Man is revealed, ushering in the Day of the Lord. There will be a false sense of security, the Christ-rejecting world saying "peace and safety" when sudden destruction shall come upon them (1 Thess 5:1-3; cf. Matt

24:38, 39).

The holocaust was on such a gigantic scale that it wiped out both the main cities and others in the plain, burnt up all vegetation and killed all the inhabitants. The indications are that there was a mighty volcanic eruption, probably accompanied by lightning and thunder. Parallel geological faults in the underlying strata extending over great distances include this area. Immense subterranean reservoirs of bitumen could explain the accumulations in the hollows of the plain (the slime (bitumen) pits) into which defeated troops fleeing from the battle blundered to their death (14:10). Josephus is said to have called the Dead Sea the Sea of Asphalt.

Considering the vast volume of inflammable gases which was imprisoned under tremendous pressure in subterranean cavities, the effect of a powerful volcanic eruption staggers the imagination. With a frightful roar accompanying the ignition of these gases, flaming pitch was hurled to a great height to fall like a terrible rain from heaven, igniting pitch deposits in the plain, consuming all combustible material in the cities in a moment (Lam 4-6) reducing it to ash, while a thick black cloud went up as the smoke of a furnace (v. 28; 2 Pet 2:6). As distinct from the meaning of brimstone in the Genesis record, the word so translated in Luke 17 originally denoted fire from heaven; it acquired the meaning sulphur probably because of the sulphurous smell left by lightning (fire from heaven). Small wonder that the overthrow ranks among the major natural catastrophes of history. The operation of what we call natural laws is in no way inconsistent with the cataclysm being attributed to the action of God by angelic agency; both angels were involved ("we" v. 13) whilst the initiative lay with one ("I" vv. 21, 22). Many scriptures draw aside the veil which conceals the spiritual realm, revealing that natural forces can be subject to spiritual forces. It is well to remember that even Satan can manipulate natural forces as in the case of the disasters which fell on Job's household, albeit not without divine permission, for reasons suggested in ch. 22.

God who can make the wrath of man to praise Him (Psa 76:10) can also overrule the malignity of Satan for His own wise purpose. Unbelievers may reject the idea of spiritual forces at work behind the scenes, but we have yet to learn that the test of truth is whether men believe it. The bird that dashes itself against a window does not believe in the solid reality of the invisible glass until it is too late. It is absurd to suppose that the Almighty God cannot control the universe. He has brought into being by His word of power. Consideration of the moral problems raised by natural disasters must be deferred.

Lot's Wife

The devastating upheaval was mercifully delayed until Lot reached the safety of Zoar, and yet it is apparent that his wife perished before Zoar was reached. At first sight a contradiction seems to be involved, but Scripture does not set out to provide the solution to every difficulty which may arise. That is far from saying that they are not susceptible of explanation. In many vast volcanic eruptions there has been preliminary activity on a smaller scale, and in this case there could well have been sporadic emissions of small quantities of burning asphalt, one of which engulfed Lot's wife who had lagged behind and looked back in defiance of the angel's warning. It was only a matter of seconds but it spelt her doom. The Saviour's injunction to remember Lot's wife has particular reference to predicted events attending the revelation of the Son of Man, but we may well ponder to what extent the story may be used in appeals to the unconverted to flee from the wrath to come.

Residence In Zoar

Her sudden and dreadful end, standing like a pillar encased in salt, must have had a shattering effect on the nerves of her husband and daughters as they hurried in terror to Zoar. The arrival of three refugees in a state of shock must have attracted the notice of some of the people of Zoar before everybody was thrown into panic by the blast of the eruption, its tremendous roar reverberating over the plain and echoing from the mountains. Their amazed relief at the miraculous immunity of their city from the general destruction would be difficult to exaggerate.

It is not unlikely that some would be able to recognise Lot as the city councillor whom they had seen sitting in the gate of nearby Sodom, and his story would arouse intense interest. When they learned that their escape was due to his presence he must have been regarded as a welcome guest. Yet, despite the angel's assurance, Lot did not feel secure in Zoar which was not far from the centre of the eruption, and we must make allowance for him, remembering the trauma he had undergone. No doubt he feared that the full force of the volcano had not yet been expended and that further eruptions were possible. The mountains, unaffected by the shock, seemed so solid in contrast to man's buildings which had so easily been reduced to ashes that he decided to take refuge there as he was told to do in the first place. The fear which, for some undisclosed reason, he had of the mountains was overcome by the greater terror which hung over him.

In The Cave

Rather than risk sheltering in some flimsy structure they took refuge in a cave where they felt safe from any danger threatened from above. The integrity of Scripture has sometimes been impugned by the critical on the wholly false principle that what is not explained must be inexplicable and therefore suspect. Thus having regard to the situation in which they found themselves, subsistence has been seen as an insuperable difficulty, but there could be a quite simple and natural solution. Lot is not likely to have left Sodom without prudently collecting such gold and valuables as were in the house. With these he could purchase from the well-disposed residents of Zoar and carry to the mountains provisions to tide them over until more settled arrangements could be decided upon. Although the curtain coming down, fittingly makes this the last scene in the drama, there is no need to suppose that the cave became their permanent home.

The view from the cave mouth in all likelihood made it possible to see the devastated plain; he could hardly have avoided contrasting this with the prospect which enchanted him on that fateful day when he had parted from Abraham. What an appalling price he had paid for his choice. But worse was to follow. No doubt Lot's case is intended as an extreme example of the perils of a worldly outlook, so as to be a more effective warning to the believer to "love not the world, neither the things that are in the world" (1 John 2:15).

Since Scripture does not draw a veil over the awful sequel we ought not to shrink from facing the facts, and forming our own conclusions. Maybe it was because he felt too weary and disorientated to care that he allowed his daughters to induce him to drink to the point of insensibility. The elder's remark that he was old is significant when we remember that as the son of Abraham's younger brother, Haran, he must have been considerably younger than his uncle; the inference seems to be that he had aged prematurely as a result of the stresses under which he had lived for so many years in Sodom, culminating in the catastrophes which had now befallen him. We need not suppose from her next remark that she imagined the human race had been wiped out; she would have known differently from her recent contacts in Zoar. She probably meant that, situated as they were, there was no prospect of forming an alliance with any man. If the sisters were genuinely concerned that their father's name should not be blotted out (a calamity in those days) it at least argues for some sympathy with him even if their conduct was inexcusable. To believe that good can come out of doing evil is a diabolic delusion, but a lifetime spent in Sodom could so have affected their moral judgment that they found it easy to persuade themselves that the end justified the means. When in due course their condition became apparent Lot must have plumbed the depths of shame, but how could he have adopted an outraged attitude when his conscience reminded him of the hideous proposal he had made to the mob outside his house not so long ago?

So he disappears from the stage. How many years were left to him we cannot conjecture, but to be obliged to live with the evidence of his shame must have been a heavy burden to bear. If he could never hope to end his days as Abraham did 75 years later, we can at least hope that God, who because He is rich in mercy has been merciful to us, took pity on His child and gave him light at eventide.

Moab And Ammon

We cannot shut our eyes to the deplorable long-term effects of Lot's shame. The descendants of the sons borne by his daughters became bitter opponents of God's chosen people, the seed of Abraham, as may be judged by such Scriptures as Num 24:17; 25:1-4; Deut 2:9. Their evil influence was seen even in Solomon's reign (1 Kings 11:1-11), and was an indirect cause of the dividing of the kingdom. The last mention of them, something like twelve hundred years later, ominously links them with Sodom and Gomorrah, testifying to God's abhorrence of them (Zeph 2:9).

Yet such is God's delight in mercy that despite the strictures in the Book of Deuteronomy that no Moabite should be allowed to enter into the congregation of Israel until the tenth generation, Ruth the Moabitess was warmly welcomed as she sought shelter under the wing of the God of Israel; more wonderful still she became one of only four women mentioned as ancestresses of the Messiah in the forty-two generations of Matthew's table. Incidentally, all four were under some cloud, the unscrupulous (though wronged) Tamar, Rahab the harlot, Ruth a Moabitess and Bathsheba who is not named but referred to as the wife of Uriah: "Sovereign grace o'er sin abounding" (Deut 23:3-4; Neh 13:1-3).

Abraham Surveys The Destruction

The Lord's promise that Sodom would be spared if ten righteous persons could be found there left the question open so that Abraham returned to his place without any definite assurance. After what must have been a restless night, he returned to the spot where he had stood before the Lord in intercession, evidently apprehensive of what he would see.

Whatever his fears were, he could hardly have been prepared for such a scene of utter destruction, involving not only Sodom and Gomorrah but other cities of the plain. The whole of the countryside was enveloped in a thick black pall of smoke like the smoke of a furnace. We are left in doubt whether Abraham was forced to conclude that Lot and his family had all perished, but as it is said that he was rescued, not so much for his own sake, but because "God remembered Abraham", it is natural to think that God allowed him the consolation of knowing that his prayers had been effective to that extent. In that case he is almost certain to have taken steps to trace Lot. Whether or not the latter ever realised what he owed to his uncle's intercession, he would have been too ashamed of his degradation to seek him out.

Whatever the truth of the matter there must have been a heavy burden on Abraham's heart. Either he mourned his nephew as perished, or, having discovered his whereabouts, he learned of his unutterable disgrace. It all seemed so futile that we need not wonder if in weariness of spirit he moved from an area associated with such painful memories (20:1).

The Moral Problem Of Natural Disasters

For the thoughtful, catastrophes of any kind, causing widespread suffering and loss of life, pose painful problems, but we confine ourselves now to what may be called "natural disasters". Much is unexplained, but in the case of Sodom and Gomorrah we are given the fundamental reason for their destruction — their iniquity had "waxen great before the face of the Lord" (v. 13).

The severe judgment may be likened to the drastic but imperative surgical operation for the removal of a cancerous growth which otherwise would affect the whole body with fatal results. These two cities were not only cesspools of immorality (on which Jude 7 casts additional light) but had acted like a moral cancer which had already infected other cities of the plain, such as Admah and Zeboim (14:2; Deut 29:23) and Zoar (v. 21), and would have spread their contagion further afield. Moral standards among the Canaanites generally left a great deal to be desired, but evidently they had not sunk as low. The Amorites were bad but their iniquity had not reached the stage where judgment could not be deferred (15:16). There were communities where conditions were a good deal better to judge by the fact that Abraham was confederate with some of the Amorites (14:13). Moreover, Abimelech and his people show up to advantage in the matter of Sarah as related in the next chapter. Again, the king of Salem was a priest of the Most High God which warrants the conclusion that his people were God-fearing (14:18). So there was still much that was worth preserving even if it was at the expense of eliminating the corrupt civilisation of the plains. Even this was not nearly so drastic as the deluge which wiped out the whole race, with the exception of eight souls, because "the earth was filled with violence" and "all flesh had corrupted his way upon the earth" (6:11-12).

God had His own glorious purposes in the creation of man and these He has pursued and will pursue until all is fulfilled in the grand climax described, for example, in 1 Cor 15:24-28 and Eph 1:9-12. In wondrous mercy He shows longsuffering towards rebellious sinners, but if His purposes are threatened, and chastisement fails, mercy must give way to judgment.

This conception of divine justice is becoming increasingly unacceptable in modern society influenced by some schools of psychology and humanism. With their shallow ideas of justice they seem at times to be more concerned with what they see to be the interests of the criminal than they are with the wider issues of the welfare of the public, both short- and long-term. Discipline has been dismissed as out-dated and unenlightened, and the baneful effect of this philosophy, escalating violence world-wide, does not seem to convince them that there is such a thing as evil.

A Warning

Beyond the immediate purpose of arresting the growth of gross perversions, the overthrow was intended as a salutary warning to future generations (Jude 7), as is made quite clear in Deut 29:22-29 written many centuries later. The many references to the overthrow in the later prophets leave the impression that the memory of it lingered on in that part of the world even longer than that. In Jonah's day, perhaps a thousand years after the destruction of Sodom, the Lord said of the great city of Nineveh: "their wickedness is come up before me" (Jonah 1:2) which almost sounds like an echo of His words to Abraham regarding Sodom and Gomorrah: "the cry of it which is come unto me" (Gen 18:21). The prophet's message from God was: "Forty days and Nineveh shall be overthrown". Had the fate of Sodom made such a deep impression on the ancient world that the threat of similar judgment seemed too possible to allow of scepticism, and led to a genuine repentance in turning from their evil ways? (Cf. Jonah 3:4-10.) This was not always the case as Amos 4:11 clearly shows, in fact those who had been mercifully "plucked out of the burning" did not return to the Lord.

Other Convulsions In Nature

Because there are clear Scriptural instances of the direct connection between sin and disaster we are not justified in concluding that every catastrophe can be interpreted in the same way. There may be many causes, and indeed various reasons, for such upheavals, but we have no warrant to assume that those who suffer are being judged for their sins. The Saviour warned us against hastily reaching such conclusions when he spoke of the Galilaeans massacred by Pilate, and the eighteen who were crushed to death by the collapse of the tower of Siloam (Luke 13:1-5).

History affords examples of wicked cities being over-whelmed but we cannot assert that it was for moral reasons. Opinions may vary, but we are on firm ground only in those particular Scriptural cases where such an explanation is clearly given. What are we to say of natural convulsions, some massive, which have occurred in remote regions where human beings have not been involved — some indeed on the beds of oceans?

It is difficult to see what moral purpose can have been served in such cases. Then again, many wicked cities have been preserved, although, maybe, retribution has taken other forms. There is reason, from Scriptural precedents, to believe that God often sees fit to visit with signal judgment the first manifestation of a particular evil to give unmistakable evidence of His grave displeasure; such occurred in the cases of Miriam (Num 12:1-10), Korah (Num 16:28-33), Achan (Josh 7:3-15), Uzziah (2 Chron 26:16-21), Ananias and Sapphira (Acts 5:1-11). It is almost certain that similar sins have been committed since, but having once made His disapproval abundantly clear He has not taken the same drastic action in every case.

The eternal and almighty God is sovereign, perfect in all His ways, and ever acts in accord with His infinite wisdom and absolute righteousness; how dare His puny creatures presume to judge how He should act (Rom 9:20)? The fact that He would have spared Sodom if there had been ten righteous persons there in no way justifies us in believing that He would necessarily do that again. It is common knowledge that cities where there have been, not ten, but hundreds of God's people have been devastated. Lot was wonderfully rescued from Sodom by angelic agency as a brand plucked out of the burning, but in many cases believers have suffered along with their fellow-citizens. Certainly there have been instances where God's people have been protected in ways too remarkable to be explained as coincidences, but we tend to overlook the fact that the ungodly have escapes which are almost miraculous. Is it not significant that the oft-quoted statement "the secret things belong unto the Lord our God, but those things which are revealed belong unto us" comes at the end of a passage which speaks of the cities of the plain being overthrown by the Lord in His anger (Deut 29:29)? Is there not a pointed hint to accept what is revealed whilst realising there is much we do not understand? Though we may learn from what is revealed to discern some of God's ways, it is well to remember that after dealing at great length with the problem of Israel's fall Paul concluded his careful analysis with the words: "O the depth of the riches both of the wisdom and knowledge of God! How unsearchable are his judgments and his ways past finding out" (Rom 11:33). Assuredly then we shall never be competent to make moral judgments in cases where we have no clear guidance from God's Word. This will save us from making the common mistake of drawing general conclusions on the basis of particular cases.

More Tolerable For Sodom

So far we have been considering divine retribution in the here and now', but there is the infinitely more solemn issue of eternal destiny. Human affairs are so complex with such great differences in privilege and opportunity that we cannot assess degrees of responsibility. Even those who maintain that the actions of men and nations can be judged at the bar of history will surely shrink from predicting the verdict at the final assize when God will judge not only the works but the very secrets of men by Jesus Christ (Rom 2:16).

Divine knowledge extends not only to the hidden springs of human actions, and not only to our very thoughts even before they take conscious shape in our minds (Psa 139:2), but also to what response men would have made to the truth had their circumstances been different. But for the Saviour's declaration, who could imagine that in the day of judgment it will be more tolerable for Sodom than for the more privileged Capernaum?

The order generally accepted in the categorisation of sins needs to be revised. Had Sodom enjoyed the same privileges and witnessed the same works of Christ it would have remained, clearly inferring (on the analogy of Tyre and Sidon) that, unlike Capernaum, repentance would have led to mercy, (Matt 11:20-24). This brings us to the verge of questions too great for us, and the subject is sufficiently solemn to smother speculation. Rather let us be like David: "Neither do I exercise myself in great matters or in things too high for me" (Psa 131:1). Sharing Abraham's faith that the judge of all the earth will do right, we wait until around the rainbow-encircled throne we see the Lamb of God in the midst open the seven-sealed book (Rev 4:3; 5:1-7).

The Judgment Of Believers

Perhaps it will not be inappropriate as we leave these great matters to turn to the very practical question of judgment on a personal level. How can we adequately thank God that the believer in Christ has passed from death into life and will not come into judgment in the penal sense (John 5:24)? Nevertheless, we may well be sobered at the thought of appearing before the Judgment Seat of Christ, where our service and the counsels of the heart will be made manifest —not merely what we did but why we did it. Let us take to heart the injunction of our Master before whom we will stand: "Judge not that ye be not judged. For with what judgment ye judge ye shall be judged" (Matt 7:1-2). If this means that He will judge us with the same degree of sympathy and understanding that we show to our fellow-servants, it should do much to curb the critical spirit. Obviously He did not mean that we should be gullible, for in the same context He warned us against false prophets and gave us the means of testing their claims (vv. 15-20).

At the same time we are to avoid the censorious spirit of the disciples who forbad one who was casting out demons in the name of Christ. They justified their action to the Lord with the repeated "because he followed not us"! Their officious prohibition is all the more extraordinary seeing that the man's success was in contrast to their recent failure in the very same matter, through lack of earnestness (cf. Mark 9:28-29 with vv. 38-40). Was it jealousy? It is not for us to decide what another servant's sphere should be — that is the Master's prerogative: "Who art thou that judgest another man's servant? To his own master he standeth or falleth" (Rom 14:4). Cf. John 21:20-22. It is enough for us to fill the sphere the Lord had chosen for us, and to serve him there faithfully and devotedly:

> Judge not. The workings of his brain
> And of his heart thou canst not see.
> What looks to thy dim eyes a stain
> In God's pure light may only be
> A scar, brought from some well-won field
> Where thou wouldst only faint and yield.   *Adelaide Proctor*

Chapter XIII

Abimelech And Sarah

(Gen 20:1-18)

Moving South Again

Comparing 18:14, "at the time appointed" (RV "the set time") with the identical phrase in 21:2, it is obvious that the incident which now claims our attention must have taken place very soon after the events described in ch. 19 and before Sarah's pregnancy had become apparent. Abraham's move to Gerah must therefore have followed closely on the destruction of Sodom, and, as we have already suggested, there may have been a definite connection between the two.

Lot's folly years earlier, in returning to that evil city after Abraham at considerable risk and effort had rescued him from the clutches of Chedorlaomer, must have been a great disappointment to Abraham and quite conceivably contributed to his mood of depression described in ch. 15. Once again Lot was a cause of sorrow. If Abraham knew that he had escaped from Sodom then in all likelihood he had learned of the shameful sequel. Either way, it was all very depressing to have to admit that his deep and affectionate interest in his nephew's welfare and his earnest supplications for Sodom had been futile. Did the devil tempt him to wonder whether his confidence in God, as the Judge of all the earth who would do right, had been misplaced? This would have been an even sorer trial. His move to the south again, although not so far as before, may have been prompted by a desire to get away from an area associated with such painful memories.

Needlessly Afraid Again

All this may help to account for his weariness of spirit which led to prejudiced judgment, faltering faith and needless fear. Even so, after making every allowance for the spiritual, emotional and physical stresses to which he had been subject,

12

it does seem strange that he should resort again to the subterfuge which, far from succeeding in Egypt, had only served to bring about the disaster it was meant to avert and from which he had been extricated only by the dramatic intervention of God. This experience should have fortified his faith, but when fear is allowed to displace faith we become irrational. His judgment became clouded and, without any evidence to justify it, he was convinced that the fear of God was not in the place. This could have been said truly of other places where he had settled and yet neither he nor Sarah had come to any harm. Faith should have assured him that the God who had so obviously protected him hitherto would protect him still, but fear argued that in those places, among smaller groups of people, his own capacity for self-defence had made him secure; the Philistines were a different proposition. They were a vigorous people, who upon migrating from Egypt had subjugated a large area of southern Canaan and had now grown to such numbers that Abimelech could rightly describe them as a nation. He had an army under the command of a chief captain implying that there were subordinate commanders (21:22). Fear told Abraham that he could easily be overwhelmed, but if he had listened to faith he would have been reminded that Pharaoh was far more powerful than Abimelech yet God had been able to deal with him.

It is true that in later history the Philistines became the implacable and formidable enemies of Israel, but this must not cloud our view of this people at this particular time. They appear in a much more favourable light, but Abraham, supposing them to be godless, was afraid that the king would use his superior strength to overcome any resistance and slay him so that Sarah could be taken with some semblance of propriety. But if the king was as unscrupulous as Abraham supposed, would he bother about such considerations?

So despite the lessons Egypt must have taught him he once more gave it out that Sarah was his sister. What was true up to a point was really a downright lie — it was equivalent to saying, "She is not my wife".

Judge Not

At first sight such behaviour after many years' experience of God seems almost incredible until we reflect on the weakness of human nature. Abraham is not an isolated case. Who would have expected that Jacob, for example, after his sacred experience at Penuel, when as a prince he had power with God, would immediately afterwards fawn on such a character as Esau in servile fear? Cf. Gen 32 and 33. If we feel confident that in similar circumstances and under the same pressures we would show up to better advantage, then we have not yet learned the painful lesson that Paul was taught after a resolute but vain struggle: "For I know that in me (that is, in my flesh,) dwelleth no good thing" (Rom 7:18). Deprived of our many advantages, and above all of the grace of God, we are capable of what the worst of men have perpetrated. Remembering the Saviour's words we should refrain from harsh criticism, and if we think that we stand we will take heed lest we fall.

Abimelech

Abimelech is not a personal name but a dynastic title, meaning father-king. He seems to have been a considerate man, concerned for the welfare of his people, and to some extent living up to his title. In taking into his harem a woman whom he believed to be unattached he was acting within the recognised rights of a king and, according to his enlightenment, without violating his conscience. It is very difficult to understand why Sarah, whilst refusing to do so in Egypt, was now willing to co-operate in the deception by saying that Abraham was her brother, especially in view of the fact that her condition would become apparent before long. Did they not foresee what problems it was going to create?

In Egypt God visited Pharaoh and his household with great plagues and, apparently without the necessity of a direct message from God, an uneasy conscience connected these inflictions with his abduction of Sarah. In the present case Abimelech and his wife suffered ill-health and the women of his household barrenness. The first would be immediately apparent; the second would not become obvious until later. Unlike Pharaoh, Abimelech saw no reason to interpret these misfortunes as evidence of God's displeasure. Consequently by means of a startling dream God revealed his error and warned him that he would pay for it with his life if he retained Sarah.

Abimelech's Integrity

The king's response is very revealing. Far from being devoid of the fear of God, as Abraham had supposed, he showed a healthy reverence and a concern for his people whom he understood to be involved. "Lord (*Adonai*) wilt thou slay also a righteous nation?" He was not, of course, claiming moral perfection but speaking relative to the maintenance of proper standards. He could plead truthfully that both Abraham and Sarah had led him to believe that she was unmarried, and he was able to speak sincerely of the integrity of his heart and the innocence of his hands. God, in fact, acknowledged his integrity: "Yea, I know that thou didst this in the integrity of thy heart; for I also withheld thee from sinning against me" (v. 6). This was a gracious tribute, and at the same time a gentle reminder that all sin is primarily an offence against God.

Abimelech Makes Restitution

The king lost no time in rectifying matters. He rose up early in the morning, gathered all his servants together and told them all these things. They likewise showed a healthy fear of God: "the men were sore afraid". The word "men" does not necessarily exclude the women. It does not appear that it was imperative for him to take them so fully into his confidence, but it throws light on his relationship with his staff. Compare his association with his commander in chief (21:22).

His next step was to summon Abraham who must have felt apprehensive as to the cause. Abimelech could justly complain that he had done nothing to offend Abraham or to deserve being deceived. How humiliating that a so-called heathen monarch regarded as "a great sin" what God's servant had condoned for expediency's sake. He classed the duplicity as something which "ought not to be done".

Abraham's Excuse

Abimelech could not believe that Abraham had seen anything in the conduct of the people to drive him to resort to deceit: "What sawest thou that thou hast done this thing?" Abraham was unable to point to anything he had seen. He could only lamely say, " I thought". How often this feeble excuse has been made when assumptions have been proved unwarranted. It is well to guard against allowing supposition to dispense with evidence. If the reader is not inclined to trace the many scriptural instances of this common weakness, he may at least be willing to ponder two cases which contain the salutary lesson that it is perilous to take important matters for granted (Luke 2:44; Acts 7:25). It is not enough to suppose.

The tone of Abraham's explanation of his conduct reveals a weariness of spirit. His mind goes back to his departure from Ur when his faith, so magnificent in many respects, was yet imperfect to the extent that he thought it necessary to take dubious precautions against possible dangers. Looking back on that momentous time when the God of glory appeared to him, an experience fraught with such significance for his own future and for ages to come, all he could say about it in his present mood was, "God caused me to wander from my father's house". Abimelech must have thought that Abraham's confession of his first impressions of Gerah was more candid than tactful, but it is difficult to assess the effect of these pathetic words interpreting God's initial dealings with Abraham.

Asaph's Nobler Example

Despondent statements made by devoted souls when weary with life's perplexities and burdens do not really reflect their true state of heart, and this was true with Abraham. Overwrought believers are fortunate if they can open their hearts to a mature and understanding Christian, but to voice their despondency to the uninitiated is to risk disturbing their faith by giving the impression that God has failed one who trusted Him.

In this respect Psa 73 will reward closer attention than would be appropriate to our present study, but a few comments may be helpful. Asaph was confronted with anomalies in life which were "too painful" to contemplate. He had tried to please God but he felt that he had "cleansed his heart in vain", for instead of being blessed he was "plagued all the day long". On the other hand the wicked seemed to prosper: "They are not in trouble as other men; neither are they plagued like other men". But he kept his bitter feelings hidden, for deep in his heart was a concern for God's glory. Involuntarily he speaks to God and says, "If I say I will speak thus I shall offend against the generation of thy children". In other words, he kept his problems and struggles to himself rather than risk stumbling some weaker soul. Eventually he went into the sanctuary which he had been neglecting — quite possibly because of the pressure of religious duties which he had allowed to interfere with his fellowship with God. There in God's light he saw life from an altogether different angle. Now he could safely recite his experience for the help of God's people. "It is good for me to draw near to God; I have put my trust in the Lord God that I may declare all thy works". But so anxious was he not to disturb their peace of mind, even for a moment, that he prefaced his story with his restored conviction: "Truly God is good to Israel, even to such as are of a clean heart".

Abimelech's Magnanimity

Abraham's unhappy mood could have left a very unhappy impression on Abimelech, but to his credit he showed a magnanimous spirit, if only from a desire to retain God's favour. Like Pharaoh he lavished gifts on God's servant who once again must have felt embarrassed and humiliated, but it would have been injudicious to risk further offence by refusing. Abimelech wanted the satisfaction of feeling that he had made ample amends. In this he was far more open-hearted than the king of Egypt. Instead of expelling Abraham as Pharaoh had done, he invited him to settle in whatever part of the land appealed to him most.

But he made a special point of mentioning to Sarah the additional gift of one thousand pieces of silver, apparently to drive home his disgust at her share in the deception. Pharaoh had rebuked Abraham by the emphasis he placed on Sarah being his "wife", but Abimelech reserved his sarcasm for Sarah by the ironic use of the expression "thy brother". "Thus she was reproved" (v. 16).

God Encourages Abraham

In all this God remained gracious to his disheartened servant. He told Abimelech that Abraham was a prophet whose prayer would be effective in saving his life. Accordingly, Abraham prayed, and God healed Abimelech and his wife and removed the barrenness of the women of the household. In all the circumstances it was a beautiful gesture on God's part to make Abimelech dependent on Abraham's intercession, when He could have shown mercy without Abraham's involvement. In this way He not only invested Abraham with a prestige which would help him in future dealings with the king, but He also thereby encouraged Abraham by allowing him to see the effectiveness of his prayers; this compensated for his disappointment that his earnest intercession for Sodom had not availed. "Who is a God like unto thee?" (Micah 7:18).

Chapter XIV
The Birth Of Isaac

(Gen 21:1-34)

It goes without saying that the birth of Isaac brought tremendous joy to Abraham and Sarah, and we are encouraged from v. 7 to think that no small element in Sarah's joy was the satisfaction brought to her husband. Sufficient material is not available to form a very clear picture of her character but she must be given credit for loyalty.

The opening of this chapter is couched in terms which serve to emphasise the faithfulness of God to His promises ("as he said", "As he had spoken", "of which God had spoken") whilst at the same time showing that He had waited until the impotence of the flesh to fulfil the purposes of God could be illustrated: "his old age, at the set time", "a hundred years old", "in his old age". Cf. Rom 4:19; Heb 11:11-12.

God not only "works all things after the counsel of his own will" (Eph 1:11) but according to His own time scale. This is not to say that He is tied to our calendar, for His plans rest on moral conditions, just as we may think of a farmer being guided not by fixed dates but by the state of the weather. Nevertheless God in His omniscience can relate His actions to our time scales, sometimes approximately, at other times with a precision expressed in days or even hours. Although this provides a fascinating scriptural study, we must content ourselves with an illustration from the life of Abraham. In 15:13-16 the precise span of 400 years is linked with a more general period of four generations and co-ordinated with moral issues relating to retribution for Egypt's oppression and the deferment of the judgment of the Amorites until their iniquity is full. Stephen, referring to what God said to Abraham on this subject, speaks of the "time of the promise" drawing near, which God had sworn to Abraham (Acts 7:17). It is easy to see the relevance of the later remark, "in which time Moses was born" (v. 20).

Waiting For God

As in all else, the Lord Jesus is the perfect example of patiently waiting for His Father to act in His own chosen time. This is very hard for restless flesh, often anxious to speed up matters by recourse to carnal means. This is the tragic mistake Sarah made in which Abraham (perhaps reluctantly) acquiesced. After waiting for more than ten years she became impatient and, relying on seemingly cogent but actually short-sighted arguments, brought about a situation ruinous to domestic harmony in the short term, and in the long term disastrous in the international realm up to the present time; such she could never have imagined. What great evils would have been avoided, and how much happier she would eventually have been had she been content to wait for God.

God purposes the best for His people even here and now, but He patiently waits the most propitious moment for the most effective action: "Therefore will the Lord wait that he may be gracious unto you". Isaiah goes on to say, "The Lord is a God of judgment", implying in this context that He can exercise fine discernment in the exactness of His timing. Since His time is always best, the prophet concludes with, "Blessed are all they that wait for him" (Isa 30:18). Habakkuk was sorely perplexed at God's apparent slowness to act on behalf of His people but he wisely decided to "watch to see what he will say unto me". He was told that the vision (i.e. the revelation of God's purposes) was for an appointed time; it would not fail. If, in human terms, that vision tarried God's people were to wait for it. It will assuredly come, and in the real sense there will be no tarrying (Hab 1:13; 2:1-3).

The Laughter Of Joy

There is a great deal of foolish laughter, but there are fitting occasions for genuine laughter (Eccl 3:4; Luke 6:21). We can enter into the exhilaration of the Jewish captives when God liberated them from the Babylonian bondage, "Then was our mouth filled with laughter ... The Lord hath done great things for us; whereof we are glad" (Psa 126:1-3).

In the present case, now that God had given Sarah real cause for the genuine laughter of joy, she must have felt ashamed of her earlier laugh of incredulity. In a state of euphoria, not uncommon with fond mothers, she optimistically imagined that everyone who heard would laugh with her. Unfortunately she reckoned without Hagar and Ishmael; probably she had forgotten them for the moment. We cannot refrain from turning our thoughts to a mother crowned with honour greater than Sarah's.

The Mother Of Jesus

In marked contrast to Sarah's unbelieving laugh at the Lord's promise of a son, the humble maid of Nazareth responded to the angel's pronouncement of a mightier miracle, "Behold the handmaid of the Lord; be it unto me according to thy word". With robust faith the most highly privileged of all women contemplated, with a quiet certainty, the birth of One whose name (also given in advance) is above every name.

Only when Isaac was actually in her arms did the excited Sarah say, "God hath made me to laugh", but this acknowledgement of God cannot remotely compare with the outpouring of Mary's heart long before the event in the exquisite doxology commencing, "My soul doth magnify the Lord and my spirit hath rejoiced in God my Saviour".

The too confident boast, "All that hear will laugh with me", falls far short of what might seem, at first sight, the more extravagant claim of Mary, "Henceforth all generations shall call me blessed". But this was spoken with charming modesty and a penetrating insight which unpretentiously accepted it as simple but wonderful truth. History has vindicated her prophecy, but it is to be regretted that some who could have happily treasured the memory of this highly favoured handmaid of God, have been inhibited by an idolatry at which she herself would have been horrified. The Saviour checked any unhealthy tendency to sentimentalise when a woman, deeply moved by listening to Him who spake as never man spake, impetuously lifted up her voice and emotionaly pronounced His mother blessed. Without contradicting the angel Gabriel ("Blessed art thou among women") He nevertheless put the matter in a very practical perspective: "Yea rather, blessed are they that hear the word of God and keep it". Here is a blessing available to all (Luke 11:27-28; 8:19-21).

Isaac Weaned

In our society the weaning of a baby is regarded as a matter of course and usually commences at a comparatively early age. In Eastern culture weaning was postponed until much later and invested with greater significance. It marked a definite stage in development from babyhood to childhood. Especially in the case of a first son his subsequent growth toward manhood was a matter of tremendous importance for its bearing on the continuance of his father's name. The circumstances of Isaac's birth and the part he was to play in the purposes of God added exceptional importance to this particular occasion and the celebrations were on an unusually lavish scale for Abraham made a "great feast". Obviously a large company had been invited including most certainly all the members of his household.

Ishmael Mocking Isaac

We have earlier seen good reason to think that relations between Hagar and her mistress had been strained ever since the girl had brazenly shown contempt for the barren Sarah when she herself was pregnant by Abraham. Matters were not improved when Abraham showed a fondness for the lad, and it seems that he even had some concern for the mother. Their close association with Abraham secured them a prominent place in the menage so that their presence at this great feast was a foregone conclusion, although we may well believe that Sarah would have been quite glad to do without their company.

Ishmael was now in his mid-teens and evidently beginning to show the characteristics which would later distinguish him in manhood according to the angel of the Lord's prediction (16:12). "Wild man" is the same word as "wild ass" in Job 39:5 which explains why the RV has so translated it in this passage. In other words, he would be as untameable as the wild asses that roam free in the wilderness. It was also said that he would be aggressive: "his hand will be against every man". If his mother made efforts to curb his wilfulness she is hardly likely to have succeeded when she set such a poor example in her disrespectful attitude to the mistress.

Instead of being awed by the auspicious occasion Ishmael poked fun at Isaac. It has been suggested that the vigorous lad was scornful of a puny child, but there is no reason to think that Isaac was in any way undeveloped. If he had been it is unlikely that in young manhood he would have been able to carry a load of wood up the side of a high mountain. No, Ishmael was acting in a spirit of mischief, probably because of jealousy at his younger half-brother stealing the limelight. Not surprisingly Sarah was furious.

Hagar And Ishmael Expelled

Having with difficulty repressed the resentment Sarah had felt for some years, it was the last straw to see what should have been a specially happy occasion marred by the impudence of this "son of a bondwoman". She peremptorily demanded that Abraham cast out mother and son, not only to be finally rid of these thorns in her side, but also to ensure that Ishmael would never have any share in the inheritance. Such a demand was very disturbing to Abraham. Earlier when Sarah had protested to him about Hagar's arrogance he was quite indifferent to the girl's welfare: "Behold thy maid is in thy hands, do to her as it pleases thee" (16:6). Taking advantage of his lack of interest she had dealt so harshly with Hagar that she fled into the wilderness, although she returned at the instruction of the angel of the Lord. However, once Ishmael was born, Abraham's attitude changed. He became very attached to the lad (17:18) and it appears that he now also had a regard for the young mother.

Consequently, Sarah's demand was now "very grievous to him, because of his son", and the underlying impression is that he was inclined to refuse his wife's wishes. There is no sign that he consulted God either about Sarah's original proposal (16:2) or when she complained about Hagar's haughtiness. On this occasion, however, God spoke to him, apparently in response to his opening his heart to God.

God's reply indicated that Abraham's grief, although primarily because of the lad, was also connected with his bondwoman, to whom Sarah had scornfully referred as "this bondwoman". If the command to comply with Sarah's wishes seems harsh, it must be remembered that God fully intended to watch over the couple in line with the pledge given in 17:20. "Hearken unto her voice" is reminiscent of what is said of Abraham in the matter of taking Hagar in the first place: "Abraham hearkened to the voice of Sarai" (16:2). It rather looks as if Abraham is being told that this unhappy situation would never have occurred but for his weakness in yielding in the first place; now he must take the consequences. He was, however, given this consolation: "In Isaac shall thy seed be called and also of the son of the bondwoman will I make a nation because he is thy seed".

Although it was a very painful step to take, Abraham, fortified by God's word, rose up early next morning to send away mother and child. As in the case of his obedience to the call to offer up Isaac, the early hour could be taken as evidence of his firm resolve in carrying out the unpleasant task, while at the same time it must be borne in mind that it meant that some distance could be covered before the sun became too hot for comfortable travel.

They were provided with "bread", which means provisions, and a skin-bottle of water. The peculiar position of the phrase "and the child" in v. 14 has caused some perplexity but the meaning is that the provisions and the water were given to both. The heavy skin-bottle was thoughtfully lifted on to Hagar's shoulders, but Ishmael was expected to help in carrying the provisions, as he was well able to do.

When it is said they wandered in the wilderness we are not to imagine them going round aimlessly in circles in a sandy desert. They were scouring the uncultivated countryside in the hope of finding some camp where they could be accommodated, if only temporarily. When Abraham spoke of wandering from his father's house he was referring to his roving manner-of-life. When a man found Joseph wandering in the field (the open country) he was trying to find where his brothers were pasturing the sheep (20:13; 37:15-16).

The supply of water ran out before mother and son found any such settlement, which left them in a desperate plight because death by thirst is much swifter than death by starvation. Unable to endure the sight of her son dying she put him in the shade of a tree and, sitting at some distance, gave way to weeping in despair. As on a previous occasion, far from being indifferent, God in the person of the angel of the Lord intervened, although it is said that it was at the cry of the lad. In their extremity they had failed to see a well close by, but God opened Hagar's eyes. She was able to replenish their supply of water and their lives were saved. This may be a suitable point at which to deal with a question which has troubled some readers of this story.

A Ruthless Proceeding?

The expulsion of a young mother and her teenage son, leaving them to fend for themselves, certainly seems harsh and unfeeling, and some find quite unacceptable the idea that God could condone such drastic action. It is difficult for us in our twentieth century culture to assess a situation totally outside our experience, especially when the present-day outlook favours the shortsighted policy of smoothing over all difficulties with temporary solutions which in the end solve nothing. In fact matters are often made worse. Papering over cracks in walls does not make a building safe. When human folly and wilfulness have created an unbearable situation, palliatives provide no remedy and radical cure is the only answer.

In the present case it is quite apparent that the continued presence of Hagar and Ishmael in the home would lead to an increasingly intolerable state of affairs harmful to all concerned. Pragmatism is unpopular to-day, but getting rid of the trouble-makers was the only way of cutting the tangled knot (Prov 22:10). It could be argued that the fault was not all on one side, but even so there was not the remotest prospect of reaching an amicable settlement. We think it may be said, in the best sense of the word, that God is realistic and deals with a situation as it exists. Far from being callous, God had shown His concern for Hagar's welfare years before and in fact later intervened again to extricate Hagar from disaster. Scripture consistently advocates the long view, and the end of the present story leaves no doubt that the drastic action taken worked out in the best interest of all concerned. Although there is a lot more we would like to know we are told sufficient to assure us that all went well.

Without any other evidence this would be guaranteed from the simple fact that, in line with His promise to Abraham (17:20), "God was with the lad" (v. 20). When he grew to manhood his mother, always an Egyptian in heart, must have felt real satisfaction in securing for him a wife from that country. Beneath the laconic statement could lie a story almost as interesting as that of Isaac and Rebekah, but as it falls outside the purpose of Scripture our curiosity is left unsatisfied. They settled in the wilderness of Paran, and the reference to his being an archer indicates that like Esau (27:1-4) he was able to provide for his family by hunting with bow and arrow. He eventually had twelve sons who became heads of nations, and who were able to establish themselves in the ancient equivalent of castles (25:12-18; cf. 17:20).

From the fact that he joined with Isaac in burying Abraham several encouraging conclusions can reasonably be drawn. Contacts with the old home must have been resumed at some point, otherwise Isaac would not have known how to get a message to Ishmael informing him of Abraham's final illness in time for him to get to the funeral, which must necessarily have taken place very soon after death. His response to that message allows us to believe that he respected his father, and was on reasonably good terms with Isaac for he had no expectations of being a beneficiary under his father's will, since all had been given to Isaac with the exception of certain gifts before he died (25:5-6). If cordial contacts had been established during the years following the expulsion of Hagar and Ishmael, we can also hope that if there had been any in Abraham's household who had been critical of their master's drastic action they had come to see that he was vindicated by events.

Spiritual Weaning

The celebrations which marked the weaning of Isaac prompt some reflections on the spiritual counterpart in relation to Christian maturity.

A babe is born with a healthy appetite, although at first able to assimilate only milk, and under natural conditions is wholly dependent on his mother who gives of herself — it might almost be said that she imparts something of her own life. Persons who put their faith in Christ become by the new birth children of God, but in their early experience are what Peter calls "new born babes". He encourages them to desire the sincere milk of the Word, i.e. the simple basic truths which they are able to digest. In this way they will grow (1 Pet 2:2).

Paul in his evangelical ministry bore in mind that those only recently won for Christ were spiritual babes. He reminded the Thessalonians that he was gentle with them as a nursing mother is with her offspring. He had been happy to impart to them not only the gospel of God but his own soul, or life. As a true minister of Christ he not only gave lucid instruction, valuable as this is, but like a nursing mother he gave of himself. By the Holy Spirit operating through his spirit he had been able to impart to the spiritually receptive what God had made real to him (1 Thess 2:7, 8).

With the new birth the regenerating Spirit of God imparts a spiritual appetite, and leaders incur a grave responsibility if they vitiate that early appetite because of the mistaken notion that the emphasis needs to be on entertaining young believers. The word of God wisely taught with warmth and freshness will not be dull and unappetising. Skimmed milk will not promote vigorous growth; the sincere milk of the Word ministered by the apostles even to those new to the faith was full cream. Babes wisely and well-nourished are likely to develop into robust adults.

Babyhood is attractive and mothers have been heard to say it is a pity they have to grow up, but these same mothers would be greatly distressed if their babies did not develop. Arrested growth is a pitiable sight whether in the natural or the spiritual sense.

This distressed Paul in regard to the Corinthians — five years after their conversion they had to be fed with milk, because they were spiritual babes who could not digest more solid food (1 Cor 3:1, 2). Like babes they were dependent on others such as Paul, Apollos or Peter (1 Cor 3:4, 5, 22). Whilst such reliance flatters some leaders these greater men, like their fellow-apostle John, would have rejoiced to see them in spiritual health able to walk in the truth without relying on crutches (3 John 1-4).

The case of some of the believers to whom the Epistle to the Hebrews was written was even more grave. They were old enough in the faith to benefit from strong meat and even to teach others, but their development had been arrested; they still needed to be fed on milk. One effect of their lack of growth was that they were dull (i.e. slothful, sluggish as in 6:12) of hearing. Had they been capable of appreciating more advanced truth they would have been taught more of the wonderful theme of the Melchizedek character of Christ's High Priesthood. How much they missed. Cf. Heb 5:10-14.

Although not in the same connection, Isaiah speaks of knowledge being taught to, and doctrine understood by, those who are weaned from the milk and "drawn from the breasts" — i.e. not now wholly dependent on others (Isa 28:9).

This does not imply that the mature despise the milk of simple and easily-digested truth. Long after weaning, milk is wholesome and acceptable to adults. Several OT Scriptures recognise this in the literal sense — indeed milk formed part of the sumptuous meal Abraham prepared for his unexpected visitors in the plain of Mamre (18:8). Mature Christians continue to enjoy the simplest of truths, but the point is that they become increasingly independent of men whilst still valuing those who can bring to them the word of God. Gideon-like they thresh the wheat of the word of God (Jud 6:11; Jer 23:28). How grateful we should be for those servants of Christ who like the wise farmer of Baal-shalisha brought to the hungry people of God loaves of bread they could eat at once and also corn which they could later thresh for themselves (2 Kings 4:42)!

Wells And Fountains – Spiritual Refreshment

Prompted by Hagar's experience at the well, we turn from the subject of nourishment to the equally important matter of refreshment. Scripture has a great deal to say about wells and fountains, springs and rivers, but the theme, fascinating and helpful though it is, is far too broad to allow of anything like adequate treatment here. All that will be attempted is to open the subject in the hope that some will be stimulated to dig again for themselves some of the old wells of spiritual refreshment which the enemy will stop up with earth if we let him (Gen 26:15-18).

Limited Supply

Abraham from his own well filled a bottle with water to tide Hagar and Ishmael over for the time being. We do not know the capacity of her bottle, but it was soon exhausted and the consequences would have been fatal had not the angel of the Lord opened her eyes to see a near-by well which strangely enough, for some reason or other, she had failed to notice before. So it is in the spiritual sense. We must be grateful for those who can refresh our souls out of their own spiritual resources; even an apostle acknowledged having been helped in this way by others (1 Cor 16:18; 2 Cor 7:13; 2 Tim 1:16). But such help can have only a temporary effect; as in obtaining nourishment for our souls, we should learn not to be wholly dependent on others.

13

Unlimited Supply

If, like Hagar, our eyes have been opened (Psa 119:18) we shall find inexhaustible sources of spiritual refreshment available to us:

> I seek the springs of heavenly life,
> And here all day they rise.
> I seek the treasure of Thy love,
> And close at hand it lies.
> *Anna Waring*

Isaiah speaks of joy in drawing water out of the wells of salvation, in other words, in appropriating in personal experience the blessings which are ours in Christ (Isa 12:3). Yet there are greater depths than the enjoyment of blessings i.e. finding our joy in God (Psa 43:4). He is spoken of in Jer 2:13 as the fountain of living water, foolishly forsaken by His backsliding people in favour of the cracked cisterns of their own making which could hold no water (cf. 17:13). David knew God to be the fountain of life and that those who put their trust in Him could drink of the river of His pleasures. Accordingly his soul thirsted for God (Psa 36:8, 9; 63:1; cf. 42:1, 2). Here, indeed, are waters out of great depths (Psa 78:15; 1 Cor 2:9, 10).

Eternal Life

When Paul exhorted Timothy to "lay hold on eternal life" he was not afraid that his "true child in the faith" and a "man of God" was in danger of perishing. Eternal life was his in Christ, but he was being encouraged to enter into the possibilities it held for him. In the same strain he, in turn, was to urge others to "lay hold on the life that is life indeed" (1 Tim 1:2; 6:11, 12, 19 RV).

The Saviour contrasted Jacob's well with the well of living water springing up to eternal life. This should be considered in the light of His definition of eternal life "to know thee the only true God and Jesus Christ whom thou hast sent" (John 4:13, 14; 17:3).

Now, as more fully hereafter, those who thirst may drink freely of the fountain of life (Rev 21:6). Cf. 7:17; 22:17.

Bondage Or Freedom

How remarkable that the story of the casting out of Hagar and Ishmael should provide Paul, nearly two thousand years later, with an allegory to illustrate the grounds on which he appeals to the Galatian believers to stand fast in the liberty wherewith Christ had made them free, and not to be entangled with the yoke of bondage. See Gal 4:19-5:1.

Judaizers' attempts to bring them to accept bondage to the law and its ceremonies as necessary to salvation imposed a serious threat to the gospel of free grace. Paul was not relying on this story to authenticate his teaching. He had been careful to make it abundantly clear that his authority was Jesus Christ (1:12). Time and time again in his letter he emphasised in various ways that the believer in Christ was not under the law; he then brought in the story, not as proving but as illustrating the point. If his readers could see that this principle lies embedded in the story, it would help them to grasp and retain the doctrine because they could relate it to the picture in their minds.

This skilful use of OT narrative does not warrant adroit and ingenious spiritualising to justify one's own ideas. Interpretation must stand the test of the clear and general teaching of Scripture.

The Covenant With Abimelech

Some few years have passed since the previously recorded contact between Abraham and the Philistine king, for in the interval Isaac had been born and weaned.

In that short time it had become evident to Abimelech that God was with Abraham in all that he did for he had become more prosperous and powerful. (God can nevertheless be with His people when circumstances might argue against it. He was "with Joseph" when, after resisting temptation, he was imprisoned on a false charge, 39:21). Abraham's increasing strength made Abimelech so uneasy about future security that he was anxious to get him committed to peaceful co-existence. Instead of expecting Abraham to respond to a summons, he paid a formal visit to him in the area he had chosen in accordance with the king's earlier generous proposal. It was a sufficiently important errand to justify taking the commander in chief of his army, accompanied no doubt with other officials. He wished to conclude a treaty with Abraham to guarantee that he would show to Abimelech and his successors the kindness that had been shown to him. It is rather sad to notice that, although the king recognised that God's hand was with his servant, so that to that extent at least he had regained his testimony, he had been so shaken by Abraham's duplicity that he felt it necessary to ask him to take a solemn oath that he would not deal falsely in this matter. Abraham agreed to swear to this effect and gave the king sheep and oxen as a sign of good-will and a witness to the compact.

The Disputed Well

Some time previously the servants of Abraham had dug a well and found water; a matter of great importance when flocks and herds had to be pastured. Some of the king's men working near that area came to know of this and coveted the well as this would make their tasks lighter. Evidently they had not taken kindly to their master's grant of land to Abraham, so they crossed into his territory and possessed themselves of the well. As it is said that they took it violently, we may conclude that Abraham's men offered ineffectual resistance. It must be remembered that Abraham's forces would be distributed over many square miles and only a small proportion would be in any particular location. He could have mustered a number of trained men in a short time, but it is easy to understand that he would be reluctant to risk a wider conflict with the friendly king. In all probability he felt that a suitable opportunity would occur to rectify the matter with a fair-minded man. This opportunity came when Abimelech arrived to seek a covenant of peace with him. Under the impression that the seizure of the well had been reported, Abraham reproved him for condoning the act, thus showing incidentally that he was in no way intimidated.

Resisting Evil

The stand he took is in contrast to the way in which Isaac complacently bowed to greater injustices without protest (26:15-22). His conduct has been highly commended by those who see in it a meek spirit which anticipated the exhortation of Christ: "Resist not evil; but whosoever shall smite thee on thy right cheek, turn to him the other side". Was Abraham then wrong to protest? The fact that Scripture records a person's words or actions does not necessarily imply approval, and where no clear indication is given either way the question has to be weighed in the light of revealed principles, whilst seeking help to discern how those principles apply in given situations.

Certainly where only our personal interests are concerned we should obey His Word by not resisting evil and following His example "who when he was reviled reviled not again; when he suffered he threatened not; but committed himself to him that judgeth righteously" (1 Pet 2:19-23). There are, however, many situations where the interest of others, whether immediately or in the long term, are involved and protests are justified. It is not always commendable to let injustice or evil go unrebuked.

When an officer struck the Lord Jesus with the palm of his hand, evidently on the cheek, His response was, "If I have spoken evil, bear witness of the evil; but if well, why smitest thou?" We cannot doubt the Saviour would have submitted had it been purely and simply a matter of His own comfort, but an important principle involving the rights of prisoners generally was at stake and a protest could have helped to check similar unfair treatment in the case of others (John 18:22-34)

Paul submitted to personal injustice at Philippi, but when the magistrates wanted to hush up matters the apostle, evidently seeing how important it was that the Christian's rights in the city should be respected, insisted that the magistrates acknowledge the miscarriage of justice by publicly conducting them out of prison (Acts 16:35-40. Cf. Acts 22:25).

Without attempting to decide the respective merits of the different attitudes of Abraham and Isaac, it can at least be noticed that Isaac suffered constant disruption (made more serious by the fact that he had turned to cultivating the soil in addition to cattle-rearing) whereas Abraham acted in a more statesmanlike way in avoiding conflict on the one hand, whilst by a well-timed protest he reached a satisfactory solution on the other. Abimelech appears to have been quite sincere in disclaiming knowledge of the high-handed action of his servants and, having acknowledged Abraham's title to the well, accepted an additional gift of seven ewes as a sort of seal and reminder of the agreement. Abimelech then vacated the area occupied by Abraham and returned to his own territory. He does not appear in the narrative again, for the Abimelech who was not so accommodating with Isaac must have been a successor who bore the same dynastic title.

Commemoration

Abraham planted a grove (RV tamarisk tree) to serve as a useful way of commemorating the occasion (as is frequently done even to-day) and also, we may believe, as a more general reminder of the way the Lord had watched over him in the vicissitudes of his eventful life. Although we cannot go about erecting memorials, it is helpful to make a deliberate mental link between special experiences of God's intervention and the associated places or circumstances.

The Everlasting God

One is tempted to conjecture why, having planted this commemorative tree, Abraham should "call on the name of the Lord" particularly in His character as "the everlasting God (El)"; there does not seem to be any satisfactory explanation available. It serves, however, to remind us that true spiritual development is marked by increasing knowledge of God. The three stages in Col 1 deserve close study: "knew the grace of God in truth" (v. 6); "the knowledge of his will" (v. 9); "increasing in the knowledge of God" (v. 10); in all three cases the knowledge of personal experience is in view rather than mental grasp.

In this connection it will be useful to refresh our memories of the advances which Abraham had made in the appreciation of the attributes of God. It was at the call of the God of glory that he left Ur of the Chaldees, but as far as we can judge it was on entering Canaan that he first "called on the name of the Lord", the word *name* implying that he had some appreciation of what the name Jehovah implied. On returning to Bethel from Egypt he again "called on the name of the Lord", evidently thankful for God's faithfulness in bringing him out of Egypt and restoring him to the place of communion. Later, entering into the good of Melchizedek's revelation he lifted up his hand unto the Lord (equivalent to calling on the Lord) in His character as the Most High God (*El*

Elyon), possessor of heaven and earth. (Cf. 24:3.) When re-action set in after his victory he learned that God was his "shield and exceeding great reward". At 99 years of age when the fulfilment of the promise of a son seemed impossible, God appeared to him as the Almighty (*El Shaddai*). By the time the threat to Sodom moved him to intercession he could plead that God was the righteous Judge of all the earth. On mount Moriah he linked the name Jehovah with Jireh because God had shown Himself as the One who could be relied on to provide what was necessary.

If we cannot assign any particular reason for again "calling on the name of the Lord" particularly as being the everlasting God (*El olam*), we can at least try to understand something of what Abraham must have felt, in an age when divine revelation was in its early stages (Heb 1:1, 2), as he pondered the ineffable mystery that the God with whom he had been privileged to walk in spirit was the unique and infinite Being self-existing from eternity to eternity. No human mind is capable of comprehending the vast implications, but our hearts *are* capable of awe which bows in worship, as no doubt Abraham's did.

Amazing Faith

Seeing that these incidents must have taken place shortly after the weaning of Isaac, it follows that the "many days" of Abraham's sojourn in the Philistine's land covers an otherwise unrecorded gap of something like 20 years before the call came to offer up his son. There seemed to be sufficient material available to picture the general character of the shorter but still-lengthy gap of 13 years between chs. 16 and 17, but in this case there is very little from which any conclusions can be drawn. It was a period during which Isaac developed through childhood to youth and then to manhood, to the delight of his parents. There was a warm relationship between mother and son (24:67) and strong ties of fellowship grew up between son and father (22:6-8). There is one great certainty, viz. that in fellowship with God Abraham's faith reached the stage where, without ever having heard of any such thing, he firmly believed that his God could raise the dead.

Chapter XV

The Sacrifice Of Isaac

(Gen 22:1-24)

God Did Tempt Abraham

The word *tempt* must not be understood as meaning inducement to evil. Certainly because of the frailty of fallen human nature it is commonly associated with evil. In that sense of the word James emphatically protests that "God cannot be tempted with evil, neither tempteth he any man" (Jas 1:13). The basic meaning is to try, to test, to put to the proof. The Hebrew word (*nasah*) is translated tempt twelve times but "prove" twenty times. Tests are intended to strengthen us spiritually so as to lead to the maturing of our character, or, in the language of Rom 8:29, "to be conformed to the image of his Son". This helps to explain much in life which would otherwise be very perplexing. Peter speaks of faith as being more precious than gold; as gold is refined by fire, so faith is refined by trials; in the end it will be to praise, honour and glory (1 Pet 1:7). In this connection the reader will find profit in considering Mal 3:1-4.

The fact that Paul several times refers to the Christian life as running in a race invites us to think of the example of an athlete who welcomes fresh challenges in order to increase his muscular strength with a view to improving on previous achievements. *Welcome* may sound a strange word in regard to trials which beset the Christian but this is the attitude encouraged by Jas 1:2, "My brethren, count it all joy when ye fall into divers temptations (manifold trials RV)". Why? Because such trials can develop patience (endurance) leading to maturity of character and a well-balanced and integrated personality (vv. 3-4). Paul writes to much the same effect (Rom 5:3-5). The extent to which this outlook seems strange to us reflects how far we fall short of NT standards, perhaps because of our comparatively easy lives. The new converts in Thessalonica, having received the word of God, became

200

imitators of the apostles in enduring affliction with joy of the Holy Spirit (1 Thess 1:6).

The serious athlete usually has an experienced trainer deemed capable of assessing how far it is wise for his charge to go in the matter of increasing strain. His judgment may be at fault — but not God's. We are assured that He knows our frame (Psa 103:14). God is faithful (absolutely to be trusted) and He will not allow us to be tempted (tried) above our strength (1 Cor 10:13). This clearly indicates that unlike a fallible trainer, He can assess our strength with absolute precision. The Lord did not need to test Abraham for His own information; years before He had said "I know him" (18:19). No doubt, in Abraham's case as in others, the trial would lead to the deepening of his faith but there are so many special features about this particular test it is difficult to avoid the conclusion that there was another issue at stake. This trial was unique in that no other child of God has been, or will be ever, put to such a test. Added to this is the quite extraordinary response of the angel of the Lord when he had passed the test (vv. 15-18). There was obviously something of profound significance involved and in due course we shall consider whether other Scriptures throw any light on the matter. Meanwhile let us look at some features of the trial.

The Moral Problem

Although the call of God to Abraham to offer up his son may present difficulties to our minds, it is a great mistake to think that it would have posed any moral problem for him. This is yet another instance where the situation must be viewed in its contemporary setting and not from the standpoint of our times. On three occasions we are reminded that Abraham dwelt among the Canaanites (12:6; 13:7; 24:3). With them it was a common practice to sacrifice children to false gods, for various reasons. Nor was this practice confined to a particular epoch; hundreds of years later some in Israel imitated them in sacrificing their sons and daughters to the idols of Canaan. This was regarded as a service to the idols (Psa 106:34-38). The king of Moab thought that the offering of his son as a burnt-offering might enlist the aid of his god in turning the tide of battle (2 Kings 3:26-27). Even as late as Micah's day the idea was abroad that such a sacrifice could atone for a father's sin (Micah 6:7). After spending over forty years among the Canaanites Abraham was quite accustomed to the idea that this practice was an accepted way of showing devotion to false gods. It would not be altogether surprising if his heart were sometimes challenged with the question as to whether he would be capable of such devotion to his, the true God, if ever the call came. Therefore when the call came, it did not seem so strange to him as it does, at first sight, to us. It was a severe challenge in several ways but it did not offend his sense of morality. We can be perfectly certain that God would never have asked him to act against his conscience. Would God be less concerned about a man's conscience than He expects us to be (Rom 14:4-16; 1 Cor 8:7-13)? It became clear a few days later that it was never God's intention that such a sacrifice should be made, but Abraham was not aware of this at the time.

The Severity Of The Trial

Even though God's call did not pose a moral problem to Abraham it was a very severe trial imposing great strain on his whole personality — mind and heart and will — at one and the same time. The sensitive reader will probably detect a gentle and sympathetic touch in the Lord's tentative approach to the subject, because He was fully aware of the mental and emotional anguish He was going to cause His servant. This is one of the only three occasions on which, as far as we know, God actually used his name in speaking directly to him, and in this instance it is all that was spoken until Abraham made his response. We do not doubt that it was uttered in such a tone as to convey His affection for Abraham and at the same time to prepare him to hear something crucial. Consider how much the risen Saviour was able to convey to a sorrowing woman by the simple mention of her name (John 20:16).

The instant response, "Behold, here I am", conveys an impression of spiritual sensitivity ever on the alert to the possibility of a communication from God. We cannot refrain from drawing attention to the use God Himself made of the phrase in Isa 58:9, where we have the wonderful suggestion that God, so to speak, keeps on the qui vive so as to respond instantly if His people cry to them in their need. Almost like a fond mother who, though busy with her household duties, keeps an ear open for her baby's cry.

Trial For The Mind

Consider how full and explicit God's instructions were, anticipating almost every question which could be raised on the matter. What? How? Who? Where? When? Yet to the one question which must have come uppermost in Abraham's mind there was no answer given. WHY? This is always the most difficult question to answer. Parents with small children know how one question leads to another, and it can be plain sailing until, when all else has been explained, up comes the inevitable, "Why?" It has been said that a child can ask a question which an archangel could not answer. Scientists can give fascinating answers to many questions about the functioning of the so-called laws of nature — the *how*, and the *when*, and the *where* — but ask them *why* it should be so! They are honest enough to admit they do not know. One eminent astronomer, after expounding at great length the theories based on the admittedly wonderful discoveries of the marvels and mysteries of this vast universe, concluded with the confession that the purpose of it all (the 'why') remained insoluble. "Something unknown to us is doing we know not what. That is what our theory amounts to." (Sir A. R. Eddington, *The Nature of the Physical Universe*, p 291.)

How Abraham's mind must have wrestled with this problem: "If Isaac has been given me by God and has been emphatically declared to be the one upon whose survival the fulfilment of His promises depends (21:12), what sense does it make to take his life away?" Such apparent contradictions have often been the hardest part of the strange paths some of God's choicest children have been called upon to tread. Why this, of all things? The anguished cry receives no answer in what seems to be a dark void, only a mocking echo. The Saviour's cry from the cross comes to mind, but that must for ever stand apart from the experience of the saints.

The Heart

One does not even need to be a parent to read Abraham's stricken heart. Depraved demon-worshippers with darkened minds and hardened hearts who have been worked up into a frenzy and impetuously offer up their children, in some cases no doubt repent of it when they return to a normal state. Abraham on the other hand had learned self control in years of walking with God. He had a specially close and affectionate relationship with Isaac upon which emphasis is laid in this chapter by the frequent use of the word *son* and the three occurrences of the phrase "thy son, thy only son" (vv. 2, 12, 16). In the first instance "whom thou lovest" is added. We are given to understand that God was fully mindful of the tremendous stress He was putting on a father's affectionate heart. If when Ishmael had to be sent from home it was "very grievous" (21:11) how must he have felt about having to plunge the knife into the breast of his much loved Isaac? It must have been an emotional struggle, beyond imagination.

The Will

Trials come unbidden and unwelcome — probably most of us would avoid them if possible, but we have no choice. They come from circumstances over which we have no control. With Abraham it was different — the decision was left to him. He could have refused to obey the call. But even granted that amid all the conflicting elements in his soul there was an underlying wish to obey would he be capable of summoning sufficient resolution to put aside the reasoning of his mind, the tumult of his affections, and steadily embark on the long path of obedience? No impulsive decision would carry him through; he must have the iron will to maintain a firm resolve as he walked with his son hour after hour day after day.

Faith Provides The Answer

"Through faith we understand" (Heb 11:3). There can be little doubt that in his perplexity Abraham reviewed God's dealings with him in the hope of seeing some ray of light in the darkness. He remembered that only recently God had promised that in Isaac and Isaac alone would his seed be called (21:12). This point is stressed in Rom 9:7, 8 and in Heb 11:17, 18. In the latter reference the fact is noted that he who offered his son was the one who had received the promises — not just one particular promise. What other promises did he think of? He remembered the great occasion when God had said that his seed would be as numberless as the stars and he believed in the Lord with such unqualified assurance that it was there recorded that it was counted to him for righteousness — a fact so significant that Paul rests a great deal on it in his masterly treatment of the subject of justification by faith (Rom 4:9). Because he believed in the Lord he rested on His word, than which there is nothing more solid in the universe. Someone has said, "Faith steps into the seeming void and finds the rock beneath its feet". He still believed it would be so, and yet if Isaac's life was to be taken how could it be so? We have noticed that he was receptive of the various ways in which God had revealed Himself; he entered into the implications of these revelations and acted in the light of them. As he went over these in his mind in relation to the paradox which faced him, would it not come home to him powerfully that the Lord had said to him before the birth of Isaac, "I am the Almighty God", and later asked the question which implied a negative answer, "Is anything too hard for the Lord?" (17:1; 18:14). Did this cause the answer to dawn on Abraham? If God was the Almighty, the All-Sufficient One, then He could raise Isaac from the dead and Abraham believed that He would do it (Heb 11:19). Never in the traditions handed from generation to generation down the long centuries had there been any mention of one person raised from the dead. In the genealogical table in Gen 5 spanning an immense period of time we read over and over again the dismal comment "and he died", and death was final. It is difficult to evaluate the faith which, without any precedent to encourage, not only believed that God *could* raise a person from the dead but was absolutely certain that He *would*. These are two different things. How many of us can improve on the faith of the leper: "Lord, if thou wilt thou canst" (Matt 8:2)?

However, there is an amazing aspect of Abraham's faith which is often overlooked. Isaac was to be a burnt-offering — his body was to be consumed to ashes. Some of the dust would trickle through the stones of the altar; almost certainly some would be blown away on the mountain breeze. It was not a faith which simply believed that God could revive a body still intact save for one stab wound, but that God could and would bring back to life a body which had been reduced to ashes. Abraham's remark to his servants at the foot of the mountain was no platitude; he was certain that he and his son would walk down the mountain together as they had walked up. What can be said of a faith like that? Pause for a while until the wonder of such a faith grips the soul.

Obedience

A great deal of light had been shed on the matter but Abraham was no nearer understanding the reason for it all. The great, "Why?" was still unanswered. Nevertheless the decision was taken; he would obey. Prompt obedience was one of his characteristics. At the very outset he had obeyed and "he went out, not knowing whither he went". When? "When he was called" (Heb 11:8). Commanded to circumcise his whole household, with all the disruption that would involve, we are told three times that he did it with all. And when? Twice it is said it was done on the self same day as God had said unto him. Cf. 17:12,13 with vv. 23-27. When instructed to do what was very grievous with regard to Hagar's son, he rose up early in the morning to do as he was bidden (21:14). Now to obey the most grievous of all commands he had ever been given, once again he rose up early in the morning (v. 3). Obedience, so hard to human pride, is precious to God (v. 18). Abraham's obedience was steadfast. He did not dally with the thought that perhaps when he got to the place of sacrifice there would not be enough wood available for the altar fire, thus providing an excuse for evading the issue. Before he set out he clave sufficient wood even though it meant carrying it for several days. He also remembered the knife. How must he have felt when he thought of taking that knife out of its sheath? By this time, apparently, he had been told the exact location, for "he went unto the place of which God had told him". We are reminded that at his first experience of God he was commanded to "Get thee out ... unto a land that I will shew thee" (12:1). That involved a vastly greater journey physically, but who shall say which was the greater spiritually? "Get thee into the land of Moriah".

Why was it necessary to go to a distant mountain? Would there not have been quite suitable spots nearer? It may have been necessary to secure absolute privacy, but is it not more likely to have been so that his resolution should be tested to the full day after day? None of his companions would have had the slightest idea of what was in store, although Abraham must have been a man of amazing self-control if they detected no signs of pre-occupation. Can we imagine how he must have felt as, after each day's long march he was conscious of his son sleeping soundly at his side with the healthy tiredness of youth? After two days of travel Abraham could see the place but it was still far off.

The Foot Of The Mountain

Presumably the foot of the mountain was reached on the third day but it is hardly likely that the ascent would be attempted immediately — a rest would be needed. However when ready to depart alone with Isaac, he told the servants to stay with the donkey while he and Isaac climbed the mountain alone. It is not at all difficult to understand the reasons for leaving the servants. Strict privacy was essential, not only because of the solemnity and sacredness of the occasion but also because the risk of Abraham's act being misunderstood was all too obvious. In any case they would undoubtedly have intervened to prevent Isaac being sacrificed. But it does seem extraordinary that the beast of burden was not used to carry the wood up the mountain. Whether there was a hidden reason for this will be considered later. Abraham's calm words, "I and the lad will ... come again to you", reflect in a wonderful way his remarkable confidence in the restoration of his son. It is more difficult to gauge the precise significance of the words "we will worship" (v. 5 RV). That the father might act in a spirit of worship is at least conceivable considering the kind of man he was, but can we think this would be true of Isaac? Was Abraham simply trying to give an acceptable reason for climbing the mountain, or was it that he was thinking that he and his son would join in worship when the latter had been received back from the dead?

The Mountain Climb

In preparation for the climb the not inconsiderable load of wood was laid upon Isaac. Although he is called "the lad" we are not to think of a boy in his early teens. The Hebrew word (*naar*) covers a wide range of ages from childhood to young manhood — in fact it is most frequently translated "young man" as in the case of those who accompanied Abraham in his assault on the four kings (14:24). Josephus the Jewish historian states, presumably with good reason, that Isaac was twenty-five years of age at this time. This is not at all unlikely, but all we can be sure of is that he was a young man sturdy enough in the eyes of an affectionate father for such a task. Lest there should be difficulty in kindling the fire on a breezy mountain top Abraham did this at the outset and himself carried it with the knife.

Purely as information, the words "they went both of them together" are superfluous as again in v. 8 because they state the obvious. The point of these remarks is surely to conjure up a delightful picture of that fellowship between a proud father and an admiring son, which has a special quality found in no other relationship. In complete rapport, each occupied with his own thoughts, they could walk steadily together in companionable silence. But something was puzzling the young man. His very capable father had foreseen the need of the wood, the fire and the knife, but how came he to have taken no thought to provide a lamb for the intended burnt offering? Such an omission was quite uncharacteristic. The question is likely to have occurred to him earlier but he probably thought that his father had some plan. But it was rather late now to expect to get a lamb somewhere. Realising that his father was evidently pre-occupied, he broke the silence very gently by a tentative, "My father", in much the same way that God had approached him in the first place with "Abraham". He responded promptly as he had done then with "Here am I my son". "My father", "My son". "Behold the fire and the wood but where is the lamb for a burnt offering?" What an amazing control the aged patriarch must have had over his emotions to reply calmly, "My son, God will provide himself a lamb for a burnt offering". It is clear that right up to this moment Abraham had, understandably, kept his son in ignorance of what was in store. The answer must have sounded rather vague, but knowing his father's intimacy with God he seems to have accepted it as satisfactory for once again we are told "they went both of them together". Was Abraham being deliberately evasive so as to postpone the inevitable explanation? Or was there some enigmatic allusion to a greater sacrifice God was going to make? Is it too much to suppose that Abraham could have gradually gained at least some dim insight into God's ultimate purpose to provide a Lamb of His own to bear away the sin of the world? He had always proved alert and sensitive to God's revelations, and let us remember that the Son of God said, "Abraham rejoiced to see my day — and he saw it and was glad".

There are two statements here implying that first of all he rejoiced because he knew he was going to see Messiah's day, and that secondly he saw it and was glad. When did he see it?

Was this the occasion? Was he beginning to feel that his own sacrifice was a dim adumbration of the greater sacrifice God was going to make in giving His only Son to be the Saviour of the world? May not v. 14 have a bearing here?

Before this possibility is dismissed it would be well to reflect that many OT saints had deeper insights than they are generally credited with. It would take too much time to elaborate on this delightful theme, but the Saviour's instruction of the two disciples on the Emmaus road will come to mind. After pointing out that it was clearly necessary that Christ should suffer crucifixion and then to enter into His glory, "beginning at Moses and all the prophets he expounded to them in all the scriptures the things concerning himself". Later in the same evening He covered much the same ground with the apostles and others (Luke 24:25-27; 44-46). Peter, perhaps recalling this very occasion, wrote many years later that the prophets speaking by the Spirit of Christ testified beforehand of the grace of salvation which would come because of the sufferings of Christ and the glory that should follow (1 Pet 1:9-12).

Isaac's Submission

Now they reached the place of which God had told him (v. 9). The altar was built and the wood laid in order thereon. The truth could no longer be withheld — obviously it had now to be explained to Isaac that he was to be the offering. The initial horror can be imagined, but what will be his reaction? A young man capable of carrying a heavy load up a mountain side could effectively resist any attempt by a man now about 120 years of age, to bind him and lift him on the altar. His submission was voluntary, and binding him was probably to prevent any involuntary reflex action which would only have prolonged the agony. Such submission strikes us as almost incredible, but we must remember that at that period paternal authority was almost absolute. We are dealing with a semi-nomadic set-up with a self-contained family structure without any judiciary. In such circumstances some authoritative control was absolutely necessary and the head of the establishment was the obvious answer. Jealousy was common especially in a large menage where children of one father would be step-brothers of varying status according to who their mothers were. Thus Ishmael mocked Isaac (21:9). Feuds

14

and vendettas were not uncommon. Esau planned to murder his brother — but notice, only after his father's death (27:41). Simeon and Levi avenged their sister in a barbarous fashion (34:25). Joseph's half-brothers plotted his murder in cold blood purely on account of their jealousy. If communities were not to disintegrate in violence some strong hand was necessary to preserve order, and the logical answer was parental authority. If Abraham's camp gives the impression of being well-conducted it was due no doubt to his moral stature and prompt, albeit firm, measures to nip strife in the bud, if we may take his treatment of the quarrel between his herdsmen and those of Lot as a sample (13:8). It is difficult to imagine such obedience as he commanded, when, for example, he subjected all his dependants to the rite of circumcision in one day (17:23). Sons usually obeyed their fathers even when they were grown men. When Isaac was nearly forty years of age his father made the arrangements for his marriage, apparently without even consulting him (24:4). Jacob was probably older than that when he obediently carried out his father's plan for his marriage (28:3, 7). Isaac's yielding in face of an agonising death was matched long after by a daughter's calm and uncomplaining acceptance of her fate (whatever it was) while supporting her father in his rash vow (Jud 11:36). When a quasi-legal system was established in Israel, the danger of a fragile society disintegrating was so great that such extremes were necessary as stoning to death an adult son who had rebelled against his parents (Deut 21:18-20).

The foregoing at least helps in some degree in understanding Isaac's unquestioning obedience to his father, but even when making full allowance for the immense power of tradition and culture in the ancient world the willingness of Isaac to accept an awful death remains a superb instance of filial subjection which has always evoked intense admiration. It has been thought that his resolution was strengthened because his utter confidence in his father's integrity and spiritual perception enabled him to accept the latter's firm assurance that, despite the perplexities, such was the will of God. Some even incline to the opinion that the strong influence of his father's unshakeable faith enabled Isaac to rest in the certainty of being restored to life. Since Scripture is silent on these questions they must remain unresolved.

Firm To The End

Now comes the ultimate test. Proof of Abraham's determination to obey God whatever the cost is seen in his raising the knife to slay his son. Of course, as became quite clear, it was never God's intention that the youth's life should actually be taken. Hitherto the divine manifestations granted to Abraham had not been specifically attributed to the angel of the Lord; now His voice is heard from heaven, not with the gentle "Abraham" as in v. 2 but with an urgent call arresting him as he raised the knife, "Abraham, Abraham". Consider other cases where the repetition of a name conveys a sense of urgent importance: Jacob (46:2); Moses (Exod 3:4); Samuel (1 Sam 3:10); Martha (Luke 10:41); Saul of Tarsus (Acts 9:4).

Abraham has not lost his spiritual sensitivity — once again there was the response, "Here am I". With what immeasurable relief he heard the command, "Lay not thine hand upon the lad". No further test was necessary. His fear of God (not a servile cringing but a filial and reverential submission to a sovereign will) had been amply demonstrated. His will was taken for the deed — to all intents and purposes he had actually offered up his son, as Heb 11:17 recognises. "Now I know that thou fearest God" does not mean that God was unsure of it before, but it is what may be called judicial knowledge. Formal notice had been taken of the fact. (Further explanation will be offered later). Although the subject of the angel of the Lord is dealt with in some detail in an Appendix, it should be noted here that the angel said, "Thou hast not withheld thy son, thine only son, from *me*".

The Ram

God had a great deal more to say to Abraham, but divine wisdom saw that he would need time to get mentally, emotionally and spiritually adjusted. Hence the interlude. As Abraham lifted up his eyes he saw what he had not noticed earlier, a ram caught by its horns in a thicket. This was no coincidence. Abraham with his life-long experience as a shepherd would see an unusual circumstance as evidence of a providential purpose. Sheep are frequently trapped by their wool becoming entangled in thorny bushes and the like, and struggles to free themselves make their plight worse. Unless a shepherd arrives in time to cut them free they are likely to die.

For a ram to be caught by its horns is most unusual; when it does happen these powerful animals are able to exert sufficient force to free themselves.

Abraham realised that·it was intended to be taken as a sacrificial victim. But for what reason? We lose a great deal of profit through failure to maintain an enquiring attitude of mind when reading the Scriptures. There must have been some good reason for this ram being provided. Leaving aside the question of any wider typical import, we suggest that there is here touching evidence of our gracious God's understanding of our inner conflicts of which we are aware but do not always understand.

An effort to assess the likely effect on Abraham's mind of the immense but sudden relief at being spared the final agony of dealing the fatal stroke will be rewarded by a greater appreciation of the Lord's tender regard for His servant in providing a valuable emotional outlet for built-up tension. A carefully-constructed altar standing unused, with the wood still laid thereon and fire ready to hand would almost certainly leave Abraham with a feeling of incompleteness as though he were in a spiritual vacuum. Something was needed to round off the whole experience in a meaningful and satisfying way.

The ram providentially caught in a thicket at the crucial time and place gave Abraham the needed opportunity to represent in an active way the reality of his heart obedience, although he had not been called upon to give the ultimate proof of it. "He took the ram and offered it up as a burnt offering in the stead of his son."

Under the Levitical system this animal, known for its tenacity of purpose, was chosen as an apt symbol of consecration (Ex 29:22-31) and was singularly appropriate as portraying Abraham's unswerving devotion to the will of God. We would not be prepared to rule out the possibility that Abraham saw something of this typical significance. There are indications in Genesis that several of the later enactments had their roots in a primeval revelation. There must have been some special reason for the remarkable particularity with which the several covenant victims (including a three-year-old ram) were so carefully specified in 15:9. Surely Abraham was expected to see some significance in the unique selection of such a variety of animals and birds. It is pleasant, therefore, to think that he saw the appropriateness of the ram as giving liberating expression in an active way, to the sacrifice he had firmly resolved upon but had not consummated.

Giving a significant name to the place, not a habit of his as it was with his grandson Jacob, reveals how much the experience meant to him. The altar had been put to use — the fire and the wood had not been carried up the mountain in vain. Abraham and Isaac rejoicing in God's provision stood and worshipped as Abraham had told the young men they would.

Jehovah Jireh

There are certain spots on earth which are of particular significance and sacredness to individuals. Some could point us to the exact spot where the light of the glorious gospel of Christ first shone into their sin-burdened hearts many years ago, or where God made Himself known in some other way leaving an indelible mark on their lives. Bethel was a place Jacob never forgot, for it was as a fugitive from the consequences of his sin he had nevertheless been promised that God would be his friend, his guard and his guide. Notice how in that narrative stress is again and again laid on the particular place (28:11-19). So here — four times is the place mentioned. To Abraham it was henceforth known as Jehovah Jireh — meaning the place where the Lord had seen a need and had provided for that need.

There is a plain link here with the cryptic remark to Isaac (v. 8), "God will provide (Heb. see for) a lamb for a burnt offering". Linking the two together and bearing in mind the emphasis on the place, may we not think of it a sign-post pointing down the long road of history until we read "they came to the place called Calvary" (Luke 23:33)? "In the mount of the Lord it shall be seen" appears to have been cited as a sort of proverb, still current many generations later (v. 14). There is a haunting sense of mystery about the saying which seems to invite us to probe for some deep underlying meaning, but we do not feel upon sufficiently solid ground to yield to the temptation to build deductions upon it. Although the identification has been questioned it is generally agreed that the mountain in the land of Moriah is the same as the Mount Moriah on which Solomon's Temple was built centuries later (2 Chron 3:1). The connection is certainly intriguing and offers scope for devotional meditation on the contrast between Abraham's simple altar of stone and the massive brazen altar described in 2 Chron 4:1, and also between the unique offering up of his only-begotten son in the privacy of the lonely mountain and the countless thousands of Temple sacrifices down through many centuries attended by a succession of priests and watched by assembled worshippers.

The Second Call From Heaven

A careful consideration of the angel's second message (again from heaven) will make it very evident that there must have been a special reason which made this particular act of obedience of unusual importance. The first indication of this is that the Lord prefaced the extension of former promises with a solemn oath, a point of sufficient significance to warrant several references to it in later Scriptures (cf. 26:3, 4; Deut 7:8; Psa 105:8-10; Luke 1:73; Heb 6:13-17). Then the words "because thou hast done this thing", stamp this particular act of obedience as something greater than previous acts of obedience, on which we have already commented. The greatness of it is seen in that God acknowledges again that Abraham had yielded up that which meant more to him than all else, using the words repeated earlier "thy son, thine only son". Then again, we can detect what might be called a note of exultation on the part of God in the use of a form of expression which, in Hebrew idiom, indicates that which is superlative: "In blessing I will bless thee, and in multiplying I will multiply". Moreover to the former promises to make his seed as the dust of the earth (13:16) and as the stars of heaven (15:5) is now added another figure, "as the sand which is upon the sea shore". In addition there is now a new element, "Thy seed shall possess the gate of his enemies". Why all this? "Because thou hast obeyed my voice". We shall venture to enquire in the next chapter what it was that made this act of obedience of such moment in God's eyes. Although Abraham was to live for another forty-five years or so, this is the last recorded manifestation of God to him, as though the climax had now been reached.

The Descent

Abraham now returns from this momentous experience to take up once more the threads of every-day practical life, although we cannot doubt that effects remained. There are high spots in the lives of all who seek to walk with God, and it is natural to feel that it would be marvellous to be able to remain on the mountain top of our experience but this is a mistaken desire. Everybody has heard of some who seem to be too heavenly-minded to be of any earthly good. The Saviour thanked His Father for those who had been given to Him "out of the world" and they were no longer "of the world", yet He went on to say that just as the Father has sent Him into the world so now He is sending into the world again those who had been taken out of it (John 17:6, 14, 18). Peter, and no doubt his companions, thought it would be wonderful to stay on the Mount of Transfiguration but there were needy multitudes in the valley below and so the Master and His servants left the mountain-top to minister to the needs of others. So Abraham returned to his young men and they made their way to Beer-sheba. Once again we get an expression similar to that used of the father and his son on the mountain climb, "they went together". But what of Isaac? Obviously he was with them, but for some reason he is not mentioned! Curious! There is another curious thing. He does not come into the picture again for several years. We cannot doubt he was at his mother's funeral something like twenty years later but his presence is not mentioned. He does not appear on the scene again until he goes to meet his bride (24:63).

Sarah's Reaction

Abraham's situation was often more complex than a casual reading of the story reveals. For example, throughout this amazing episode no mention is made of Sarah, although as Isaac's mother she would have been profoundly affected. The party could hardly have set out from Beer-sheba without her knowledge but possibly in view of his complete confidence that her son would return safe and sound he felt justified in keeping secret the real reason, so as to save her distress. There is, however, one distinct possibility which would have saved Abraham from any immediate embarrassment on this score. As his base was at Beer-sheba it is natural to assume that they set out from there but this may not have been the case. Large flocks and herds would not be likely to be concentrated in one area, and Abraham no doubt had out-stations which he would need to visit from time to time, just as the flocks of Laban and Jacob involved their absence from home, and as was the case with Joseph's brethren (30:34-36; 31:4, 19-22). An indication that this sometimes happened with Abraham is the fact that when his wife died at Hebron some years later he was away from home, for we read he *came* to mourn for her (23:2).

May it not be that the call to offer up Isaac came to him when he was at some outpost from which he could set out for the land of Moriah without any one at Beer-sheba being any the wiser? Even if this supposition is correct Sarah would surely know, sooner or later, what had happened; conjectures about her reactions will vary according to opinions of her character and temperament.

News From A Far Country

Some time after the offering up of Isaac a message reached Abraham that his brother Nahor had twelve children. Evidently this was news to Abraham so there could have been no exchanges between them since they parted in Ur perhaps more than 50 years before. Yet news must have reached Nahor from time to time, otherwise Abraham's whereabouts would not have been known. Although means of communication were then primitive by our standards there was no insuperable difficulty. See 27:42-45. The conclusion seems to be that Nahor had been lacking in sympathy with his brother and hitherto had not bothered to respond, but now that he had mellowed with the approach of old age he felt the urge to make some sort of contact. See paragraph headed *Arrival At Haran* in chapter 19.

Bible genealogies, although always of great importance to Jews, are of little interest to a modern reader. Nevertheless they often repay study with points of interest and profit. In the present case the list of Nahor's children seems, at first sight, to have little relevance beyond leading up to the birth of Rebekah, the future bride of Isaac and mother of Jacob from whom sprang the twelve tribes of Israel.

However it is worth looking into the links between Abraham's lineage and that of Job and his friend Elihu. The first born of Nahor, Abraham's brother was Uz (v. 21 RV) and the book of Job opens with the statement that Job lived in the land of Uz. The second son was Buz who appears to have been an ancestor of Elihu, who is said to be the son of Barachel, the

Buzite, of the kindred of Ram, who was probably the Aram of
v. 21 (Job 32:2). This will add interest to our later comparison
of the character and experience of Job with that of Abraham.

Chapter XVI
The Trial Of Abraham
(Gen 22:1-24)

Is There An Explanation?

Consideration has already been given to unique features of the test which point to some deep but undisclosed reason going beyond the normal purposes of trial. Whilst there is much in the ways of God which will remain hidden from us while we are in this world, we are, nevertheless, invited to enquire into other matters which may not at first sight be clear (Deut 29:29; Prov 25:2; 1 Cor 2:9, 10). Therefore acting on the encouragement and promise of Prov 2:1-5 it will be well worthwhile to emulate the worthies of old (1 Pet 1:10) and enquire and search diligently into a question which has such important practical bearings on the government of God in relation to the painful and perplexing experiences which befall His children.

Comparisons With Job

Links between the families of Abraham and Job have been noticed in the genealogy of 22:21-24, and these in conjunction with the parallels mentioned below prompt us to look for help in finding a solution by comparing the two cases.

God named both as His servants	Gen 26:24	Job 1:8
God said that both feared Him	22:12	1:1,9
Concern for their families is prominent	18:19	1:5
Both had great substance	12:5	1:3
	13:6	1:10
Both were men of consequence	23:6	1:3
Both were blessed	14:19	1:10
	24:1	1:21
and specially after trial	22:17	42:12
Both died old and were full (satisfied)	25:8	42:17

Both are outstanding examples of enduring unique trials.

218

It can safely be said that no believer has ever been called upon, or ever will be, to face Abraham's ordeal, and we may be almost equally certain that one has never had to suffer the devastating blows which fell on Job in such rapid succession. Neither of them knew the explanation, but one great difference was that whereas the decision was left to Abraham, Job had no choice. It should not be overlooked that Job's burden was accentuated by his well meaning friends' complete lack of understanding, and instead of being a help they even essayed, quite unjustifiably, to attribute his misfortune to some secret sin. This cruel and false assumption is occasionally made even today, mostly by those who enjoy comparative immunity from trouble. It is small wonder that Job in exasperation said, "I have heard many such things. Miserable comforters are ye all" (16:2). What a warning to us not to incur God's displeasure as they did by impugning His servant. God vindicated him and made them indebted to his prayers (42:7-9).

The Curtain Lifted

In the case of Job the reason for his afflictions is revealed by the partial lifting of the curtain which hides the spiritual world from the eyes of men. There are some points which remain unexplained but upon which other Scriptures throw a good deal of light. Having regard to the far-reaching issues involved, it will be worthwhile taking the trouble to get as complete a view as possible of the background by piecing together scattered glimpses of the spiritual realm. Particularly relevant to our enquiry is Paul's conception of life being lived out on a stage of a theatre where behaviour under stress is watched not only by human but by angelic spectators: "We are a spectacle (theatre, as in Acts 19:29) unto the world and to angels and to men" (1 Cor 4:9ff). For other illuminating references to the genuine interest which angels take in our affairs see 1 Cor 11:10; Eph 3:10; 1 Tim 5:21; 1 Pet 1:12.

The Government Of God

It is always very desirable to get the right perspective on any matter and this is specially important on such a subject as the government of God. Surely no thoughtful person can suppose that this unimaginably vast and complex universe exists for no useful purpose. Until the light of eternity dawns the believer is satisfied with the explanation of Scripture that all things were created by (through) Christ and for Him, and that in the dispensation of the fulness of times God will gather together in one all things in Christ, both which are in heaven and which are on earth (Col 1:16; Eph 1:10). What that will mean in detail is beyond our present powers of comprehension, but we may be sure that every part of the universe will fit into the grand over-all divine purpose stretching through immeasurable aeons. God "worketh all things after the counsel of his own will" (Eph 1:11). Even the most effective business executives have to work within the narrow limits of their time and capacity and are therefore obliged to employ numerous assistants to share the load, but omnipotence and omniscience make it quite unnecessary for the eternal God to depend on anything or anyone (Acts 17:25). He is self-existing and self-sufficient with no need outside Himself except that eternal love must find expression. That love found its completest demonstration in the gift of His Son to be our Saviour (Rom 5:8), but finds further evidence in a multitude of ways. Let us now consider one of those ways.

Co-operation With God

The love of God finds expression in His gracious desire to give His creatures, human and angelic, the privilege of co-operating with Him, not only for present purposes but as training in preparation for the enjoyment of greater privileges and responsibilities in His coming kingdom (Luke 19:17; Eph 3:8). We must confine our present attention to one aspect of God's employment of angels as His ministers (Psa 103:20). Some have judicial roles in regard to the human race. A careful reading of Dan 4:8-27 reveals that holy ones, or watchers, having observed the behaviour of Nebuchadnezzar had decided that he needed chastening. It is instructive to notice that what in v. 17 is said to be the decree of the watchers, is said in v. 24 to be by the decree of the Most High, from which it may be inferred that decisions needed to be submitted to God for endorsement. In the same strain is the example of the rich but self-centred and God-forgeting farmer, where a more literal rendering of Luke 12:20 is, "this night they demand thy soul".

Judge Of All The Earth

Nothing detracts from the over-all authority of the supreme and sovereign Judge of the whole universe. He is answerable to none, and no one has any rightful claim to question His decrees. We share Abraham's conviction that He will do right (18:25) though He is never arbitrary in the capricious sense. "Justice and judgment are the habitation (foundation) of thy throne: mercy and truth shall go before thee" (Psa 89:14).

Free societies recognise as a sound principle in the administration of law that not only must justice be done but that it must be seen to be done. Thus we have open courts where members of the public can listen to the evidence on which decisions are reached. Indications are not lacking that the Almighty has His reasons for demonstrating the righteousness of His judgments to angelic hosts and even to the powers of evil.

Heavenly Courts

Although there is ceaseless activity in the government of God, the opening chapters of the Book of Job give the impression that there are what could be called regular sessions in the heavenly realm at which certain cases are examined, as we may say, in open court. This is implied by the two occasions when "there was a day when the sons of God came to present themselves before the Lord" (Job 1:6; 2:1). The expression "sons of God" applies to angels, not in the NT sense, but as beings who owe their creation to the direct act of God in contrast to human generation. Cf. Job 38:7 where God says the sons of God shouted for joy when earth was being prepared as a habitation for man. So important is the principle that justice must be seen to be done that even Satan himself is allowed to put in an appearance and is invited to have his say. His object in attending may be safely inferred from the very fact that his name means *an adversary*, and when linked with the title "the devil" in Rev 12:9 he is exposed as "the accuser of our brethren", in the sense of maligning or slandering them. He does not confine his accusations to special occasions but "accuses them before God day and night". Although his activities will eventually be terminated, it is clear that for the present he is allowed a degree of liberty, and that God over-rules his activities so that in the end they are turned to the glory of God and the blessing of His people.

He adopts various guises, ranging from a roaring lion to devour and an angel of light to deceive (1 Pet 5:8; 2 Cor 11:14). If he can, he will even intervene as an adversary to object to God's blessing being bestowed, as in the case of Joshua the high priest for which he was rebuked (Zech 3:1-5). Cf. Jude 9; 1 Thess 2:18; Dan 10:12-13. To say that the language used is sometimes figurative is saying no more than can be said of our everyday conversation. Since divine wisdom uses this method to make intelligible to us realities which otherwise would be beyond our comprehension it is absurd to suppose that it can be improved upon.

Sifting As Wheat

The words of the Lord Jesus recorded in Luke 22:31, 32 throw additional light on this theme. The expression "Satan hath desired to have you" implies far more than a passive wish, it carries the force of a formal application and suggests that he claimed the right to put the disciples' devotion to Christ to the test, thinking to sift them as wheat. It is both stimulating and comforting to realise that even when on earth the Saviour knew what was taking place in the courts of heaven and could put in His plea as an advocate; how much more wonderful to know that now He actually appears in the very presence of God for us (Heb 9:24). On that occasion He did not pray that Satan's application be refused for He knew that the disciples needed to be taught their frailty. In relation to Peter his faith was Satan's special target and therefore the Lord prayed that it should not fail. The Lord, in the confidence that Peter's faith would be maintained, told him that when he had learned his need of divine power he would be able to strengthen his brethren (2 Pet 1:3). Satan seems to have imagined, rather foolishly, that sifting would get rid of the wheat (i.e. what was of value in the disciples) and leave only the chaff. In the event he succeeded only in winnowing out the chaff and leaving the wheat. Again and again the devil repeats the same kind of mistake almost as if he fails to learn by experience. No doubt burning hatred of God and therefore of His children (the converse of 1 John 5:1) has perverted and twisted an intellect which, before his fall, was brilliant.(Ezek 28:12). Evil can never be truly wise (Jas 3:14-18). We need to take the lesson to heart, for if we allow hatred to replace love in our hearts we are in danger of becoming spiritually and morally blind (2 Pet 1:7-9; 1 John 2:9, 10).

Job's Trial Explained

The sidelights given in the various Scriptures considered above will help us in examining the two sessions referred to in Job 1:6; 2:1. Satan's appearance was acknowledged by the Lord's enquiry, "Whence camest thou?" This was not seeking information but giving Satan the opportunity of having his say. Satan's reply "from going to and fro in the earth" brings to mind Peter's words, and helps us to understand Satan's object in thus going to and fro: "your adversary the devil ... walketh about seeking whom he may devour" (1 Pet 5:8). The Lord certainly knew all about this for He watches the adversary's moves —witness the angel's assurance to Zechariah: "The eyes of the Lord which run to and fro through the whole earth" (Zech 4:10). The same words in 2 Chron 16:9 bring the added assurance: "To show himself strong on behalf of them whose heart is perfect toward him". Yet Job was prominent among the perfect and upright as the Lord Himself acknowledged: "there is none like him in the earth, a perfect and an upright man" (Job 1:8). The immediate sequel may seem to throw into doubt whether He was showing Himself strong on behalf of Job, but that is because we are naturally shortsighted. God takes the long view and His timing is exact: "Therefore will the Lord wait, that he may be gracious unto you ... blessed are all they that wait for him" (Isa 30:18).

Now, what was behind the Lord's question, "Hast thou considered my servant Job"? This seems a sudden transition — the connection of this question with Satan's statement is not explained, but the Scriptures we have been considering offer a satisfactory explanation. Satan had been going to and fro observing and considering God's people, and the Lord knew perfectly well that, consistent with his character as adversary and his role as accuser, he would seize the opportunity to slander them. Satan as the hater and enemy of God strives to dishonour God and he delights to reproach God by alleging that His people are no credit to Him. Possibly he was here insinuating that there was no real example of genuine devotion to God, in other words God's work of grace had been a failure. Well, here was a challenge flung down in open court before the assembled angels. Has God an answer? Yes, His servant Job: "A perfect and an upright man that fears God and eschews evil". Satan's reply in effect is that Job fears God simply because he has discovered it pays him handsomely. You have built a protective hedge about him and about all he has. The work of his hand has been blessed and his substance has been increased. If these rewards are withdrawn it will be seen how hollow his profession is — he will curse you to your face (1:9-11).

Could God accept this challenge? He knew and trusted His servant (despite what Eliphaz said, 4:18) and was confident not only that his devotion was genuine and disinterested, but also that he could trust Job to remain faithful even in severe trial. The Lord does not trust all profession — consider how Christ, with His perfect knowledge of all men, would not commit Himself to those whose faith was shallow (John 2:23-25). On the other hand, think of Paul's abounding gratitude that he had been trusted with the revelation and propagation of the gospel (Eph 3:8; 1 Thess 2:4; 1 Tim 1:12).

Satan was given liberty to afflict Job, the only qualification being that his actual person must not be touched. Satan, determined to prove his point, eagerly used his licence to the utmost in stripping Job of all his possessions and his children as well. It did not turn him against God. "The Lord has given and the Lord hath taken away. Blessed be the name of the Lord. In all this Job sinned not, nor charged God foolishly" (1:21-22).

A Second Attempt

It might have been thought that such a thorough exposure of his slanderous accusation would have silenced the devil. But no; at the next hearing he was there again as the accuser. God could answer him by repeating His appreciation of Job and adding that despite the calamities that Satan's malice had inflicted on him he had held fast to his integrity. Despite the evidence, Satan would not desist — he complained that he had not been allowed to test Job thoroughly. If he were allowed to touch his person and destroy his health he would curse God to His face (2:1-6). God was willing to trust Job even to this extent and with the same result. Despite Satan's despicable use of a distraught wife who would rather see her husband die than continue to suffer such agony, his attitude was, "What, shall we receive good at the hand of God and shall we not receive evil? In all this did not Job sin with his lips". Although it is not actually stated, obviously Satan was silenced and no more is heard of him in the book, even though Job's affliction continued for some time as if Satan was still hoping his fortitude would break down. Listen to Job's later statement, "Though he slay me, yet will I trust him" (13:15). When God intervened He showed His delight in His servant, vindicating him, rebuking his three critics, and declaring he had rightly represented God and made them seek his intercession. As a reward the Lord gave him twice as many possessions as he had before and a new family, precisely corresponding to the children he had lost — seven sons and three daughters. It has been suggested that his children were also doubled because in answer to his early prayers those who had died were in God's keeping (42:12-17). Like Abraham he "died being old and full" — the word *full* being the same in both cases — *sabea*, satisfied (Gen 25:8).

The Application To Abraham's Case

The reader must be left to judge whether the explanation given for Job's affliction has some light to shed on Abraham's agonising trial. Does not Satan's general behaviour, and more especially in the case of Job, make it quite possible that at another session he had boasted of servants who would sacrifice their children to him, his object being to suggest that such devotion could not be found among the worshippers of God? Where could any servant of God be found who could show the same measure of devotion? God had the answer. He knew He could trust Abraham, so the court was invited to listen while He called on him, and to witness his prompt and obedient response. In contrast to the impetuous and frenzied demon-worshippers, he quietly and resolutely set out on a sustained course, all unconscious of the rapt attention of witnessing angels and demons (1 Cor 4:9). As day succeeded day Satan had to cling to the thought that even such amazing devotion would crumble when the real crunch came and the fatal blow had to be struck. But no; Abraham raised the knife to slay his son, ready to sacrifice not merely one of his children but his unique and loved Isaac — in a sense, his only son. It was enough. What further proof was needed? To all intents and

15

purposes he had actually offered up his only son as Heb 11:17 acknowledges. His renunciation was not known by others for some time, but was immediately appreciated in heaven. There have been many noble souls through the generations who in the secret of their own souls have renounced, for Christ's sake, what was dear to their hearts, and the knowledge has been hidden from all but themselves and God, to be revealed and rewarded only at the Judgment Seat of Christ.

Judicial Verdict

Why should the Lord say, "Now I know that thou fearest God"? He had not needed proof. It was, we suggest, a judicial statement, for the benefit of Abraham certainly, but also for the court of heaven from whence the pronouncement came (v. 11). The judge in a court of law sometimes has private and personal knowledge of some of the issues at stake in the case before him but he does not base his judgment on that. He allows all the evidence for and against to be presented and on that evidence alone sums up the case. So it was here; God knew His servant would be equal to such a sacrifice, but that was not enough — it must be demonstrated to the satisfaction of the court. He could now pronounce judgment on the evidence and, as in the case of Job, express his gratification in saying, "In blessing I will bless thee". Cf. the remarks on 18:21 in relation to God's investigation of Sodom's iniquity.

The Friend Of God

Abraham is called the friend of God on three occasions in Scripture, although evidently it became an accepted idea, else how came Jehoshaphat in prayer to God to speak of "Abraham thy friend"? (2 Chron 20:7). Moreover, speaking through Isaiah the prophet, God owned him as his friend (Isa 41:8). This is not saying that God was Abraham's friend, although that was true; it is saying that he was God's friend. It is surely very significant that James links the bestowal of this honoured title with the sacrifice of Isaac (Jas 2:21-23). May we not say that, faced with Satan's challenge, God needed a friend upon whom He could rely and that friend was Abraham? He is the only person so called by name, although it is said that God spoke to Moses "as a man speaketh unto his friend" (Exod 33:11).

We feel honoured if some notable man refers to us as one of his friends, but what a transcendent honour to be regarded as a friend by the Most High God. The Lord Jesus called his disciples His friends and indicated how that honour can be enjoyed: "Ye are my friends if ye do whatsoever I command you" (John 15:14, 15).

The Lesson For Us

Do not these considerations throw light on one of the great mysteries of life viz. that some of the severest trials and the most perplexing situations fall to the lot, not of easy-going believers, but of the most devoted and dedicated servants of God? Is it because these are the men and women who can be trusted to remain loyal not only before the eyes of men but in the sight of spiritual hosts whether good or evil? The testings of Abraham and Job were unique but may not the principle have a bearing on our lesser trials? Satan has not changed. Maybe there is more than appears on the surface in the appeal of Prov 27:11, "My son be wise and make my heart glad that I may answer him that reproacheth me". (Psa 119:42 is an interesting parallel.)

God does not in this age express His approval by material reward, but "Blessed is the man that endureth temptation (trial) for when he is tried (has been approved) he shall receive the crown of life which the Lord hath promised to them that love him" (Jas 1:12, cf. 2:5). Rev 2:10 makes it clear that this is a future reward, but we incline to the view that it also involves a sort of crowning now in the sense of enrichment of the quality of life in the enjoyment of closer fellowship with God. Notice the inference that they who endure are those who love Him. Love to God is not proved by the luxury of religious emotion but by our desire to please Him by obedience. As in all else Christ is the perfect example: "I love the Father and as the Father gave me commandment, even so I do" (John 14:31), and "He that hath my commandments and keepeth them he it is that loveth me, and he that loveth me shall be loved of my Father and I will love him and will manifest myself to him" (John 14:21). Would that not be crowning life?

Chapter XVII
Offering Of Isaac

(Gen 22:1-24)

A Shadow Of Things To Come

No situation in human life can exactly reflect spiritual and heavenly realities, but there is no denying that the OT abounds in material which lends itself to a spiritual application in terms of NT doctrine. This is clearly stated in such passages as Rom 15:4; 1 Cor 10:11; Heb 9:8; 10:1. It is foolish to attempt to force a typical meaning on every detail, and dangerous to draw conclusions not adequately supported by other Scriptures. The reader will judge for himself whether the offering up of Isaac has spiritual parallels with the greatest of all sacrifices. One of the incidental benefits of such studies is that confidence in the divine inspiration of Scripture is strengthened.

His Only Begotten Son

Attention has been drawn earlier to the emphasis in this chapter on God's own recognition of the special relationship between Abraham and Isaac in the frequent references to "thy son" and the three mentions of "thine only son". Abraham had other sons and there were many things common to Isaac and his half-brothers, so obviously the word 'only' is intended to indicate that in some way Isaac was unique. Isaac stood alone in being the one and only child of Abraham's true wife, in the circumstances of his birth (Heb 11:11), in the foremost place in his father's affections, and in his special destiny: "In Isaac shall thy seed be called" (21:12), cited in Rom 9:7; Heb 11:17-18. The use of the expression "only begotten" in the latter passage is of interest in view of John's fivefold use of the title in relation to Christ: John 1:14, 18; 3:16, 18 and 1 John 4:9, passages affording a wealth of material for soul enrichment. Our present purpose is simply

228

to stress that this quite remarkable link is ample justification for seeking other comparisons and contrasts.

Before The Foundation Of The World

Abraham's special love for Isaac ("thine only son whom thou lovest") went right back to Isaac's birth and continued through the years to the end (24:36; 25:5), but it was a love we can comprehend because it was the affection of a human father with its limitations; but how can we hope to grasp what is implied in that eternal and infinite love to which the Saviour referred in speaking to His Father: "Thou lovest me before the foundation of the world" (John 17:24)? If Abraham's love made his decision to yield up his son so astonishing, who is sufficient to comment on the amazing revelation that whilst the Father loved the Son from all eternity, yet at the same time the Son was foreordained (marked out) before the foundation of the world" as the Lamb of God by whose precious blood we would be redeemed (1 Pet 1:20)? The offering of Isaac was not an impetuous act but the carrying out of a resolution formed in the secrecy of Abraham's heart days before, and maintained during the long journey to the appointed place, which after two days travel was still "afar off". The cross at "the place called Calvary" (Luke 23:33) was no emergency measure suddenly decided upon to meet an unexpected situation, but part of a plan decided upon in the counsels of God before time began. The strength of Abraham's resolve was tested by the few days' journey, but God held to His purpose through untold ages until at last, to use Peter's words, Christ was "delivered by a determinate counsel and foreknowledge of God" (Acts 2:23). To a limited degree we can understand what it must have cost an affectionate earthly father to offer up his son, but we shall never understand what it cost God to give His Son. This is an aspect of the plan of salvation which is not sufficiently considered, although John saw in it evidence of the depth of God's love for us, as is evident from his use of that expressive little word *so* in one of the best known of Bible verses: "God so loved the world that he gave his only begotten Son" (John 3:16). Clearly he means that this is the demonstration of a love which cannot be measured: "Herein is love, not that we loved God but that God loved us and sent his son to be the propitiation for our sins" (1 John 4:10). That is the one all-embracing and incontrovertible evidence of God's heart toward us and the ultimate shield against the devil's fiery darts of doubt when trials perplex us: "He ... spared not his own son (Rom 8:32).

Now we turn from faint comparison to striking contrast. Isaac was spared the knowledge of what awaited him until the last possible moment, but Christ was fully aware of the Father's purpose whilst in "the glory that I had with thee before the world was" (John 17:5). With this in mind let us seek some light on Paul's sublime introduction to his letter to Titus. There he speaks of a promise made by God "before the world began", the literal phrase being an interesting variation but conveying the same truth, "before times eternal". A promise must be made to some one. To whom could it have been made "before times eternal" except to the Son of God? But this cannot mean that He was promised eternal life, for He himself is "that eternal life which was with the Father" (1 John 1:2). Paul's meaning becomes clear as he proceeds to say that in due time the promise was manifested through preaching. (The student will profit from considering the frequent use of the word *manifestation* in connection with this wide subject.)

This preaching proclaimed that the grace of God bringing salvation had appeared to all, the grand result being that Christ would have a people for His own peculiar possession (Titus 2:11-14). That this promise meant a great deal to Christ is evident from His seven-fold mention in the so-called high priestly prayer (John 17) of those whom the Father had given Him. Compare Titus 1:2, "in hope of eternal life ... promised before the world began", with John 17:2, "that he should give eternal life to as many as thou hast given him". See also John 10:28, "I give unto them eternal life". They were His Father's love-gift and were "chosen in Christ" (Eph 1:4), and once more we get the phrase "before the foundation of the world". Clearly then, in contrast to Isaac, He was in the Father's counsel from eternity — He knew all things.

We have seen that the cost of our redemption involved the marking out of Christ as the Lamb of God — but there was an awful price to be paid. Now we have the further revelation that Christ was willing to pay it. Long before Adam's fall made redemption necessary Christ "through the eternal Spirit offered himself without spot to God" (Heb 9:14). So it was in the full knowledge of His Father's will and in fulfilment of His voluntary consecration that He came into the world in the "fulness of the time" (Gal 4:4), sent of His Father: "I came down from heaven not to do mine own will but the will of Him that sent me" (John 6:38); "A body hast thou prepared me ... Lo I come to do thy will O God ... by the which will we are sanctified through the offering of the body of Jesus Christ, once for all" (Heb 10:5-10).

Knowing All Things

The foregoing relates to His preincarnate knowledge of what redemption's plan involved, but the Gospels reveal how very detailed was the Saviour's knowledge of what awaited Him in human experience as He made His journey through this world. Those who know that He suffered for them will be impressed with the advance information that He was able to give His disciples, and with His concern to see that all that the prophets had foretold should be fulfilled to the letter: "Behold we go up to Jerusalem and all things that are written by the prophets concerning the Son of Man shall be accomplished" (Luke 18:31-33). When all other things had been accomplished He fulfilled the prediction of Psa 69:21 and only then uttered the triumphant cry, "It is finished" (John 19:28-30).

Thy Will Be Done

Nothing is revealed of Isaac's state of mind and heart when faced with his ordeal, but we know that when the shadow of the cross lay across the Saviour's path, His perfect understanding of all that would be involved in bearing our sins distressed His soul and spirit, but He did not ask to be spared; "Now is my soul troubled, and what shall I say? Father save me from this hour: but for this cause came I unto this hour. Father glorify thy name" (John 12:27, 28). The only occurrence of the word *agony* in the NT is reserved for the Saviour's request to be spared a certain cup. To assume that this was a request to be spared the cross involves a difficulty for which no satisfactory explanation can be offered. Must it not have been a certain aspect of His humiliation which was not an integral part of His atoning work? Even here, however, He bowed to God's will: "Nevertheless not as I will, but as thou wilt" (Luke 22:42-44). If we are right in this it must have been something more bitter than the mindless brutalities and indignities heaped upon Him, for with regard to those we have this prophecy: "I was not rebellious, neither turned away back. I gave my back to the smiters and my cheeks to those who plucked off the hair. I hid not my face from shame and spitting" (Isa 50:5, 6).

Obedient To Death

We may be confident that Isaac always displayed an obedient spirit to patriarchal authority, but even so we cannot help being amazed at his acceptance of death, when he could have offered effective resistance if so minded. It was the greatest conceivable test of his obedience. We have been considering the Saviour's life of absolute compliance with His Father's will, but the final test was the acceptance of the cross and the bearing of our sin. His uniformly righteous life was crowned by this one supreme act of righteousness (Rom 5:18 RV). He became "obedient unto death" not in the sense of obeying death, but in the sense that His obedience went as far as submitting to death, and that no ordinary death but such a death as "the death of the cross" which meant for Him the bearing of sin's penalty. Who can fathom what "bearing away the sin of the world" involved? Like Isaac He was under no external compulsion; all the power of the mighty Roman Empire and the greater power of the kingdom of darkness could not have bound Him to the cross. "I lay down my life. No man (no one) taketh it from me but I lay it down of myself" (John 10:17, 18). Powerful bullocks intended for sacrifice were bound to the altar against their wills by ropes to prevent resistance, and Isaac was bound to avoid reflex action making matters worse. The Saviour was bound to the cross not by nails but by the twin cords of His devotion to the Father's will and His compassion for us (Psa 118:27).

Spared Not His Own Son

It was never God's intention that Isaac should be slain. The angel intervened in time to spare him the final stroke: "Lay not thine hand upon the lad". It is not at all unlikely that Paul was thinking of this when he said that God "spared not his own Son but delivered him up for us all" (Rom 8:32). God not only spared Isaac, but He also spared the father the final agony of slaying his loved son. He did not spare His Son and He did not spare Himself. What it cost the Father and Son we shall never know. If ever the Father's purpose to secure our salvation could have wavered surely it would have been when the moment arrived to "make to meet on him the iniquity of us all" (Isa 53:6). We can dimly enter into Abraham's feeling when he laid upon Isaac the burden of the wood, but what was that load compared to the load the Saviour carried in bearing our griefs and carrying our sorrows (Isa 53:4)? But the divine resolve stood firm. There is nothing more certain than that Abraham willingly laid down his knife, but God called upon the sword of divine justice to awake against His shepherd, the Man who was His Fellow (Zech 13:7). Note the Saviour's reference to this passage in Matt 26:31.

The Father Is With Me

A thoughtful reading of the mountain-climb will impart a sense of the tender atmosphere of fellowship between father and son as they climbed in companionable silence, except for the affectionate exchange of question and answer: "My father", "Here am I, my son". The repetition of something obvious in itself is surely significant: "They went both of them together" — a not-inadequate definition of fellowship, reminding us of Amos 3:3, "Can two walk together except they be agreed?"

Were it not that Scripture itself often employs the most homely of illustrations to set forth sublime truth we would not venture to see in the understandable pleasure Abraham found in Isaac at least some faint reflection of that divine intimacy of fellowship within the Godhead in a past eternity and of its perfect counterpart in the uninterrupted communion of Christ with the Father during His earthly pilgrimage. Does not the present tense in John 1:18 "is in the bosom of the Father" (i.e. the privileged position of special affection, John 21:20) suggest that the transition from heaven to earth involved no interruption of that eternal fellowship?

How beautifully Whittier's hymn speaks of those frequent private prayer-sessions which are a feature of Luke's Gospel (5:16; 6:12; 9:18, 28; 11:1):

> O Sabbath rest by Galilee,
> O calm of hills above
> Where Jesus knelt, to share with Thee
> The silence of eternity,
> Interpreted by love.

What a pleasant sight it is to see an admiring son imitating his father, happily joining in the same task, and even repeating with a confident air of authority what he has heard his father say. Who can doubt that as Isaac grew up Abraham had often been touched with such traits in his beloved son, as the latter learned the skills of sheep and cattle rearing. Paul affectionately used this homely situation to describe Timothy's happy relationship with him: "As a son with a father he hath served with me in the gospel" (Phil 2:22). Provided we use due reverence and caution may we not think in this connection of the Saviour Himself doing what He had seen His Father do and saying what He had heard His Father say (John 5:19; 8:26, 28; 15:15)?

Abraham and Isaac withdrawing from the servants to approach the place of the altar alone can serve to remind us that as the cross drew nearer so Christ became more and more detached from His disciples. He even anticipated being left alone as a result of their desertion, and yet not alone: "Ye shall be scattered every man to his own and shall leave me alone, and yet I am not alone for the Father is with me" (John 16:32). Truly it could be said, "They went, both of them together". The central cry from the cross, "My God, my God, why hast thou forsaken me?" involves depths into which it would be inopportune to go now, but the significance of the first and last cries being addressed to the Father will not be lost on the thoughtful reader. It is important to quote and refer to these passages correctly (Luke 23:34, 46; Matt 27:46). Without a doubt Isaac further endeared himself to his father by his submission. Would anyone dispute that never was the Lord Jesus dearer to His Father than when yielding the supreme act of obedience? "Therefore doth my Father love me because I lay down my life" (John 10:17). God's delight is quite evident from the fact that on account of His voluntary suffering of death He was "crowned with glory and honour" (Heb 2:9), elsewhere described as being "highly exalted" and being "given a name which is above every name" (Phil 2:8, 9). When He gave Himself for us it was "an offering and a sacrifice to God for a sweet smelling savour" (Eph 5:2).

I Will Rise Again

As mentioned earlier, Scripture does not enlighten us as to Isaac's state of mind as he surrendered himself to death on the altar. We are therefore unable to judge whether he was able to share his father's amazing faith and so rest in the confidence of being restored to life. As it turned out, of course, he suffered only a symbolic death and was likewise raised to a symbolic resurrection. Abraham received him even from the dead ... in a figure (Heb 11:19).

It was very different with our blessed Lord. His announcements of His coming death were constantly linked with confident assurances that He would rise again, specifying the third day, and even saying that He would thereafter go before them into Galilee. We cannot refrain from referring to the beautiful words put into His mouth, as it were, by the prophetic Spirit in Psalm 16. Even without Peter's explanation in his speech on the day of Pentecost (Acts 2:26-28) it would have been evident that the passage could refer only to Christ. Who else could say, "Thou wilt not suffer thine holy one to see corruption", or speak of being "at the right hand of God" — the place reserved for Him alone (Heb 1:13)? How blessed then to ponder the words, "Thou wilt show me the path of life, in thy presence is fulness of joy, at thy right hand are pleasures for ever more". He looked with the calmest and firmest confidence beyond the sufferings to the glory that should follow (1 Pet 1:11). It was for the joy set before Him that He endured the cross and despised the shame, and He has been anointed with the oil of gladness above His fellows (Heb 1:9; 12:2).

Isaac was simply restored to his former standing as Abraham's heir, but Christ could speak not only of being restored to the incommunicable glory He had with the Father "before the world began" but of another glory given Him — that of glorified humanity which He would share for ever with those given Him out of this passing world (John 17:5, 22). Even in the darkness of Golgotha He could see the new and splendid path of life stretching before Him, which like the path of the just, commencing with a morning without clouds, shines more and more unto the perfect day (2 Sam 23:3-4; Prov 4:18; Acts 3:14).

Chapter XVIII
The Death Of Sarah

(Gen 23:1-20)

All we know of the interval of not less than 12 years between chs. 22 and 23 is that soon after the offering up of Isaac, Abraham received news of the children and grandchildren of his brother Nahor whom he had not seen for more than 50 years (22:20-24).

Sarah, the only woman in Scripture whose age is given, died at the age of 127, at Kirjath-arba or Hebron, where Abraham dwelt at different times over the years.

Here he settled for a while after Lot left him and built his third recorded altar unto the Lord (13:18). Whether he had been elsewhere in the interval we cannot say, but he was there, confederate with three prominent Amorites, when he received news of Lot's capture (14:13). It was in the plains of Mamre, adjacent to Hebron, that he received the three visitors on the day prior to Sodom's destruction (18:1). We know from 35:27 that at some time he dwelt there with Isaac, the impression being that the latter was then of a responsible age. Soon after the death of Sarah, they moved to Lahai-roi, at least until Abraham died (24:62; 25:11). It is therefore quite likely that Jacob is speaking of the period in which Sarah died. Perhaps this is why Isaac's presence at the funeral is not mentioned, because in the circumstances it could be taken for granted.

It appears, however, that Abraham was away from home when his wife died, for it is said that he came to mourn for her. Had it been apparent that she was likely to die we can hardly think that he would have gone away, so we conclude that she died suddenly and unexpectedly. His absence from home raises no problems, for with an establishment of such a size, his flocks would be spread over a very wide area and his presence at some distant pastorage would often have been necessary. For example, there was a three days' journey separating the flocks Laban looked after personally, and those

236

which were under Jacob's care (30:36; 31:19-22).

Negotiating Land Purchase

In the aggregate, Abraham must have spent a great deal of time in Hebron over the years, and this helps to explain his acquaintance with the people living there and his knowledge of the lie of the land. It was common for people to select their sepulchres well in advance, and this practice persisted even to NT times. Joseph of Arimathæa must have gone to enormous trouble to hew out of the rock a new tomb, which remained unused awaiting the time when it would be needed, but it was needed much sooner than he had expected for the burial of the body of the Lord Jesus (Matt 27:58-60).

It is not at all unlikely that Abraham had given some thought to this question and in his own mind had tentatively ear-marked the cave of Machpelah, but thinking there was plenty of time had made no move. However, when the death of his wife took him by surprise he was not completely at a loss.

With his understanding of the local set-up he sensed that the wisest course would be to acknowledge the sons of Heth by first of all making a general request for a burying-place. He tactfully and modestly described himself as a stranger and a sojourner, thereby enlisting their sympathy in his sudden bereavement and the plight in which he had been placed. This approach brought forth an effusive response. He was addressed as "my lord" and acknowledged to be a mighty prince among them; although flowery language was common in such cases, there cannot be any doubt that there was genuine recognition of his considerable prestige.

This is not surprising when we consider that even a king some years earlier had thought it politic to make sure of his friendship (21:22-23). We think sadly of the poor impression Lot had made in Sodom where, despite his municipal status, he was scornfully referred to as "this fellow" (19:9). In view of the importance attached to the possession of one's own tomb, the open-hearted response to Abraham's request is really amazing: "In the choice of our sepulchres bury thy dead; none of us shall withhold from thee his sepulchre" (v.6).

They had evidently been sitting together in conference, but now Abraham rose up and courteously bowed to the sons of Heth to express his deep sense of gratitude for their truly magnificent offer. This broad invitation gave him just the opening he needed to make the request which he had in his mind at the first, although he left it to the sons of Heth to put it to Ephron.

He was contacted, and as there was business to be discussed and witnesses needed, they repaired to the gate which, as we noticed in the case of Sodom, was the usual place for such purposes.

He, too, addressed Abraham as "my lord", but we need not take too seriously his offer to present the desired property to Abraham as a free gift. This was simply a gambit in the game of bargaining which the oriental loves so much, although in view of the solemnity and urgency of the occasion Ephron had the grace to come to the point more quickly than normally would have been the case. He would have been flabbergasted if this rich man had closed with his offer, but of course Abraham was not so gauche as that. The readiness with which he closed in with Abraham's insistence on paying would be enough to show the most naïve that this was what he had intended to do.

He made out that the matter of four hundred shekels of silver was neither here nor there between men like themselves, but the second reference to this figure would be consistent with the idea that it was quite a sum to pay. It may have been a perfectly fair price to judge by Abraham's prompt acceptance of the figure unless the explanation is that this was no time for bargaining.

The careful definition of the property, the field which was before Mamre, the cave which was therein, all the trees that were in the field, that were in all the borders round about, the mention of witnesses and the repetition of "made sure", have the ring of a legal document. The title was indeed made sure for it was recognised by both sides in subsequent generations. About 200 years later Jacob in Egypt revealed that he knew all about the purchase of the field and the cave from Ephron the Hittite, and he charged his sons to bury him in the same cave where not only Sarah and Abraham had been buried but also Isaac and his wife and then Jacob's own wife, Leah. He had no fears of the descendants of Ephron questioning the title. Attention has been drawn to the highly organised civic life in southern Mesopotamia, but here we have a valuable insight into the stage reached in legal processes in the less-advanced Canaan.

Memories Of Ur

The death of his wife broke the only direct link Abraham had with the now far-off days in Ur of the Chaldees. Soon after, he moved with Isaac to Lahai-roi and here his thoughts turned to a bride for Isaac. Canaan was still an alien land: "Thou shalt not take a wife to my son of the Canaanites in whose land I dwell" (24:37). "But thou shalt go unto my country and to my kindred" (24:4) and "my father's house" (24:40). If this seems incompatible with the God of glory's call to "get out of thy country and from thy kindred and from thy father's house", we must remember that apart from a burial-plot, for which he had paid the full price, he could not, as Stephen said, claim enough ground so much as to put his foot on (Acts 7:5). This is not to say he had any desire to return to his own country as he might have done. He knew that Canaan was where God wanted him to be and that one day it would be the possession of his posterity. This was afar off, but faith brought it within his spirit's reach so that he could embrace the promises and confess that he was a stranger and pilgrim on the earth. He desired a heavenly country and looked for a city which had foundations and whose builder and maker was God (Heb 11:10-16).

But there was nothing wrong in cherishing affection even for those with whom he could have no spiritual affinity. The lack of such affection for those close to us by ties of nature is looked upon as a feature of the depravity of the last days (2 Tim 3:3). The AV and RV have supplied the word "natural" to bring out the latent thought that such affection is in the proper order of things. It is to be feared that a commendable resolve to walk a path of separation with God has sometimes been accompanied by a coldness toward unsaved relatives which has, humanly speaking, reduced the likelihood of winning them for Christ.

Chapter XIX
A Bride For Isaac

(Gen 24:1-67)

Charming though the story is, it is not immediately apparent why so much more space is given to it than to any other episode in the book but since all Scripture has been given by inspiration of God and for definite purposes (2 Tim 3:16), it will be well to consider possible reasons after the story has been studied.

Master And Servant

One of the many interesting features is the prominence given to master and servant — the words appear 21 and 14 times respectively. The relation between the two was delightful. We take the "eldest servant" to be none other than the Eliezer mentioned in 15:2, in which case he had been Abraham's steward for over 55 years by this time. Long experience had given Abraham such complete confidence in the man's ability and integrity that he had been given control of Abraham's large establishment, and all of his goods were in his hand (vv 2, 10). Cf. Joseph (39:4-6). Abraham also had such a high opinion of his discernment and discretion as to entrust him with the delicate and important mission of finding a bride for Isaac.

In the early days he himself had been Abraham's heir presumptive, but the arrival of Ishmael as a more likely candidate for such an inheritance, and later the birth of Isaac as the undoubted heir, destroyed any hopes he may have cherished. But he showed no bitterness at everything going to Isaac. On the contrary his many years in Abraham's service had developed an affectionate and intelligent loyalty to his master and to the cause of Isaac. To attempt to reduce the evidence to a formal tabulation would be like taking the bloom off the rose, rather should we let the following story speak for itself. It will be as pleasant to observe the natural unfolding of the marks of this ideal servant as it will be profitable, if we are challenged to display, on the spiritual level, like faithfulness and devotion in our service for God in the cause of His Son, our Lord and Saviour Jesus Christ (1 Cor 4:1-2). His behaviour shows distinct signs of having been influenced by the example of the master he admired. See vv. 26-27, 52 and compare with 18:2. Cf. also Eph 5:1 where "followers" carries the idea of "imitators" (RV).

Isaac's Future Planned

Isaac was now 40 years of age (25:20), so it follows that his father was about 140 years old. Although he actually had another 35 years left to him (25:7) he is described as "old and well stricken in years" from which we gather that he was beginning to fail (cf. 18:11). His full and active life, but especially the strains and stresses, were taking their toll, and the death of his life-partner must have left him feeling very lonely in what was still an alien land, with Isaac as his only near kith and kin. Although mistaken, he seems to have felt that his end was near, and he naturally wanted the satisfaction of seeing his son married since the fulfilment of all God's promises depended on Isaac having a son. This was assured by the word of God, but there is no inconsistency in making sensible plans as a proper balance between divine sovereignty and human responsibility. In the event, as so often, God was better than his fears, and he was spared long enough to see two grandsons grow to the age of 15 years. Cf. 25:20 (40 years) with 25:26 (60 years).

Since he would not contemplate his son marrying a woman of the corrupt Canaanites among whom he dwelt, he decided the best thing was to find a bride among his own people, who were now settled in Haran. As he and Isaac were living at Lahai-roi in the south of Canaan this meant a journey of about 500 miles each way. This being far too great a journey for him to contemplate in his frailty, we might have supposed that he would send his son to Haran to make his own arrangements. He preferred to rely on the more experienced Eliezer. Even if the latter had been appointed steward when a very young man he would now be something like 80 years of age, but bearing in mind the normal life-span at that period there is nothing exceptional in his making such an expedition. Jacob was well past 90 when he undertook the far more

16

difficult task of transferring his huge flocks from Haran to Canaan (31:18).

The Solemn Charge

He was asked to put his hand under Abraham's thigh, a recognised way of solemnising an oath, that he would not take a wife for Isaac from the Canaanites but go to Abraham's people (cf. 47:29). Abraham's use of the word *woman*, which Eliezer repeated, is interesting as indicating that, although girls were often married at an early age, they had a mature person in mind.

We need not be surprised to find Abraham in a somewhat reminiscent mood common to old men. Haran, although far from Ur, was nevertheless in Mesopotamia, and now as he was thinking of a link being formed with relatives he had never seen and would never see, he thought of it as "my country" (v. 4) and the "land of my nativity" (v. 7 RV). He was dwelling among the Canaanites (v. 3) and recognised it as their land (v. 37). The only plot he possessed in Canaan was a burial ground (23:20). But we are not to think that he was indulging in nostalgic regrets. True, he was still only a sojourner in a strange country (i.e. a country belonging to another), but by faith it was to him the land of promise, and he had never desired to return to his native land, though he could have done so had he wished. Heb 11:9, 13-16 will repay careful reading.

The form of the oath he required ("by the Lord, the God of heaven and the God of earth") suggests that he was still living in the good of the revelation brought to him by Melchizedek many years before (14:19). If the Most High God was possessor of heaven and earth then Canaan was at His absolute disposal in His own good time.

The Servant's Forethought

Eliezer was a cautious man and not ready to take the oath without due thought. What would be his position if the woman he selected was unwilling to come? Ordinarily, the proper time for such a question would be if and when he returned having failed in his mission. But he shared his master's fear that the days left to him were few and, although the journey would not take more than a couple of weeks, he thought it possible that Abraham would be gone by the time he returned. As a man anxious to see his master's wishes carried out he was prepared to make the journey again, this time to accompany Isaac to Haran in the hope that he would be able to find a suitable bride for himself. It is extraordinary that he should take it for granted that a grown man would need to be accompanied. He certainly was not a very forceful character, and the contrast between Abraham's firm stance and Isaac's preference for the line of least resistance in almost identical circumstances is illuminating (cf. 21:25 with 26:19-22).

Abraham's Confidence

Abraham was in a contented and confident mood. We recall how disheartened he seemed in Gerah when wearily and almost complainingly he spoke to Abimelech of God causing him to wander from his father's house (20:13). Here his language is quite different: "The Lord God of heaven (before whom I walk, v. 40) which took me from my father's house, and sware unto me saying, Unto thy seed will I give this land". He was quite assured that his servant need have no concern. That same God would send His angel before him (and with him to prosper his way, v. 40), and he would be able to take a wife for his son. However, to put his mind at ease Abraham made it clear that if the woman would not follow him, or if her family would not let her go (v. 41), then he would be clear of his oath. That anxiety removed, the servant gave the required undertaking and set about preparation for the journey.

Setting Off For Haran

He had no resources of his own from which to fit out such an expedition, but he could draw on the immense resources of his master (1 Cor 9:7; 2 Cor 3:5). As all of Abraham's goods were in his hand, and as he ruled over the household, the details were left to him. So he chose his assistants out of the large staff, and ten camels to carry the party and such things as he thought necessary, as well as to bring back the woman with attendants as propriety would require. The luggage included gifts, jewels of gold and silver as well as raiment for her, and other "precious things" for the family (v. 53). This is eloquent testimony to his master's confidence in his honesty and integrity (1 Cor 4:1, 2). His faithfulness was much more than a matter of duty; his affection made the happiness of his master his great concern (vv. 12, 14, 27, 49).

The long trek of 500 miles or so is passed over without comment, but it does not need a very lively imagination to follow the route in thought and to estimate the rigours and the risks involved in such a small party carrying so many valuables. But if over three hundred trained and armed men were available to meet the crisis occasioned by Lot's capture (14:14), he would have no difficulty in selecting a few who could give a good account of themselves. Moreover he had a greater safeguard than an army could provide for he had the angel of the Lord (v. 7), (Psa 34:7).

Arrival At Haran

After many days of weary travel Eliezer and his companions reached the outskirts of Haran at eventide.This is an appropriate point at which to summarise the situation there, although little of this was known to the servant until later.

As the place is here referred to as the city of Nahor, we can only conclude that at some time subsequent to Terah's death and Abraham's departure sixty five years previously, his brother who had been left in Ur had been sufficiently impressed with what he had heard of conditions there to leave Ur and settle in Haran. According to a message which reached Abraham after the offering up of Isaac (and therefore about 15 to 20 years ago) Nahor had eight children by his wife Milcah, and four by his concubine Reumah (22:20-24). That he was still alive cannot be asserted, but it cannot be doubted that many of his family were there. Bethuel, his youngest son, may have been born there; the latter's daughter Rebekah almost certainly was. As Laban was not mentioned when Rebekah's birth was reported to Abraham, we conclude that he was younger. He cannot have been more than a youth but was evidently a very capable one. On the occasion we are now considering Bethuel is mentioned only once, with Laban taking precedence (v. 50). The house is said to be the mother's not Bethuel's, and even she took little part in the proceedings; she is mentioned but once again and even then Laban takes precedence. It has been conjectured that the father was incapacitated in some way or another and unable to handle affairs.

The family lived in a house in the town not in tents; the

extent of the accommodation available at short notice (v. 31) coupled with the indications of a large staff (v. 61) argue for a considerable degree of prosperity. Among the incidental sidelights on Rebekah's character we may note that, despite her brother's forcefulness, she was able to hold her own and to have her say both in household matters and in her personal affairs (vv. 25, 58).

It seems that Nahor had brought his idolatry with him. There is no hint that it was practised in Rebekah's household, but it has to be remembered that only a comparatively fleeting glimpse is given of the home. There is no sign at any time that Rebekah attempted to bring false gods into Isaac's household; even if she had Abraham would certainly have stamped on it. It is clear that when Laban was established in his own home he had his false gods, and that his daughter Rachel surreptitiously took some of his idols into Jacob's household; *he* was too weak to act until God called him to return to Bethel (31:34; 35:2).

Eliezer At The Well

Eliezer halted outside the town where there was a well linked with a fountain or spring. The well is referred to in vv. 11, 20, but elsewhere in this chapter a fountain is meant. It would have been natural if his first concern had been to secure accommodation for the night. On the contrary, having a good man's care for his beasts (Prov 12:10), he first made his still-laden camels kneel down for rest, then immediately gave his mind to his errand and betook himself to prayer, (inaudibly — in his heart, v. 45). The fact that he addressed his petition to "the Lord God (Jehovah Adonai) of my master Abraham" encourages us to think that he had enjoyed spiritual fellowship with Abraham. Cf. 15:2, and note on v. 27.

He was anxious to get the business settled with the minimum of delay, having a sense of urgency because of his master's frailty and his concern for the proper management of affairs at Lahai-roi. It was a late hour, but he prayed for good speed that very day. He hoped to find a suitable bride that evening! Although his discernment and astuteness had earned the confidence of his master, he did not rely on his own judgment. He desired to be guided to the woman whom God had "appointed" for Isaac. How wonderful when life-partners are able to enjoy the assurance that they were appointed for each other; hence the vital importance of young people putting such an important matter into the hands of God for His direction before their affections become involved.

He sought a circumstantial token of God's will not because he needed to bolster up a feeble faith, but because he wanted to make absolutely sure of making the right choice. He did not suggest something haphazard or arbitrary but showed his shrewdness by imposing a test which would give a valuable insight into a person's character and disposition. This is more important than beauty, which is too often the deciding factor. Before continuing with the narrative it may be well to look at the subject of guidance by tokens.

Guidance By Tokens

Some take the view that it is a mistake for a Christian to seek guidance by a token, on the grounds that, possessing a completed revelation of God's will in the Scriptures, it should be possible to determine the course of one's action by applying the principles enunciated there to the situation in question. No doubt the Saviour's stricture on the scribes and Pharisees in asking for a sign largely accounts for this view. For that reason we use the term token. But the two cases are quite different. They demanded that the Saviour should give them some spectacular display of miraculous power to authenticate His claims which they rejected. He knew full well that miracles do not change the hearts of those who are not willing to believe. This was proved abundantly when the outstanding miracle of raising Lazarus from the dead, far from leading to faith, only incensed the chief priests and the Pharisees, increased their hatred of Christ and crystallised their determination to kill Him (Matt 12:39; John 11:53).

On a less serious level, it is both futile and insulting to ask God to make His will clear so that we can then decide whether it suits us to obey. Moreover, it is quite incongruous to ask God for a token of His will when the point is covered by a clear injunction in His Word.

But it does not follow that it is wrong for a believer, sincerely anxious to do God's will in a situation not covered by Scripture, to seek such guidance, so long as the token has a significant bearing on the matter and is supported by other confirmatory circumstances. Cf. Jud 6:37. To ask for some odd or curious token totally unrelated to the problem is childish.

Eliezer's Token

Here was a man old enough and wise enough to know that, as we have already suggested, the really important considerations were character and temperament. Accordingly, the token he submitted to God was one which would be very revealing in these respects.

Apparently he intended to watch the maidens who would be coming to the well at that time of day, and he would ask the first who favourably impressed him for a drink and nothing more. If she not only responded readily to that simple request but also of her own volition offered to draw water for the ten camels, he would take it that she was the one appointed by God, provided that another vital condition was fulfilled.

To appreciate the sagacity of the chosen token it is only necessary to remember a thirsty camel's capacity for water. It would not be fair to blame any girl for being reluctant to undertake such a laborious task, especially if there were chores awaiting her at home, and certainly not when the men responsible for the camels were there to do it. It would take a girl with very rare qualities and a care for animals, and a very willing and helpful spirit, to take on the task so readily without even being asked.

Rebekah Arrives On The Scene

Eliezer had been praying inaudibly, and before he had done Rebekah arrived at the well carrying a pitcher to draw water preparing the evening meal at home. Since we know from v. 61 that she personally had at least two serving girls, there must have been several others on the household staff. The fact that she undertook this menial duty quite naturally shows that she was free from petty pride. In all probability this was routine with her, and it never occurred to her that this occasion would be any different from any other of the many times she had done the same thing. Little could she have dreamed what tremendous issues would depend on her behaviour on this particular occasion. So it is often in life — a day which begins with the established pattern may well have in it a circumstance comparatively trivial in itself but having the potential for changing the course of one's life. Thus Moses took his father-in-law's flock day by day for thousands of times, but one day on the mountain slopes he found himself face to face with God and called to be the spiritual shepherd and leader of God's flock (Exod 3:1 ff). Or think of the Samaritan woman whose daily trip to the well had become routine; on that special day the stranger at the well turned out to be One whom she came to accept as the Saviour of the world and thereby became a channel of blessing to her townsfolk (John 4:6ff). Since we never know what may hang on the seemingly trivial in life it behoves us to acknowledge the Lord in all our ways and commit everything into His hands (Prov 3:5, 6).

Rebekah had probably left her home just before the man had begun his short prayer and had arrived at the well just before he had concluded (vv. 15, 45). Here is one of the many examples in which events apparently unrelated are beautifully co-ordinated by God's over-ruling, in this case illustrating the double promise in Isa 65:24, "before they call I will answer (i.e. in the departure of Rebekah at the right moment) and while they are yet speaking I will hear" (i.e. in her arrival at the well).

Now the moment arrived for the first test. Eliezer watched her descend the steps to the spring and then come up with a pitcher full of water on her shoulder. His simple request was met with ready response: "Drink my lord", which showed that she was discerning enough to recognise his standing and respectful enough to acknowledge it. Her readiness is seen in her hasting to lift the pitcher down from her shoulder and offer it to him. Then instead of tentatively volunteering she declared her already formed intention of watering the camels as well. Still acting swiftly and decisively she emptied the one pitcher full of water into the trough and then, still running, she went down to the spring and up again time after time until she had drawn what she considered enough to satisfy the thirsty camels.

As this was going on the man wondered at her, as well he might, seeing a beautiful and well-to-do girl displaying such vigour in willingly undertaking such humble but arduous labour. He was already reaching a conviction, but with admirable restraint he "held his peace" as Rebekah, despite having been already considerably delayed, waited patiently to make sure that she had drawn enough water to satisfy the animals completely.

Taking v. 22 with v. 47, the present of a golden earing and two bracelets, and the asking of the vital question, "Whose daughter art thou?" were simultaneous. It is almost as if he had now reached the conclusion that his quest was ended.

The value of the ornaments was out of proportion to the service she had rendered, which suggests that in his own mind he was symbolically claiming her for Isaac. With the same breath he asked whether there was accommodation in her father's house. In view of the fact that he hoped to complete his mission that same evening it would seem safe to conclude that he felt sure he had found the right family.

Nevertheless he must have waited with bated breath for the crucial answer to his first question. She gave a full and frank answer whilst at the same time probably wondering why this should be of interest to a stranger. The effect on Eliezer when he learned that she was Bethuel's daughter, and therefore the grand-daughter of Abraham's brother, may be judged by the pouring out of his heart in his thanksgiving as he bowed his head in worship and blessed the Lord for His kindness to his master. Are we reading too much into his words "mercy and truth" if we see in them some indication that he appreciated the difference between the sovereign grace which reached Abraham in Ur when he had no claim on God, and God's fidelity to His covenant promises which gave Abraham a claim on God?

Rebekah answered the second question without hesitation being sufficiently confident of her standing in the home to assure him there was no problem of accommodation. He could hardly fail to be slightly amused, and perhaps even pleased, when she mentioned straw and provender for the camels (cf. vv. 31-32) before room for him and his men. This, with the practical concern she had already shown for the welfare of animals, was an encouraging sign of her suitability as the mistress of a cattle-owner's establishment.

Unlike his earlier prayer, his thanksgiving was not merely in his heart: "He said, Blessed be the Lord God of my master Abraham". Rebekah no doubt heard this before, running again, she sped to her mother's house to tell them these things.

The Lord's Leading

Before going into the effect of her news on the family let us give a little thought to something else the servant said in his thanksgiving, "I being in the way the Lord led me". These words have often been quoted as pointing to a very necessary lesson that we need to be walking in the way, in the path of obedience to the known will of God, if we are to expect His further leading, and also that it is better to be able to say in retrospect that the Lord has led us rather than make the claim beforehand that we are being guided to say this or do that. A claim like this has to be judged by its sequel, and it has too often been the case that individuals who have been bold enough to declare that the Lord has told them to say or do certain things proceed in a way which raises serious doubt whether it was indeed the Lord's will. Even the apostle in his plans observed the principle laid down by James: "If the Lord will, we shall do this or that". See, for example Rom 1:10.

Laban's Invitation

Whilst Rebekah was reporting on the interview at the well, Eliezer was properly waiting there for her spontaneous invitation to be confirmed rather than acting too precipitously on the word of an enthusiastic girl. We have seen reason to think that Laban, though young, had the chief say in household affairs, and he entered enthusiastically into making the provision his sister had promised. It is difficult to avoid the suspicion that he had a mercenary motive, for the sight of the valuable golden earing and bracelets is linked with his ready response.

His heartless treatment of his own sister's son, Jacob, in later life reveals him as a grasping and scheming man. Cf. 29:25; 30:27; 31:6, 7, 14, 15. In the light of this one wonders how sincere was his effusive welcome and his show of piety in addressing Eliezer as "Thou blessed of the Lord". His acquaintance with the divine name *Jehovah* is difficult to explain unless he had been astute enough to take advantage of his sister's report of the man's use of the divine name (cf. v. 50).

Eliezer Enters The Home

"The man came into the house" (v. 32). It is worthwhile trying to visualise the homely scene. The tired camels were taken to some outbuildings, their loads removed, fodder provided to satisfy their hunger and straw laid down on which they could rest. Then the guest's feet were washed and a meal was set before them. But whatever his men thought of it, he was so full of his message that he declined to eat before he had told his errand. His manner carried such weight that there was no protest from his hosts, who no doubt were eager to learn what was so important about his errand that the meal must wait.

He told them nothing about himself beyond what came within the scope of his opening words, "I am Abraham's servant". That was all they needed to know about him, although they could draw some inferences from the fact that he had been entrusted with such a mission as they were going to hear about. He could have spoken of his long years of service, of the pre-eminent position he held, ruling over the establishment with everything in his hand, but he was not there to speak about himself. We need only to read 1 Cor 3:5; 2 Cor 4:5; 12:6 to see that he and Paul were of kindred spirit.

The listener sensed the pleasure he found in describing, in a few well-chosen words and with an eloquence unconsciously imparted by his affection for Abraham, his master's greatness and wealth, nevertheless being careful to attribute this, as his master would have done, to the Lord's blessing. His own position would have justified expectations, but without any trace of complaint he went on to say that Abraham had given to his son Isaac all that he had. Cf. Eph 3:8.

Now came the crux of the matter. He was here, as perhaps they were now beginning to suspect, to win a bride for this loved son. He gave a full account of the circumstances in which he was solemnly entrusted with this commission, and it is worth noticing that, having already become well acquainted with Rebekah, he still used the word *woman*, recognising that she appealed to him as a mature person. Next, he explained how he had sought for divine guidance and how events had provided just the token for which he was looking.

Up to this point all was new to his listeners, but he then continued to recount in detail the facts with which they had been acquainted already from Rebekah's report when she returned from the well. It leaves us with the impression that he found pleasure in recalling the behaviour of Rebekah. It reveals a proper modesty when he refrained from referring to her use of "my lord" in addressing him.

A Decision Called For

Having explained the whole matter briefly but clearly,

without further ado he appealed for a definite decision there and then. This was not due to impatience; probably anxiety about Abraham's health made him feel that no time must be lost if he were to be sure of giving him the satisfaction of seeing his son united to a suitable bride: "And now if you will deal kindly and truly with my master tell me". Divine over-ruling in the whole affair was so evident that Laban and his father felt that the matter was out of their hands — they could say neither bad nor good. He could take Rebekah. His relief was immense, and once again he worshipped the Lord. At the well, to avoid the appearance of ostentation in the public eye, he had simply but reverently bowed his head. Now in the hushed atmosphere of the home he could express his deep emotion by bowing to the ground.

It is not difficult to imagine the effect on all gathered when, in addition to the ornaments given to her at the well, Rebekah was presented with jewels of gold and silver. His inclusion of raiment in the valuables he brought from home and now gave to her could well be an example of his judicious foresight in forestalling a difficulty which he anticipated could arise when, as he intended to do, he insisted on immediate departure. Her brother and her mother received precious things, but the omission of any mention of the father is perplexing. The evening meal must have been pervaded with an atmosphere of excitement, but eventually all retired to rest.

The Morning After

Although no doubt breakfast was taken the family must have been somewhat taken aback by Eliezer's request to be allowed to leave at once with Rebekah. Laban and his mother had talked things over after the pronouncement that he and his father had made whilst under the deep impression made by the story they had heard. Looking at things more calmly they felt that this had been too impetuous, and now they wanted the departure delayed until suitable celebrations had been held. It would take at least ten days to stage a worthy farewell to one they would be unlikely to see again. The sort of thing they had in mind may be gathered from Laban's complaint to Jacob that instead of stealing away with Rachel he should have afforded an opportunity to have a merry time with songs and tabret and harp (31:27). This would not have been to Eliezer's taste in any case, but quite apart from that he was resolved not to brook even a day's delay, welcome though a restful break would otherwise have been. Not being strong enough to resist his determination, they temporised by saying they would consult Rebekah, no doubt feeling sure she would shrink from leaving at such short notice.

Rebekah's Decision

They must have been astonished at her prompt and decisive reply, "I will go". Nor can we fail to be impressed with the courage and resolution in the ready abandonment of the many and varied preparations which would normally have been considered essential before setting off on a long journey to make a new home in a distant country from which she could never expect to return. The visitor was the kind of man to inspire confidence, and the wealth he could distribute so far confirmed his story, yet she had to take a good deal on trust in agreeing to become the wife of a man she had never seen. All this is of a piece with the qualities she showed on a lesser scale in her decisive and unhesitating handling of a simpler situation at the well the evening before.

Evidently as a child she had been in the care of a nurse whose name, we learn from 35:8, was Deborah. An attachment between the two led to her being kept on the staff when her charge grew up, and to her accompanying Rebekah on her journey. The faithful soul outlived her and was taken into the household of Rebekah's son Jacob, who so lamented her death that the burial place was given a name which reflected that sorrow; Rebekah was also accompanied by two serving maids. Many a lesser woman would have demanded sufficient time to set herself out in a manner befitting her station but, as suggested earlier, she had no false pride and was ready to leave at very short notice. We can nevertheless believe that she felt grateful to her guide who had anticipated the need by bringing for her raiment in which she need not be ashamed when she met her husband to be.

She was not motivated by the prospect of leaving a poor home for a life of luxury — in fact she was giving up a comfortable house in a town for a semi-nomadic life in tents, despite the wealth her bridegroom inherited from his father. We cannot think she was kept in ignorance of this, so we are surely safe in concluding that she felt strongly attracted by what she had been told about Isaac.

The Journey

Again we have no details of the long journey, but it can be safely said that it was not a comfortable one. Riding on camels, not without reason called the ships of the desert, is not a very comfortable form of travel especially for the inexperienced. The inconvenience of having to bed down for the night again and again need not be enlarged upon here, but we will endeavour to draw some lessons from the journey when the typical aspect of this story comes under consideration. But the most tiresome of journeys come to an end and there came an evening when their destination was in sight.

Isaac Re-appears

It is quite remarkable that the record does not mention Isaac's descent from the mount of sacrifice (22:19), nor does he appear again until we now read of his leaving home to walk in the field (the open countryside) for a quiet time of prayer. Had he been able to estimate that, if Eliezer's mission had been successful, he would be returning about now, or had he received advance notice?

Be that as it may, he lifted up his eyes northward and "behold the camels were coming". At the same time she lifted up her eyes and saw a man who was obviously coming to meet them. She was riding closely enough to her guide to be able to ask who this man was, although it is more than likely that she had drawn her own conclusions. Having repeatedly spoken of Abraham as his master the servant now describes Isaac in this way. This surprising reply shows that Eliezer accepted that now that Isaac had come into his father's wealth and was about to set up his own home, the old relationship had changed. Considering that he had been steward before Isaac was born and was now about twice his age, his prompt and willing recognition of Isaac's new status speaks volumes for his loyal spirit.

Rebekah had evidently had the position explained to her beforehand for she quite understood, and, observing the proprieties, she veiled herself before alighting off the camel. How some writers would have revelled in dramatising the first meeting of two who were destined for each other, but Scripture leaves us to visualise the scene.

Relieved to find that all was well with his old master, and

faithful to the end, he renders to his new master a full account of all that he had done, the recital of which would later delight Abraham's heart and cause thanksgiving to the God who had so wonderfully over-ruled it all. Isaac was a strange man if his heart was not moved on learning that this beautiful and capable young woman had readily left her home and kindred at short notice to become his bride.

Abraham had vacated the main tent in favour of the young couple, and here Isaac installed his wife. It occasions no surprise that she filled the void left in his heart by the death of the mother who had meant so much to him, nor that he, on his part, loved her in return.

Eliezer drops out of the picture, but who can doubt that Isaac found in him not only a faithful servant but a friend and experienced adviser? He had not the remotest idea that his record would be forever preserved in holy Scripture and that the captivating story of his faithful service would become a source of pleasure and profit to countless generations of appreciative readers. If a book of remembrance was written before the Lord to commemorate those in Malachi's day who had feared the Lord, and if He has promised not to forget those who have shown their love to Him by serving His people, we should be sobered by the thought of what is written in heaven concerning us. Cf. Mal 3:16; Heb 6:10.

One question is worth raising before we leave the subject. Why is it that Scripture is so often very sparing in the treatment of much that would be of immense interest to us, whilst at the same time laying great stress on other aspects of the narrative? In the present case we have a full account of Eliezer's experience and of the part that Rebekah played, with a good deal of repetition which some would regard as needless. Various answers may suggest themselves; upon these we offer no comment because we wish to invite consideration of the possiblity that the inspiring Spirit reflects the pleasure God found in a man happily devoted to his duty and in a young woman whose beauty did not make her vain nor position make her haughty. If this is so it is a heart-warming thought for all who wish to honour God in the every-day things of life.

Chapter XX

The Typical Aspect

(Gen 24:1-67)

Extravagances in spiritualisation have unhappily raised prejudice against typical teaching but few would refuse to see correspondences between the offering up of Isaac and the sacrifice of Christ, and between the search for a bride for Isaac and the NT truth of Christ and the Church. Some, seeing a typical significance in the report of Rebekah's birth coming after the account of the sacrifice of Isaac, have linked it with the "birth" of the Church on the day of Pentecost following upon the death and resurrection of Christ. Certainly because no human situation can adequately portray spiritual realities analogies are bound to break down at some points, but even then contrasts can be thought-provoking.

The Father's Purpose

The uniqueness of Isaac in his father's eyes, his love for him (acknowledged by God) and the ties of fellowship between them have all been considered in ch. 22; this close and happy relationship should be kept in mind as we turn to the plans Abraham made for his son's future, as faintly reflecting the unity of the Father and His only begotten Son, and the Father's purpose for the eternal glory and joy of Christ.

As the first step Abraham turned everything over to Isaac as heir (v. 36; cf. 15:4), and certainly it was a substantial inheritance, but the purposes of God regarding His heir were settled before the foundation of the world — a timeless state which we are incapable of conceiving. Christ was appointed heir of all things before God, through Him, made the worlds — the ages and all they contain (Heb 1:2). This is elaborated in Col 1:16, "By (in) Him were all things created, that are in heaven and that are in earth, visible and invisible, whether they be thrones or dominions, or principalities or powers". Then it repeats "all things were created by (through) Him" but adds the illuminating words "and for Him". Here we have in one verse what would otherwise be two of the greatest mysteries — the origin of the universe and its ultimate purpose. How vast then are the implications of the Saviour's words "all things are delivered unto me of my Father", uttered, incidently, when everything seemed to be going wrong. In the light of this we can better see the aptness of His next statement: "No one knoweth (fully comprehends) the Son but the Father".

When we consider how a little power can make a puny man proud how like the Heir of all to add: "I am meek and lowly in heart" (Matt 11:27, 29). In perfect accord with this is His gracious act when, in the full realisation "that the Father had given all things into his hand" He rose to wash His disciples' feet (John 13:3-5).

> The high mysteries of His Name
> An angel's grasp transcend
> The Father only — glorious claim
> The Son can comprehend.

Christ's Future Glory and Joy

In the light of God's promise that his seed would be innumerable, Abraham realised that his plans had a bearing on many future generations but he did not know how long God's purpose would take to work out. In contrast God's programme for Christ takes in the majestic sweep of what are sometimes called, in the search for some meaningful phrase, the unending ages of eternity. Leading up to that we are told that "in the dispensation of the fulness of times he might gather together in one all things in Christ, both which are in heaven and which are on earth".

The situation with which Abraham was dealing called for measures beyond endowing his son with all his wealth. Although from the divine standpoint he had the promise of God confirmed by an oath (22:16; Heb 6:13-17), from the human standpoint it was obvious that Isaac would need to have a son. Accordingly he took steps to provide a bride for him, and the care and concern he showed proved clearly, what in any case we would naturally expect, that he was anxious also to secure his happiness with the right woman.

For reasons too profound to venture on, God saw,

17

inadequate as language is to express it, that provision needed to be made, not only for the Son's destined glory but also for His complete and everlasting heart satisfaction and fulness of joy. To save repetition, the reader is invited to refer to the comments on Psa 16 under the sub-heading "I Will Rise Again" in ch. 17 and on Titus 1:2 under the sub-heading "Before The Foundation Of The World".

The suggestion is that the Saviour's "fulness of joy ... and pleasures for evermore" has a connection with the "hope of eternal life". Since Christ is Himself "that eternal life which was with the Father" (1 John 1:2) that promise must relate to His words to the Father in John 17:2, "Thou hast given him power (authority) ... that he should give eternal life to as many as thou hast given him". This gift of a people for Himself who would share His life was highly prized for He refers to them as the Father's gift again and again in this prayer (vv. 2, 6, 9, 11, 12).

The immediate reference was to those who up to that time, drawn by the Father, had come to Christ and put their trust in Him, but happily for us He definitely embraced all who would thereafter be brought to Him: "Neither pray I for these alone, but for them also which shall believe on me through their word" (v. 20; cf. John 6:37; Matt 16:16-17). We need not hesitate either to take to ourselves the statement in John 13:1 "having loved his own which were in the world he loved them unto the end".

The Church The Bride Of Christ

The Father's gift, then, comprises all those He has given to Christ and thus constitute the Church; this has often been described as "The Father's love-gift to His Son".

It will be well at this point to consider reasons for seeing the simile of a bride as representing an important aspect of the Church.

The idea comes out clearly in Paul's concern for those he had won for Christ in Corinth and were in danger of being beguiled by the devil from the simplicity and the purity that is toward Christ (2 Cor 11:2, 3 RV). He speaks of being jealous over them with a godly jealousy (Gr. a jealousy of God) because he had espoused them to one husband that he might present them as a chaste virgin to Christ. This passage refers to individual believers, but later Paul applies the concept to the Church as a whole (Eph 5:23-33). In this short passage he refers no fewer than six times to the relationship between Christ and the Church as a model for husbands and wives, and after quoting Gen 2:24 ("Therefore shall a man leave his father and his mother, and shall cleave unto his wife: and they shall be one flesh"), he adds "This is a great mystery but I speak concerning Christ and the church".

Other Scriptures could be adduced but the foregoing seems ample justification for seeing typical significance in Rebekah as Isaac's bride.

The Father's Initiative

It is evident that in the matter of providing a bride for his son Abraham took the initiative, while Isaac as a submissive son was content to leave all to him, although he would naturally have been taken into his father's counsel along with the servant.

Similarly in the counsels of the holy Trinity purpose is attributed to the Father as is very definitely brought out in the work of redemption by such expressions as "according to his good pleasure which he hath purposed in himself" and "according to the purpose of him who worketh all things after the counsel of his own will" (Eph 1:9, 11; cf. Jas 1:17, 18).

The Son is in the Father's confidence "for the Father loveth the Son and sheweth him all things that he himself doeth" (John 5:20; cf. 15:15). The same is true of the Holy Spirit (John 16:13; 1 Cor 2:9-11).

The Servant Sent

When plans for finding the bride appointed by God (v. 12) had been settled, attention is focussed on the servant sent by the father on behalf of his son to carry out the father's will. He is unnamed but described as the eldest servant, probably in the sense of having been longest in Abraham's service; there can be little doubt that he was the Eliezer who was born in the house (15:2-3). His mission, so faithfully carried out, has some parallels with the work of the Holy Spirit sent by the Father in the name of the Son (John 14:16, 26; 15:26).

The activities of the Holy Spirit, a prominent theme in the Acts, has largely to do with reaching those who are destined to form the Church, although He operates in and through those who already belong to Christ. Both aspects are brought out in Peter's words: "them that have preached the gospel unto you with the Holy Spirit sent down from heaven" (1 Pet 1:12; cf. Acts 4:31-33).

Rebekah Marked Out

On arrival at the well, where a number of young women could be expected at that time of day, Eliezer would need to single out the one who impressed him most and he would then judge whether she was the one appointed by her response to a request for water. When Rebekah arrived she attracted him at once. It is worth noting the stress put on the fact that she was a virgin, especially in view of Paul's use of the word in 2 Cor 11:2, to which attention has already been drawn. The choice by the servant illustrates one aspect of the work of the Holy Spirit in sanctification or, as it means, setting apart for God. It is interesting to see, incidentally as evidence of inspiration, this operation of the Spirit in sanctification is similarly described by two very different apostles writing to two very different classes of people. Peter addresses the scattered believers to whom he is writing as "Elect according to the foreknowledge of God the Father, through sanctification of the Spirit unto obedience and sprinkling of the blood of Jesus Christ" (1 Pet 1:1, 2). The Spirit had separated them from others, with the object of leading them to obey the truth whereupon the efficacy of the blood of Christ would be made good to them personally. The point is illustrated in Exod 12 where the shed blood of the lamb in the bason would not have protected the household; it had to be applied to the door by the bunch of hyssop. Paul, after speaking of those who "received not the love of the truth", thanks God that He had "from the beginning chosen them (i.e. the believers) to salvation through sanctification of the Spirit and belief of the truth" (2 Thess 2:10-14). As Eliezer judged by Rebekah's response, so Paul knew that the Thessalonians were elected of God, because of the way in which they responded to the gospel which came to them in the power of the Holy Spirit (1 Thess 1:4-6; 2:13). These believers did not realise when they first heard the gospel that they had been singled out by the Holy Spirit. Similarly Rebekah had no idea that she had been marked out, nor could she have dreamed what consequences would follow her appropriate response. Whilst she was still ignorant of the significance of it all bracelets were put on her hands, symbolically claiming her for one of whom she had not yet even heard.

In The House

It was not until all were gathered in the house that the servant explained the purpose of his mission. Of necessity he had to say something about himself in order that his role should be understood but his main concern was to put forward the claims of Isaac. Some have misunderstood the Saviour's words in John 16:13 to mean that the Holy Spirit would not speak *about* Himself, which is manifestly incorrect because in the revelations He has imparted as promised by Christ, we learn a great deal of His Person and work. The meaning is that the Spirit would not speak *from* Himself as confirmed by the words which immediately follow: "whatsoever he shall hear that shall he speak ... he shall glorify me". That aptly applies to the discourse of Eliezer repeating what he had heard from Abraham and drawing attention to the glory which belonged to Isaac in virtue of his vast inheritance (vv. 35-36). Remarkably enough the Saviour went on to say, "All things that the Father hath are mine; therefore said I that he (the Spirit) shall take of mine and shew it unto you". Eliezer certainly could not have taken all that had been handed over to Isaac, but he did take part of that wealth and not merely showed but bestowed it on Rebekah and her family (vv. 22, 53). It was to Rebekah a token of what was yet to come. The things which God has prepared for those who love Him cannot be seen or heard or understood by the natural man but God has revealed them to believers by His Spirit (1 Cor 2:9, 10). Even so the believer cannot yet realise, much less actually enter into, the full extent of his inheritance in Christ but he has been given an "earnest" or a token as a foretaste (Eph 1:13, 14).

Rebekah's Decision

The position having been explained it was now for Rebekah to make up her mind as to how she would respond to the challenge. Her brother and mother would have postponed matters but Eliezer was insistent on the urgency of the matter and would brook no delay. Evidently they themselves did not suppose that Rebekah would consent to an immediate departure, but under pressure they agreed to call the damsel and put the question to her probably expecting her to ask for time to make preparation. "Wilt thou go with this man?" Having regard to all that was involved her courageous and resolute reply "I will go" must have astonished her family as much as it moved the servant's heart.

Here we have the interplay between the appointment of God and the exercise of free-will. Her right of choice was taken into account from the beginning as is clear from the servant's words to Abraham, "Peradventure the woman will not follow me" (v. 5). The parallel truths of divine sovereignty and human responsibility will never be rationalised to the satisfaction of human philosophy and such attempts as have been made to explain the paradox have never succeeded in doing more than shift the emphasis. The believer holds firmly to both, content to wait until the parallel truths meet in infinity when we shall discover how limited our earth-bound thinking has been.

Rebekah's spontaneous and dramatic decision finds its spiritual counterpart in those not infrequent cases where individuals, powerfully confronted for the first time with the convicting Spirit's effectual call, have decisively abandoned their former manner of life for a new and entirely different life in which Christ is owned as Lord and Saviour. Such cases can be sensational, but there should be a sympathetic understanding of those believers, often among the most devout, whose assurance is sometimes shaken because the devil plays on the fact that they have no remarkable story of conversion to relate, their lives having always been sheltered. This is particularly true of many who genuinely trusted Christ at such a tender age that they cannot even remember having made a conscious decision. Certainly some children have been put in a false position because of pressure brought to bear on them to make some sort of profession, but there are a great number of genuine believers, some of them now faithful servants of Christ, whose hearts were opened when very young. A living faith in Christ now is proof enough that there was at some time a turning to Him. Such should be encouraged to see that they are being offered the opportunity to gain a victory over doubt, which can be just as real as the victory some have had over sin and the world which once enslaved them.

Rebekah never forgot the evening when the stranger she later came to know so well arrested her attention, and certainly not the moment soon after when her decision changed her life for ever. Believers deprive themselves of a great deal of blessing if they neglect to meditate frequently on the wonder and deep significance of their conversion, irrespective of whether their story is such as to arrest the interest of others or whether it conforms in its outward form to the simple pattern with which we are all familiar. Every true conversion is a miracle of grace for it means that just as God broke into human history in the fulness of times in the person of Christ, so He broke into the life of the individual by His convicting and regenerating Spirit. The true wonder of this should grow on us but the full realisation of all it involved must wait until we stand in the light of the throne.

The Journey To The New Home

Like the outward journey the return journey is passed over in silence. There was a good deal to interest an intelligent young woman as she passed through various territories, new to her, and observed different peoples and their way of life. Not without reason is life often thought of as a journey through changing scenes and experiences. Of one thing we may be quite certain — her main interest was to learn all she could about the man with whom she was going to spend the rest of her life. This was certainly the attitude of Paul who commenced his Christian life with the question, "Who art thou Lord?" and near the end counted all that he had surrendered and suffered for Christ as refuse compared with the deeper knowledge of Christ. He defined his ambition in a number of ways but in this context it was, "That I may know him" (Phil 3:7-10).

We know sufficient of Rebekah's guide to be assured that he was only too pleased at her interest and delighted to tell her all she wanted to know. One wonders what her reaction was if among the things she heard was the story of Mount Moriah.

As is so often the case the Scripture here draws our attention to a fact by repetition amplifying a remark as though to ensure that the point is not overlooked. We are told, not only that "Rebekah rose and ... followed the man" but also that "the servant took Rebekah and went his way". He was ready to be her guard and guide but she, for her part, had to be ready to follow, which should serve to remind us that what is available for us in the ministry of the Holy Spirit can be appropriated in experience only so long as we are ready to yield to His guidance.

Eliezer had revealed sufficient in the home to enable Rebekah to come to a decision, but there was a great deal more to impart as they made their way together day by day. The Holy Spirit has been given to guide us into all truth — that is, the full range of what may be learned during our pilgrim journey through this world to our eternal home. It does not mean that we shall be able to learn all there is to know; even Paul did not claim to have done that (1 Cor 13:12). Nor is this what is meant by "Ye have an unction from the Holy One and ye know all things". As in some other contexts "all things" must be understood as referring to the matters under discussion (1 John 2:20).

Our enlightenment is limited by the degree of our desire. On three occasions Daniel was told that he was "greatly beloved" (Dan 9:23; 10:11, 19). In the first two passages the margin offers the alternative "a man of desires". Taking the context into consideration it appears to be justifiable to understand the two phrases as expressing the pleasure which God found in Daniel's earnest desire to understand the mind of God.

If Eliezer's willingness to instruct her in the matters affecting her future bridegroom was matched by her eagerness to learn we may be sure that not only did it give great pleasure to him but also resulted in her beginning to feel that she almost knew Isaac. How well do we know the One with whom we are going to spend eternity?

Journey's End

The meeting of bride and bridegroom on that last evening of the journey, before darkness set in, has appealed to many as a beautiful picture of Christ coming from heaven near the close of this age and before the darkness of the day of wrath, to meet His people in the air. Cf. Joel 2:1, 2 and especially vv. 28-32 quoted by Peter in Acts 2:16-21. He did not say that the day of Pentecost was a fulfilment of that prophecy — years later he spoke of the day of the Lord as still future (2 Pet 3:10). See 1 Thess 4:15-17 where the differences are obvious.

We have read of the father's plans for Isaac and of the

servant's testimony but he himself has not figured in the story at all in the interval between his being offered up on Mount Moriah and his leaving home to meet his bride. In fact his descent from the mountain is not mentioned, although of course he did return with his father. This omission is certainly so curious as to seem intentional. Would it be too fanciful to see in this a shadow of the truth that after the cross the Saviour was not seen publicly but only to His own circle (Acts 10:41: "Not to all the people but unto witnesses chosen before of God") and, having returned to heaven, is hidden as it were in His Father's house until the appointed time for Him to appear again (Acts 1:11; 3:21)?

Rebekah had been informed that she was drawing near to Lahai-roi and she was on the qui-vive of expectation anxious to miss nothing. A man like Eliezer would certainly have sent on one of his men in advance to give notice of their approach and the expected time of arrival. Isaac was therefore expecting them when he left his home in the camp for the field — that is the open country. He was meditating and it is not difficult to imagine the thoughts which were running through his mind as he tried to picture Rebekah from such details as the messenger had given.

"Lifting up his eyes" he saw the camels coming and made his way toward them. Rebekah too had "lifted up her eyes" to watch him approaching and each caught the other's flash of recognition. Beyond the fact that she covered herself with a veil and lighted off the camel nothing is said of the actual meeting and it would be insensitive to make a futile attempt to capture the drama of it in words. The greater impossibility is to form even an adequate mental picture of that great event when our eyes will meet our Lord's for the first time — a sight which will transform us into His likeness (1 John 3:2).

Up to this point the story has been told in such detail that there has been little need to make deductions but after Rebekah's meeting with Isaac, we have only the following bare facts:—

1. The servant told Isaac all that he had done;
2. Isaac brought Rebekah into Sarah's tent;
3. She became his wife;
4. He loved her;
5. He was comforted.

The reader will probably agree that the conclusions drawn are quite safe and perfectly in accord with what would quite naturally happen; however when we turn from these to their spiritual counterpart we are on absolutely firm ground.

The Servant's Report

Seeing that Eliezer gave such a full report ("all things that he had done") it must have taken some time and there was hardly opportunity for this until the preliminaries were over. Isaac must have been struck with Rebekah's beauty as soon as he saw her ("she was very fair", v. 16) but his appreciation of her must have been greatly enhanced when he heard of her magnificent behaviour at the well, followed so soon by her brave and resolute decision to respond immediately to the call and, forsaking all, to link her future to a man she had never seen but to whom she had lost her heart on the testimony of the servant.

Of course there is no such thing as Christ needing a report of His people — if proof is needed the Acts and Rev 2 and 3 abound in evidence that He is well aware of what is happening here below. Whilst still here Himself he disclosed that there is joy in heaven, in the presence of the angels of God over one sinner who repents (Luke 15:7, 10). Beyond doubt then every believer has brought Him joy by acceptance of His claims.

The quotation in Heb 1:8, 9 makes it clear that the king in Psa 45 is Christ, so when we read "Hearken O daughter ... forget thine own people and thy father's house; so shall the king greatly desire thy beauty" we cannot help remembering that this is substantially what Rebekah did, and it would be strange if Isaac was not moved by what he heard.

The Lord expressed His appreciation of those who followed Him in His path below and, indeed, of every one who makes sacrifices for His sake (Matt 19:28-29) and He pronounced Peter blessed when he, in contrast to the various estimates men formed about Christ, confessed, "Thou art the Christ, the Son of the living God" (Matt 16:16-17). Peter must therefore have been somewhat puzzled when the more striking confession of Thomas was met, not with blessing on him but on those who believe "without seeing" (John 20:28-29). To whom was the Lord referring? Years after Peter was writing to scattered believers who loved the Lord though they had never seen Him. Was he recalling the special blessing pronounced on such when he went on to say, "Ye rejoice with joy unspeakable and full of glory" (1 Pet 1:8)? We need not envy the disciples their privileges for it has been granted us to receive the witness of the Holy Spirit and give our hearts to the One whom we must wait to see (John 16:7).

A Place Prepared

Rebekah was brought into the tent once occupied by Sarah but now Isaac's home and henceforth hers for ever. Considering Abraham's wealth and status ("a mighty prince", 23:6) it was a tent of considerable size and well furnished by the standards of that day, in contrast to the humbler tents around. Even so, no bridegroom could refrain from making some special preparations to give his bride a suitable welcome. We have our heavenly Isaac's assurance that we shall be with Him in the place He went to prepare among the many abodes in His Father's house (John 14:2-3; 17:24). "So shall we ever be with the Lord" (1 Thess 4:17). If we knew no more about heaven than that, it should be enough for us as it was for Asaph, whose understanding went far beyond his time (Psa 73:24, 25).

Because of a widespread but mistaken impression that every aspect of the universe can now be investigated by the sophisticated means available, some Christians are wary about speaking of heaven as a place; instead it is vaguely described as a state, or mode of existence. This nebulous conception is an unsatisfactory and unsuccessful attempt to avoid the issue.

Every advance in our exploration of the universe shows that our previous understanding was incomplete and there are no grounds for supposing that at last everything is known. Scientists are willing to admit that there are still unsolved mysteries. The constitution of familiar matter once seemed a simple concept but such comfortable ideas have had to be drastically changed and the reality is quite different from what it appears to our limited vision. Heb 11:3 expresses a fact which was inconceivable to our forefathers, "things which are seen are not made of things which do appear". It is quite absurd then to hold that there can be no realities beyond our means of detecting.

If the Saviour in His wisdom chose to use terms we can understand we shall not succeed in finding a better way of describing the ultimate reality which in any case is beyond our present powers of comprehension. Similarly, despite all that has been revealed about the child of God's future glory, it has to be said, "it doth not yet appear what we shall be" (1 John 3:3).

She Became His Wife

The return of the party from Haran with their master's bride most certainly excited a good deal of interest among the numerous servants in the camp; we cannot doubt that they were given some share in the celebrations. We have no means of knowing what form heaven's celebrations may take but if any think it strange that such an idea should be associated with the heavenly scene they need only remind themselves of the astonishing picture the Saviour painted of the scene in the father's house when the prodigal returned. The note of exuberance is unmistakeable: "They began to be merry"; "music and dancing"; "It was meet that we should make merry and be glad".

But this does not match the voice of that great multitude in heaven, like the sound of great waters and mighty thunderings saying, "Let us be glad and rejoice and give honour to him; for the marriage of the Lamb is come and his wife hath made herself ready". Are we right in thinking that the raiment the servant provided for Rebekah, with the jewels of gold and silver, was with a view to her being suitably arrayed for the wedding ceremony he anticipated with such pleasure? The Lamb's wife is seen arrayed in fine linen clean and white as a symbol of the righteousness of saints (Rev 19:8).

Rebekah certainly shared Isaac's considerable inheritance but how can this compare with being joint-heirs with Christ, in an inheritance incorruptible and undefiled and that fadeth not away (Rom 8:17; 1 Pet 1:4)?

Settled At Home

It is a pleasant task to try to construct a picture of life at Lahai-roi, whilst guarding against the romanticism which ignores the inability of human nature to reach even its own ideals. Nevertheless seeing that Isaac loved his bride and (as we shall see) she made her contribution to his happiness we need not hesitate to visualise a very pleasant situation. However we can cast reserve aside when thinking of that heavenly home where perfected saints are united in the closest fellowship with Christ, "present (at home) with the Lord" (2 Cor 5:8).

As mentioned earlier the first mention of love in the Bible is the love of Abraham for his son — the second is that of the son for his bride. Whether one was matched by the other we have no means of knowing, but we do know that the Saviour said that as the Father loved Him so He loved His people (John 15:9). In that case He loved us before the foundation of the world (John 17:24). This accords with Eph 5:25 —Christ loved the church before it actually came into being and gave Himself for it, first in eternal intent and then in the fulness of time on the cross (Heb 9:14; 10:12; Eph 5:2). It is thrilling to find the phrase which in Eph 5:25 is applied to the church corporately as comprising all believers repeated in a very personal context: "The Son of God loved me and gave himself for me" (Gal 2:20). We are individuals in His eyes and will not lose our identity when with Him for ever —indeed there will be a special link between each saint and the Redeemer symbolised by the secret name He has for each (Rev 2:17).

Rebekah's beauty had an enduring quality for if the move to Gerah took place after their two sons had grown up (25:29) it was 30 years or more later when it is said of her that she was still "fair to look upon"; not only did this attract attention but the relaxed and light hearted spirit between them both was noticed by others (26:7, 8). No one however resists the relentless march of the years and superficial beauty fades like the flower of the field; but the bride of Christ is going to be a glorious church not having spot or wrinkle or any such thing and that beauty will never lose its first lustre. This in fact is the glory which the Father gave the Son and which in love the Son in turn imparts to His people — the glory of the perfection of glorified humanity, to be distinguished from that incommunicable glory which He had with the Father before the world was (John 17:5, 22).

Despite the felicity of Isaac and Rebekah in their personal relationships we all know, from our experience of the realities of life, that the atmosphere of the home would have been marred if there had not been a harmonious rapport with the father; on this score there was no cause for concern. The favourable impression Rebekah made upon Eliezer when he first set eyes on her is likely to have had the same effect on Abraham who, as is not always the case with parents, met her without any unfavourable prejudice — indeed, seeing that he had himself set in motion the chain of events which had brought her to Lahai-roi, he was all too ready to welcome her. When he heard of her readiness to forsake her home and family for Isaac's sake, and then saw the change which came over his son who had been mourning his mother's death, he could not but be drawn to his daughter-in-law. It is unthinkable that the omission of any further reference to Eliezer implies that, after so competently and faithfully carrying out his mission and bringing it to such a happy conclusion, he was ignored. The appreciation of all three would be a great recompense to him and we may believe that he enjoyed a privileged position in the household, all contributing to making it a place of deep contentment.

If we have used the eye of imagination to look into that home we can leave supposition, however strong, entirely behind us when we look into the saints' eternal home in the light of revelation, a light so bright that there is a great deal which even faith's vision cannot bring within our comprehension.

We have thought of Abraham as being pre-disposed toward Isaac's bride because her arrival was the result of his planning toward that end, but it is only for want of any adequate way of worthily expressing it that we hardly venture to raise our thoughts to an infinitely higher plane and reflect on the amazing truth that it was not because the Father had pre-destinated us that He was disposed to love us, but that it was in love that He predestinated us (Eph 1:4, 5). His purpose was not only to take us into His family ("unto the adoption of children") but to conform us to the image of His Son (Rom 8:29). All this was potential before the people for Christ's possession were actually "called" but now His love has an additional angle — He loves them because they love His Son, "He that loveth me shall be loved of my Father". But the Saviour's words went farther than that: "My Father will love him and we will come unto him and make our abode with him" (John 14:21-23). It is not easy for us, who have long been familiar with such a transcendent theme, to enter into the feelings of the Thessalonians, those one-time worshippers of unfeeling and capricious false gods, when they first learned that the living and true God was "even our Father who hath loved us and hath given us everlasting consolation and good hope through grace" (1 Thess 1:9; 2 Thess 2:16).

If Rebekah was gladly accepted into that circle of fellowship for Isaac's sake, we on our part can take to heart the assurance that we are accepted in the beloved (Eph 1:6) and may know the fulness of joy which comes from fellowship with the Father and with his Son Jesus Christ (Eph 1:6; 1 John 1:3, 4). Then the oft-used doxology of 2 Cor 13:14 will not lose its grip by repetition: "The grace of our Lord Jesus Christ, and the love of God, and the communion of the Holy Spirit be with you".

The intimate consultation which took place between Abraham and Eliezer involving Isaac, which was solemnised with an oath before the search for a bride was launched, is completely overshadowed by that eternal counsel when, in the absolute unity of three Persons in the one Being of God, there was the sublimest fellowship of infinite wisdom, love and power engaged in the most exquisite accord for the ultimate glory and joy of the Son through the ages of the ages. That perfect unity in the Godhead by its very nature can never be disturbed and the believer will never be God, yet the Saviour used some expressions which suggest a fellowship so beyond our comprehension that none dare to speculate what possibilities are open before us in that perfect state. Caution will allow no more than simple acceptance of the Saviour's words and patience to wait until there dawns the light of that eternal morning without clouds. When we read, for example, "At that day ye shall know that I am in my Father and ye in me and I in you" and "That they may be one, as thou Father art in me and I in thee, that they also may be one in us" we neither venture nor wish to say more than, "With thee is the fountain of life: in thy light shall we see light" (John 14:20; 17:21; Psa 36:9).

Christ is said to present to Himself a glorious church not having spot or wrinkle or any such thing but there is also the action of God who will present us faultless before the presence of His glory, not grudgingly, but with exceeding joy (Eph 5:27; Jude 24).

The Bridegroom's Joy

Rebekah's right of choice had been respected ("Wilt thou go with this man?") and her emphatic decision to become his wife made Isaac a happy man, whereas it would have been very little satisfaction to him had she been coerced. This might well suggest at least one of the reasons for mankind's endowment with the great privilege yet awesome responsibility of free-will. The automatic response of robots however precise could bring no satisfaction to the heart of our Redeemer. True, without the gracious constraints of the Holy Spirit we would never have yielded to the Saviour's claims, yet we were called upon to exercise our wills. Some do that in the wrong direction; Christ did not say that the Jewish leaders *could* not come to Him. He had sadly to say "Ye will not come to me that ye might have life" (John 5:40). His church will be His joy throughout eternity in a way which would not have been possible unless her heart had been won.

It was "for the joy that was set before Him he endured the cross and despised the shame" (Heb 12:2). The first chapter of the same epistle tells us that God has anointed Him with the oil of gladness above His fellows (Heb 1:9). This is a further extension of the quotation from Psa 45 which speaks of the one chosen to be the king's bride. The metaphor may rest on the analogy of the anointing of Aaron the high priest and his sons, although the Psalm introduces the concept of gladness. The anointing oil was liberally poured over the head of Aaron so that it ran down over his garments to the very skirt whereas it was only sprinkled on the dress of the sons who were appointed priests to serve under him (Exod 29:7, 21; Lev 8:12; Psa 133:2). The phrase "oil of gladness above thy fellows" clearly emphasises that however great is the joy of His people, His own joy will be immeasurably greater. In view of His immense sacrifice which made all possible no saint will hesitate to say "He is worthy". When He stands in the midst of that vast throng redeemed by His blood out of every kindred and tongue and people and nation surely then it will be that He shall see of the travail of His soul. Our hearts may well leap at knowing that when all that heavy burden and deep darkness is reviewed and then placed against the background of the infinite results achieved, the verdict is: "He shall be satisfied" (Isa 53:11).

Chapter XXI

In Retrospect

(Gen 25:1-11)

Keturah

A casual reading of vv. 1-4 leaves the impression that Abraham took Keturah soon after Isaac's marriage, and therefore when he was more than 140 years of age. Yet she bear him six sons. Seeing that over 40 years earlier he was able to beget Isaac only because of divine intervention (Heb 11:12) poses an obvious problem which it would not be right to ignore.

The difficulty disappears if it can be shown that this passage is in the nature of an appendix inserted out of chronological order, possibly to avoid interrupting the even flow of the main story. It is worth noting that the RV substitutes "and" for "then again" while the NIV suggests "Abraham had taken".

The use of the word *wife* need not imply that Abraham as a widower took her by a regular marriage, after Sarah's death three years previously. Although often used of one who is a wife the word is actually more general and is frequently translated "woman" where the idea of wife would be quite inappropriate. In Jud 19:27 it is applied to a concubine: "the woman, his concubine". The same word is used of the handmaiden whom Rachel gave to her husband Jacob, as it is also of the maid Leah gave to him (30:4, 9). Most conclusive of all is 1 Chron 1:32 which definitely refers to Keturah as "Abraham's concubine", effectively ruling out any idea that she was his wife in the real sense.

There are indications that a much earlier period in his life is in view. V. 5 reads, "And Abraham gave all that he had unto Isaac". This is clearly an echo of Eliezer's declaration in the home of Rebekah (24:36), showing that it had happened before he was sent to find a bride for Isaac. The gifts Abraham gave to the sons of his concubines must have been distributed before he gave all that remained to Isaac. If Keturah was not one of these concubines then Abraham would have no reserves left to make adequate provision for her six sons.

We conclude, therefore, that when he had decided to hand over all to Isaac, knowing his son's compliant character, he thought it prudent to remove first all other claimants after he had done them justice by providing for them. It could be significant that the sons of Keturah, and their sons and grandsons are listed (vv. 2-4) before the generations of Ishmael (vv. 12-18) and Isaac (vv. 19-23). Furthermore in 1 Chron 1:29-34 these are given in the order of Ishmael, Keturah and Isaac. On the whole it seems safe to conclude that our passage is an appendix which chronologically belongs to the period between the end of ch. 16 and the beginning of ch. 17. Here we have one of the several large gaps in the story which deals in detail only with those portions of Abraham's life which suffice to illustrate how he developed in the school of God.

Abraham's Last Years

When Abraham was 99 years of age he was "well stricken in age", but he must have been granted a renewal of health and vigour to judge from the activities in which he continued to engage. More than 20 years later he was able to take a three-day trek on foot to Mount Moriah (22:4).

Three years after the death of Sarah it is said again that he was "well stricken in age" (24:1) and we have seen reason to think that feeling his end was near prompted him to settle all on Isaac and make plans for finding a bride for him. If he thought his days were few he was mistaken for he lived another 35 years, although it is likely that his strength was failing.

We read nothing of any activity of his after Isaac's marriage, but we know that 20 years after the marriage his two grandsons, Esau and Jacob, were born. It must have been a great satisfaction to the old man to be spared to see them develop up to their 15th year.

They all remained in the same camp (Heb 11:9) and, remembering that God knew that he would "command his children, and his household after him, and they shall keep the way of the Lord, to do justice and judgment" (18:19), it is safe to picture him in his leisurely old age seeking to implant in their hearts a reverential fear of God. Times have changed, but not human nature, and it is easy to imagine the boys listening to the wonderful stories he could tell them of the way that God had led him in the hope of encouraging them to trust the same God.

Privileged Children Can Disappoint

It may have struck the grandfather that Esau differed from Jacob in much the same way that Ishmael had differed from Isaac. Esau was impulsive and restless, roaming from home in hunting, using bow and arrow as Ishmael did (25:27-29; 27:1-3; cf. 21:20). Jacob loved a quieter kind of life and did not go far from home — he "was a plain man, dwelling in tents". Abraham was undoubtedly aware that the Lord had said that the elder should serve the younger (25:23) but could he have anticipated how this would turn out?

Jacob's name given him at his birth means "supplanter", and to achieve his ends he became a schemer, provoking Esau's angry complaint, "Is he not rightly named Jacob, for he hath supplanted me these two times" (27:36). Perhaps he was not a very attractive character in the early days, but at least he valued what was spiritual and coveted the birthright for the sake of the privileges it involved, but which Esau despised (25:34).

Lacking his brother's submissiveness, Esau married two Canaanitish women much to the grief of his parents; we suspect that Rebekah, for her own ends, exaggerated somewhat when she complained to her husband that these women made her weary of life, and that if Jacob should follow Esau's example her life would not be worth living (26:35; 27:46). When Esau saw that he had distressed his parents, his way of trying to retain their good-will was to take, in addition, a daughter of Ishmael, which would hardly strike them as a great improvement (28:9).

Whether Abraham, with his long experience of people, had been able to form a shrewd idea as to the kind of men they would become is only a matter of conjecture. Could he have foreseen that despite the twist in Jacob's character God would patiently discipline him until at last he became a prince with God, and was given his new name Israel (32:28; 35:10)?

It is remarkable how these two men appear in close proximity in the same epistle in the last mention of them in Scripture. Esau is described as a profane person and a fornicator, a warning to any in danger of failing of the grace of God; Jacob is spoken of as dying in faith worshipping on the top of his staff (Heb 11:20-21; 12:15, 16).

Judge Not

That twins, brought up together under the influence of a grandfather who was a man of faith and the friend of God, and a God-fearing father whom God blessed and before whom he walked as his father did, turned out so differently should make us cautious of assigning reasons for the behaviour of the children of believers who bring sorrow to their parents (25:11; 26:24, 28; 31:42, 53; 48:15). It is quite clear from scriptural history that good fathers and evil fathers alike have had sons like them and sons very different from them. God Himself lamented that He had brought up children and they had rebelled against Him (Isa 1:2).

Length Of Days

If mankind did not have an instinct for self-preservation the human race would not survive; life is precious to all of us and generally long life is regarded as a boon. Even the Christian, who rejoices in the prospect of eternal glory, sees length of days as affording further opportunities for usefulness in the service of Christ which will never recur (Phil 1:23-25).

In the OT longevity was regarded as a sign of God's blessing. He who set his love on God was given the promise, "With long life will I satisfy him" (Psa 91:14-16). The man who desired life and loved many days was told the conditions under which he may expect to enjoy it (Psa 34:12-15). Peter quotes this passage for the benefit of Christians (1 Pet 3:10, 11).

At the same time it is well to keep in mind that, whilst this is a general rule, allowance must be made for exceptions. God has His own good reasons, at present unperceived by us, for calling some of his devoted servants home at a comparatively early age; it would be monstrous to assume that this was because of some failure on their part. On the other hand, wicked men have sometimes been allowed to reach advanced years. Believers are often perplexed because of situations which seem inconsistent with scriptural promises, through failing to distinguish between those promises which are absolute and those to which God may be pleased to make exceptions. To hold a balanced view it is important to discern the general tenor of the teaching of Scripture instead of basing one's whole outlook on a single passage. For example, Psa 145:16 declares that God opens His hand and satisfies the desire of every living thing, yet we know that some creatures perish from starvation. Another Psalm recognises the fact that young lions lack and suffer hunger (Psa 34:10; cf. Job 4:11).

In contrast to a general promise, admitting of exceptions, Abraham had a specific promise from God that he would die in a good old age, and in accord with that promise he was given 175 years (15:15).

Peace At Eventide

He was also told that he would die in peace. What a beautiful close to a long and chequered career. Who can doubt that he shared Simeon's sentiments: "Lord now lettest thou thy servant depart in peace according to thy word, for mine eyes have seen thy salvation"? Simeon actually held the infant Christ in his arms and had faith to see in that Babe the future light of the nations and the glory of Israel. He had the benefit of all the glowing prophecies of the completed OT, but Abraham, with only the dim light of early revelation, saw Christ's day far in advance and rejoiced (Luke 2:29-32; cf. John 8:56).

Satisfied In Retrospect

But there was more. Our text says he died "full *of days*" which certainly seems a somewhat unnecessary stress on a fact already sufficiently indicated by, "in a good old age, an old man". Italics indicate that the translators thought it necessary to supply the words "of days". The true sense is that he died "full". The Hebrew word really means "satisfied" and is so translated frequently elsewhere. He died in peace, a satisfied man. Men as a whole are never really satisfied, but Abraham had no complaints to make (Prov 27:20; Eccl 1:8, 11; 4:8).

Of course, he was not satisfied with himself. He would recall his failures of faith and courage, but he did not indulge in morbid introspection — he looked outward and upward to the God who had shown him mercy and truth (24:27) and had been his companion, guard and guide. Despite everything he might regret, he was satisfied that God had done all things well (Mark 7:37). With God's countenance shining on him, his shadows fell behind him. God did not remember his sins. When He pronounced His blessing on Isaac He said it was "because that Abraham obeyed my voice and kept my charge, my commandments, my statutes and my laws" (26:5; Heb 10:17).

Perfect Satisfaction In Prospect

The greatest satisfaction God's people can experience on earth can never be perfect and complete. That will be our portion hereafter. Abraham looked forward to the heavenly country and city, so clearly he believed in resurrection, as did many OT saints (Heb 11:35), but perhaps it is too much to expect that he shared David's amazing insight: "I will behold thy face in righteousness, I shall be satisfied when I awake with thy likeness" (Psa 17:15; 1 John 3:2).

Abraham's remains lie in the cave at Machpelah, but his spirit is with the One who is not ashamed to be known as the God of Abraham, of Isaac and of Jacob, all of whom will sit in the kingdom of heaven (Matt 8:11; 22:31, 32).

This God is our God and He will guide us by His counsel not only along life's pathway, but through death itself and receive us to glory (Psa 48:14; 73:24):

> The God of Abraham praise,
> Whose all sufficient grace
> Shall guide us all our pilgrim days
> In all our ways.
> He calls a worm his friend,
> He calls himself our God,
> And he shall save us to the end
> Through Jesus' blood.
> > *Thomas Olivers*

Appendix A
The Angel Of The Lord

From Eph 3;10 and other Scriptures we learn that there are degrees of dignity within the innumerable hosts of angels: "principalities and powers in heavenly places". Quite distinct from all these there is One who stands alone, "the angel of the Lord". He is also called the angel of God (21:17), the angel of his presence (Isa 63:9) and the messenger (angel) of the covenant (Mal 3:1). What is recorded of him makes it quite clear that his appearings were manifestations of God.

Hagar

His first recorded appearance was to Hagar, to whom he makes the promise "I will multiply thy seed exceedingly", language inappropriate for any creature however exalted. Hagar sensed this for "she called the name of the Lord that spake unto her, Thou God seest me". Fourteen years later, speaking from heaven, he promised to make of Ishmael a "great nation"; a promise which God had made in the same terms to Abraham some time before (16:7-13; 21:17-18; 17:20).

Abraham

When Abraham was about to slay his son the angel of the Lord called out from heaven to prevent him, the reason being "Thou hast not withheld thy son, thy only son from me" (22:11, 12. Cf. vv. 15, 16).

Jacob

On his flight to Haran Jacob spent a night at Bethel where God revealed Himself as the Lord God of Abraham and the God of Isaac. There he made a vow to God. When the time came to return home "The Lord said unto Jacob, Return to the land of ... thy kindred". In reporting this to his wives he said,

"The angel of God spoke unto me ... saying ... I am the God of Bethel ... where thou vowest a vow to me ... now arise, return unto the land of thy kindred" (28:13-20; 31:3-13).

At Penuel there wrestled a man with Jacob, who when questioned withheld his name, seeming to imply that Jacob ought to have known it. Cf. Jud 13:18. Jacob named the place Penuel (i.e. the face of God) for he had seen the face of God and expressed surprise that his life had nevertheless been preserved. Referring to this incident Hosea says Jacob "had power with God: yea he had power over the angel and prevailed" (32:24-30; Hos 12:3, 4). In blessing Joseph, Jacob linked God with the angel (48:15, 16).

Moses

At the burning bush the angel of the Lord appeared to Moses but it was the Lord who saw that he turned aside and God called to him. He hid his face for he was afraid to look upon God. Just as Jacob wanted to know the name of the one who wrestled with him, so Moses wanted to know what name he should give to the people of Israel. He was told to say "I AM hath sent you" (Exod 3:2-6, 13-14).

Gideon

An (RV the) angel of the Lord sat unseen under the oak at Ophrah before becoming visible to Gideon, yet it is said "The Lord looked upon him". The Lord thereafter is regarded as the speaker although Gideon was actually listening to and speaking with the angel, without knowing that he was the angel. Only when the angel of the Lord, also called the angel of God, caused fire from the rock to consume the offering, did Gideon realise who he was, whereupon he feared for his life until assured by the Lord that he would not die (Jud 6:11-23).

Manoah And His Wife

When the angel of the Lord appeared to Manoah and his wife he was regarded as a man of God, although his countenance was like that of an angel of God, very terrible. As was the case with Jacob and Moses, Manoah was concerned to know the name of the visitor. The angel's reply was similar to his reply to Jacob: "Why asketh thou after my name, seeing it

is secret (or wonderful)?" Cf. "And the angel did wondrously".
It was only then that Manoah realised he was an angel of the
Lord whereupon he said to his wife, "We shall surely die
because we have seen God". Manoah's wife was more logical
than her husband, or Gideon, for she saw clearly that the
promise given to them precluded the idea of death (Jud 13:1-
23).

Seeing God

In all five cases it is clear that seeing the angel of the Lord
was regarded as equivalent to seeing God. Yet in none of these
instances did death ensue, despite the Lord's plain statement
to Moses: "Thou canst not see my face; for there shall no man
see me and live" (Exod 33:20). John declares that "no man hath
seen God at any time". Paul elaborates on this: "Who only
hath immortality dwelling in the light which no man can
approach unto, whom no man hath seen nor can see". Earlier
in his letter to Timothy he had described God as "the King,
eternal, immortal, invisible" (John 1:18; 1 John 4:12; 1 Tim
6:16; 1:17). Yet Jacob was conscious of having seen God face to
face (cf. Deut 5:4; Exod 33:11).

How can these apparent contradictions be resolved? John
points the way when after saying, "No man hath seen God at
any time" he adds, "The only begotten son who is in the
bosom of the Father, he hath declared him". This ties in with
his earlier statement, "The Word was made flesh and dwelt
among us, and we beheld his glory, the glory as of the only
begotten of the Father" (John 1:14). Man cannot see God as
He is in His eternal and almighty being. It is impossible to gaze
at the sun shining in its strength and any one foolhardy
enough to attempt it would pay for his rashness with his
sight. So no man can see God as He is in His essential deity.
What can be seen of God is seen in Christ. He is "the
brightness of his glory and the express image of his person"
(Heb 1:3. Cf. 2 Cor 4:4).

The Name

Mention has already been made of the importance Jacob,
and Manoah attached to the name of the angel of the Lord.
Jacob did not receive an answer on this point but Manoah was
told that the angel's name was secret. The word translated

"secret" means "wonderful" and is akin to the name "wonderful" given to the coming Messiah: "His name shall be called Wonderful" (Isa 9:6).

God said of His angel whom He would send before the Israelites, "Beware of him and obey his voice; for he will not pardon your transgressions: for my name is in him" (Exod 23:20, 21). Link with this the fact that Christ took to Himself the title by which Moses was to identify the God who sent him to the people of Israel: "Thus shalt thou say, I AM hath sent me unto you". Cf. "Before Abraham was I AM" (Exod 3:13, 14; John 8:58). We conclude then that the appearances of God were in fact appearances of Christ and that He was the angel of the Lord.

Myths?

The appearance of God in human form in OT times certainly presents problems to the natural mind, although they are no more mysterious than the appearance of angels in the NT. It is just a question of whether we are prepared to believe what we cannot understand, which is something we all have to do at times, even in relation to the operations of nature. Critics relegate such appearances to the realm of myths and some see the OT narratives as being parallels with the pagan myths of false gods. It would however be passing strange if such crude myths had been refined into sober narratives fitting in with natural human situations, yet serving a divine purpose. It would be much more in accord with natural tendencies if the crude pagan myths were the result of traditions becoming increasingly perverted as they were transmitted to other lands in the course of generations.

Miracles

Scepticism refuses to accept the possibility of miracles but to those who believe in an eternal and almighty God they present no problem. There are multitudes of marvellous processes constantly occurring in the ordinary course of nature, which if they occurred only once, or rarely, would be regarded as miraculous. The term natural laws means no more than ways in which science has been able to define the orderly courses of natural forces. These processes can be described and appropriate names found for them but all this falls far short of explaining why things happen the way they do. All we can say is that this is the way that God has decreed His universe shall work. To claim that certain happenings are contrary to natural laws does not prove that such things are impossible. Before such a claim is warranted it would be necessary to be sure that all natural processes are known. This is a tremendous claim to make. Many of such laws which we are able to detect to-day were quite unknown to even the acutest minds in the relatively recent past and no doubt further discoveries will be made. But even if all natural laws were known it would be absurd to suppose that the God who created the universe is a prisoner within the forces He himself has set in motion.

Are we to dismiss as simpletons those prophets and apostles who accepted the scriptural record without question? They lived in that part of the world with which we are now concerned, and very much nearer in time to the events in question, and probably possessed sources of information denied us. To those whose faith does not stand in the wisdom of men but in the power of God (1 Cor 2:5), and have reached the solid conviction that the Scripture is indeed the word of God, such considerations as have been mentioned above are of no more than passing interest. We are quite content to follow our Lord's example when rebutting the devil's suggestions: "It is written" (Matt 4:3-11).

Appendix B

Psalm 110

The Order Of Melchizedek

The brief but dramatic intervention of Melchizedek, the king-priest, played an important part in the spiritual development of Abraham, but there the matter seemed to end. However the writer of the Epistle to the Hebrews sees the omission of any mention of Melchizedek's ancestry, and Abraham's acknowledgement of his superiority, as illustrating his grand thesis of the superiority of Christ's high priesthood over the Levitical system. The weight of his argument rests on the few pregnant words of Psa 110:4, "The Lord hath sworn and will not repent, Thou art a priest for ever after the order of Melchizedek".

The psalm is well known but if privileged familiarity is not to rob us of appreciation of its several remarkable features, an effort must be made to approach it as if for the first time.

The prominence given to it in the NT attests its importance. The opening verse was quoted in full by our Lord (as noted in all three of the synoptics, Matt 22:41-44; Mark 12:35, 36; Luke 20:41-43) and also by Peter on the day of Pentecost (Acts 2:34-35). It is quoted almost in full in Heb 1:13; 10:12, 13, and is reflected in Heb 8:1; 1 Cor 15:25-27; Col 3:1 and 1 Pet 3:22. Then again v. 4, which now chiefly concerns us, is appealed to no fewer than seven times in the Epistle to the Hebrews: 5:6, 10; 6:20; 7:15, 17, 21 almost as if to force it on the reader's attention.

The Lord frequently made it clear that He accepted the OT Scriptures as the word of God but in regard to this psalm He explicitly said that David spoke in the Holy Spirit (Mark 12:36). It provides an outstanding example of the inspiring Spirit's illumination of a prophet's mind on matters beyond the range of even the keenest perception. How else could David possibly have known what had passed in the divine counsels so as to be able to reveal what the Lord had said to his Lord, the promised Messiah?

The invitation to sit at the Lord's right hand is linked with kingly rule, which subject takes up by far the greater part of the psalm and is in line with numerous other prophecies, but David is able to reveal by the Spirit what was hitherto unsuspected. Only one of the seven verses is devoted to this revelation but its importance may be judged by the oath, "The Lord hath sworn and will not repent, Thou art a priest forever after the order of Melchizedek". This was an altogether new concept.

The two offices of king and priest were never held by any save Melchizedek and Christ. In Israel kingship belonged to the tribe of Judah and priesthood to the tribe of Levi. Uzziah as king had been marvellously helped until he was strong but his presumption in daring to exercise a priestly function was instantly visited with severe judgment (2 Chron 26:16-21). This was such an emphatic line of demarcation that even Christ could not have been a priest in Israel because He sprang from the kingly tribe (Heb 7:14). "If he were on earth he should not be a priest" but the glorious truth is that "we have such a high priest who is set on the right hand of the throne of the Majesty in the heavens" (Heb 8:1, 4).

That the revelation that Christ's perpetual priesthood was not after the Levitical order but after the order of Melchizedek should come through David is all the more striking as we remember that up to the very end of his life he was deeply committed to the Levitical system, evidently regarding it as a permanent institution. Under his zealous patronage and direction it was restored to a prestige it had not enjoyed since the days of Moses and Aaron. The evidence is too bulky to handle here but we need think only of the exuberant joy he showed in both stages of bringing the ark to the temporary tent he had prepared although he had set his heart on building a temple which was to be "exceedingly magnifical of fame and glory through all countries". He organised the service of the Levites on an unprecedented scale and brought the temple choirs to a high degree of perfection.

And yet in a brief isolated reference to Melchizedek, which broke the silence of a thousand years and was then left without any further comment for another thousand years, the whole Levitical system, although ordained by God, was ignored. On this one cryptic but pregnant sentence the writer of the Epistle to the Hebrews builds his tremendous exposition of the high priesthood of Christ, showing its divine perfection in contrast to the inadequacies of the now defunct order. (Nevertheless it would be wrong to overlook the wonderful way in which the Aaronic priesthood and its ordinances can beautifully illustrate many important aspects of Christ's ministry from on high.)

The spiritual wealth of that time is readily available to all who will give time and prayerful thought to the Hebrew Epistle. We linger only to point out that whereas Melchizedek ministered to Abraham on but one occasion and then only for a brief time our great High Priest "after the power of an endless life ... hath an unchangeable priesthood. Wherefore he is able to save them to the uttermost that come unto God by him, seeing he ever liveth to make intercession for them" (Heb 7:16, 24, 25).